Austin Lovegrove examines the sentencing of offenders appearing on multiple offences, and how judges, having fixed a prison sentence for each offence, determine an overall sentence for each offender. Analyzing judges' verbal protocols for sentencing problems and sentences for fictitious cases, he is able to offer, first, a model of judicial sentencing in the form of a decision strategy comprising working rules deduced from the given responses of judges as they attempted to apply sentencing law, and, second, a numerical guideline in the form of an algebraic model quantifying the application of the working rules. On the basis of this empirical data, Dr. Lovegrove furthers understanding of the nature and place of intuition in sentencing and of how the cumulation of sentence can be integrated into a system of proportionality related to the seriousness of single offences.

The framework of judicial sentencing

Cambridge Criminology Series

Editors
Alfred Blumstein, *Carnegie Mellon University*
David Farrington, *University of Cambridge*

This new series publishes high quality research monographs of either theoretical or empirical emphasis in all areas of criminology, including measurement of offending, explanations of offending, police, courts, incapacitation, corrections, sentencing, deterrence, rehabilitation, and other related topics. It is intended to be both interdisciplinary and international in scope.

Other titles in the series

Simon I. Singer
Recriminalizing delinquency: violent juvenile crime and juvenile justice reforms

J. David Hawkins (ed.)
Delinquency and crime: Current theories

Scott H. Decker and Barrik Van Winkle
Life in the gang: Family, friends, and violence

The framework of judicial sentencing

A STUDY IN LEGAL DECISION MAKING

Austin Lovegrove

University of Melbourne

CAMBRIDGE
UNIVERSITY PRESS

Published by the Press Syndicate of the University of Cambridge
The Pitt Building, Trumpington Street, Cambridge CB2 1RP
40 West 20th Street, New York, NY 10011–4211, USA
10 Stamford Road, Oakleigh, Melbourne 3166, Australia

First published 1997

Printed in Great Britain at the University Press, Cambridge

A catalogue record for this book is available from the British Library

Library of Congress cataloguing in publication data
Lovegrove, Austin.
The framework of judicial sentencing / Austin Lovegrove.
  p.   cm. – (Cambridge criminology series)
Includes bibliographical references and index.
ISBN 0 521 58427 2 (hardcover)
1. Sentences (Criminal procedure) – Great Britain – Decision making.
2. Judicial discretion – Great Britain.
I. Title.   II. Series.
DK8406.L68   1997
345.41'05–dc20
[344.1055]   96–36778   CIP

ISBN 0 521 58427 2 hardback

This is one of the great lessons of science. It is often necessary to resort to the abstract – to formal mathematical manipulations – to make sense of the world. Ordinary experience alone can be an unreliable guide.

Paul Davies. (Davies, 1983:16)

Contents

Figures

Tables

Acknowledgments

I could not over-emphasize the generous and open spirit of the eight County Court judges who agreed to undertake the extensive series of sentencing exercises upon which this research project is founded. To them and to the Chief Judge who countenanced the study, I am most grateful.

Deep appreciation is also due to Trish Dutton and, particularly, Jean Rodrigues who under trying conditions typed the scripts for the fictitious cases and the manuscript for this book so diligently.

Finally, I should like to thank the staff at Cambridge University Press (UK) for their willing assistance in the publication process.

The Criminology Department and the Faculty of Arts at the University of Melbourne generously provided financial assistance in order to facilitate the completion of this project.

CHAPTER ONE

Judicial decision making and sentencing policy: continuation of a study

In sentencing, the judge's task is to determine the type and quantum of sentence appropriate to the facts of the case, and this judgment must be made in accordance with the relevant statutory provisions and appellate principles. But in Australia, as in England and elsewhere, sentencing law speaks in only general terms so that it is left to the sentencing judge to develop and apply the working rules required to give detailed effect to these provisions and principles in actual cases. What is not known is how individual judges have responded to this challenge. The present monograph is the second report from a continuing study of this matter. The first, Lovegrove (1989), examines how judges in Victoria scale and combine the seriousness of the offence characteristics, such as organization and violence, of a single count and use this to determine what is appropriate by way of sentence (quantum of imprisonment) for that count. The product of this work is a model offering both a decision strategy and a numerical guideline; since it takes no account of legally immaterial considerations or distortions in thinking arising from the limitations of human information processing, it represents an account of ideal (cf. actual) decision making in sentencing.

The present study extends that enquiry, being concerned with multiple-count cases: how in Victoria the judge, having fixed an appropriate sentence of imprisonment for each of the comprising counts, determines an effective sentence appropriate to the overall seriousness of the case.

One goal of this report is to present a decision strategy – a body of principle consisting of working rules – apparently relied on with varying awareness and comprehension by the judges for the purpose of determining effective sentences in cases comprising multiple counts; the strategy is general with respect to offence type, covering comprising counts both of the one offence type (e.g., multiple burglaries) and of a variety of offence types (e.g., burglary and armed robbery), and applies where the counts are properly regarded as separate transactions and the sentences fixed for them are appropriately sentences of imprisonment.

The second goal is to develop a prototypal numerical guideline by quantifying the judges' application of the preceding working rules: this takes the form of an algebraic model relating quanta of sentence for comprising counts to the effective sentence, so that the latter can be generated from the former.

Taken together, the decision strategy and numerical guideline have the potential to give rise to a decision structure or framework in the form of a comprehensive sentencing guideline comprising written policy statements and a numerical decision aid for the application of that principle to the sentencing of the multiple offender. With this there is the opportunity for sentencing judges to ensure they share a common policy, for the fairness and soundness of that policy to be open to appraisal, and for judges to refer to a decision aid when implementing that policy in individual cases.

These are the descriptive components of the study. Yet more than description was sought; the investigation has theoretical pretensions over and above the rather weak theoretical base required to facilitate description. In one of the two broad conceptual analyses, a solution is offered to the problem paramount in the sentencing of the multiple offender, as it has been identified by Ashworth (1983, 1992a), namely, the problem of integrating the seriousness of two or more offences of the same or of a different kind into a coherent system of proportionality principally related to the seriousness of single (principal) offences or classes of (principal) offence. Underlying the posing of this problem is a concern that the cumulation of sentence should not be untrammelled: that an effective sentence imposed for a multiplicity of minor counts should not be condign and more appropriate to a serious single count. The solution was not found in sentencing policy or in the sentencing data collected in the present or the previous study, but was formulated by the author. It involves the linking of the author's two decision models. The model in the present study covers the cumulation of seriousness, operationalized by quantum of sentence, of counts belonging to one or several varieties of offence category, but provides no principled basis for constraint on cumulation. The first (1989) model deals with not only the scaling of seriousness associated with offence factors characterizing single counts, as intimated above, but also the determination of the overall seriousness of a case comprising multiple counts of the same kind; moreover, its components are so defined and structured that there is a principled basis for constraint on cumulation. This first model directly addresses Ashworth's problem for multiple counts of the same kind; it can provide a principled limit on the cumulation of sentence for the second model's coverage of multiple counts of a different kind (and, of course, of the same kind) by means of its common coverage with that model of counts of the same kind.

It will be clear now that the present study not only extends the first study, it is also complementary. In the first study a decision structure was developed for the determination of sentences for single counts in respect of their offence characteristics. The decision structure from the present study covers the aggregation of already-determined sentences for single counts comprising a multiple-count case. Finally, it is only by means of the first decision structure that it is possible to introduce in a principled way a limiting component into the second decision structure. Together, these two decision structures can be regarded as providing the armature underpinning the judicial determination of sentence. While the armature is largely derived from the description of current practice, it nevertheless has a normative character to it. This follows from its reliance on models of ideal decision making and the limit on cumulation being a theoretical formulation rather than an empirical discovery. Yet it is, of course, very much a circumscribed rationality, requiring a coherent logic only within the current general judicial approach to sentencing.

The point was made earlier that it has been left to the sentencing judge to work out in detail what is correct by way of approach to the sentencing of the multiple offender in individual cases. For some policy matters raised by this sentencing problem a particular judge may be guided by rules derived from and consistent with broad principle, for other matters the same judge may rely on unprincipled heuristics – what experience has shown are acceptable appropriate sentences for particular combinations of comprising sentences – and yet other policy matters may not be regarded as significant or even enter the judge's mind and for this reason be ignored; and, of course, the content and mix of this principle and heuristic and the areas of ignorance may vary across judges. When decision making in sentencing is viewed in this light there are inescapable implications for the methods of data collection; the consequence of this view for the method is that it should be characterized by the following three features: (1) the individual judge as the unit of analysis; (2) a data base of the judges' more or less conscious thoughts as they determine sentence (verbal protocols); and (3) a decision modelling process consistent with a requisite solution. The point is that care must be exercised that the techniques adopted for the purpose of studying the decision making are appropriate to the phenomenon and problem. A review of the empirical sentencing literature relevant to guideline development suggests that careful thought has not been given to this. Each of the preceding three method characteristics is dealt with in turn, but is not independent of the other two.

If the judges share a comprehensive body of principle and apply it reliably, a group analysis would be informative. But should these conditions not hold – should, say, there be only a few judges with a principled and shared understanding of this problem, the rest having little idea about what is correct by way of approach, or should there be a number of judges with their own limited understandings, but these to a considerable extent not being common in regard to element or content – then the averaging process in a group analysis would blur the researcher's view of this principle and favor the erroneous conclusion that there was little or no principle to be discovered.

In an area of study rich in theory, there is much to be learned by testing and comparing the ability of the various models to predict behavior, in this case the behavior being judges' effective sentences and the independent variables being case facts. But where the topic is largely uncharted conceptually, as in the sentencing of the multiple offender, it is a different matter: where hypotheses were unsupported, it would be helpful if there were clues to alternatives; and the testing and support of only a few hypotheses leaves the possibility of there being significant elements of the decision making yet to be uncovered. A record of the content and sequence of individual judges' thoughts may provide a means of moving beyond these unproductive and uncertain outcomes.

In circumstances where sentencing decisions may not be in regard to a settled, detailed and comprehensive approach, a research strategy aimed at discovering policy is inappropriate since, should that policy not exist, the strategy is doomed to failure: a crude and simple model must then be regarded as an end in itself or the search for a valid model must continue on, albeit fruitlessly. Now, these circumstances may hold in regard to the sentencing of the multiple offender; for this reason what is wanted is an approach aimed at fostering policy development by judges. From this viewpoint the task of the researcher initially is to tease out the part-approaches adopted by the various judges and to look for common and disparate aspects. The common elements may be regarded as a first draft of what after judicial consideration may come to be regarded as correct by way of approach, and the disparate elements are grist for judicial debate in the process of policy development. This describes the first steps in "requisite" decision modelling, a term introduced by Phillips (1984), a decision theorist. Clearly, this process would be facilitated by verbal protocols and would require the individual as the unit of analysis. Moreover, on matters on which there was not a detailed policy, the requirement to give a verbal protocol might prompt the judges to be deliberative and to attempt to work out how to apply the general policy in individual cases, and the protocol would provide a record of their thoughts as a basis for policy development.

The policy and quantitative analyses in this present study do not go further than these initial steps towards the development of a decision framework and comprehensive sentencing guideline for the multiple offender. Consequently, the decision strategy identified should be treated as no more than tentative and incomplete, and the numerical guideline as only illustrative, yet both can be regarded as ripe for development.

How a decision model is to be put to work should be a critical consideration in its development. Since this is an apparently little-appreciated point in sentencing research, it is important to ventilate it in this overview of matters of importance in the present study. The point has already been made that here the model is to be the basis of a policy statement and a decision aid for working judges. In view of this, a profitable distinction can be drawn in the model's content between the legally material case characteristics and the combination of these elements. It is one thing to establish that, say, the number and the seriousness of the comprising counts are significant factors in the sentencing of the multiple offender; whether the combination of these factors in the effective sentence is determined according to a simple linear-additive function or something more complex is another matter. In respect of both matters, Lovegrove (1989) has argued that in sentencing the content of the model must faithfully represent judicial thought. In general, empirical sentencing research does not satisfy this criterion; the importance of this point has been recognized in regard to the search for legally material case factors (Vining and Dean, 1980) and combination (Lawrence, 1988), but not as it applies to guideline development. It is this aspect which is the more important one in the context of the present study and needs to be explained. There are several cogent reasons for analyzing sentencing data in accordance with a decision model faithful to the structure of judicial thought, rather than by means of an atheoretically and directly applied standard descriptive statistical technique (see, generally, Lovegrove, 1989, 1995).

First, it has the potential to offer a more accurate, detailed and comprehensive description of judicial decision making in sentencing, in respect of the critical factors and their lines of influence, since the story data tell is partly a function of the type of analysis used to interpret them. The statistical model adopted by Wilkins, Kress, Gottfredson, Calpin and Gelman (1978), multiple regression, represents the combination of the individual case information by, as it were, adding the average effects of each element on sentence. Although this may be appropriate for describing the combined effect of various elements on the seriousness of the offence characteristics of a case (e.g., how the seriousness of the organization of a burglary, the value of the property stolen, the violence experienced by the victims and the damage to their property during the offence, contribute to the overall seriousness of the circumstances of that burglary), it is clearly inappropriate for representing certain aspects of the determination of sentence. The fact that a judge may have to achieve more than one goal in the sentencing decision provides one illustration of this point. In part the punishment must be proportional to the culpability of the offender, but it may have to be tempered so as to allow for the offender's favorable rehabilitation prospects. Some factors like remorse are involved in both decisions – in the first as a factor in the scaling of seriousness, in the second as an indicator of reform. If present, it will always carry weight in the first decision and, hence, affect sentence, but its effect on sentence by way of the second decision may depend on the presence of other factors suggestive of rehabilitation, and if, but only if, they are present, it may count a second time in the determination of sentence. Two difficulties associated with the validity of the regression equation as a representation of actual sentencing policy follow. First, in the above example, the factor of remorse would be under- or over-weighted in a particular case depending, respectively, on whether or not according to policy weight should be given to the goal of rehabilitation. Secondly, the approach to sentencing implicit in the equation – the addition and subtraction of factors so as to allow for the effects of aggravating and mitigating factors – is at variance with the orderly sequence of steps required by sentencing policy (see Chapter 2). The problem here is that the multiple regression model is incompatible with the structure of judicial thought and, consequently, some of the complexities of judicial thought processes could not be adequately represented. In these statistical approaches to the modelling of decision processes, the impression is given that the use of a statistical analysis is atheoretical in the sense that it allows the researcher to find the structure of the decision maker's thought in the data. This is not correct; it belies the fact that in such an analysis the data are organized around the structure of the statistical model. Now, a researcher cannot analyze data in a vacuum; data must be interpreted in relation to some sort of model. It is a model faithful to the structure of judicial decision making that has the potential to provide the most valid representation of the determination of sentence.

Secondly, as intimated above, sentencing policy may require development. Now, it would be expected that a description of current judicial decision making mirroring the structure of the judges' thought would provide the conditions most favorable to judicial reflection with a view to policy development, because the description could be understood and contemplated developments linked directly to the judges' existing decision scheme.

Finally, it must be appreciated that no guideline, particularly a numerical decision aid, can be expected to take account of the less important and less common factors and patterns of influence. Accordingly, a numerical decision aid is to be regarded as providing a standard or reference sentence against which the sentencer must allow for the additional influence on this quantum of punishment of the less significant and the innovative considerations bearing upon a particular case. Again, and for the same reason of intelligibility offered under the preceding point, it would be expected that a numerical description of sentencing policy analyzed and presented in terms of a structure faithful to judicial thought would facilitate the ready and accurate allowance for matters not provided for in the guidance. While this point has been made in the decision-making literature (see Cohen's, 1993, concept of user-driven and prescriptive decision aiding), unfortunately sentencing guideline developers have not shown a regard for it.

A question remains over how to set about building the first draft of a requisite model, faithful to the judicial approach, with the potential to describe the working rules to be used by judges in applying the broad legislative provisions and appellate principles to the sentencing of individual multiple offenders. What is required in requisite modelling is a picture of the current judicial approach, one capable of accurately portraying its likely diversity and sparseness of thought, yet able to facilitate a move towards uniformity in a comprehensive and detailed approach. A review of the empirical literature showed that it held little for the present study: the range of factors included in these analyses was found to be extremely narrow and the combination of these factors was not treated as a part of the policy to be discovered but simply left to be represented by the structure of a standard statistical model. Fortunately, two English academic lawyers (Ashworth, 1983, 1992a; Thomas, 1979) have analyzed judgments of the Court of Appeal in an attempt to discern a decision strategy followed by the courts, and their analyses cover both legally material factors and the aspect of combination. Nevertheless, this work is fairly characterized as qualitative and limited in scope; happily, the two contributions are supplementary, not contradictory. To take these analyses further, the author considered possible implications of them, this step including aspects not covered directly by them, and in this way generated a detailed and comprehensive decision model. This, then, was used to derive predictions regarding how judges would sentence in a variety of cases, each case illustrating a different element of the sentencing of the multiple offender. The responses of the judges to these cases were used to test the validity of the model and to give clues to alternatives and to additional aspects of the judicial approach. This process seems to be compatible with the idea of requisite modelling.

This introduction now turns to the other of the two broader conceptual questions canvassed: the nature of judicial intuition and the vexed problem of the proper place of intuition and deliberation in sentencing. Common judicial wisdom is that a system of individualized justice requires finely honed judgments for which intuition is a necessary condition; deliberation in the form of a conscious series of structured steps would make for almost certain error; moreover, since in a system of individualized justice there is infinite variation between cases in terms of the factors material to sentence, and differences on these factors and potentially relevant combinations of them for sentence, it is not possible to set down in more than general terms how these matters, and, indeed, how the considerations relating case facts and sentencing goals, should determine what is appropriate by way of sentence. Nor, it is said, can the sentencer profitably apply mathematical rules to the task of quantifying sentence; there are principles, but they are few and broad, and judgments about the facts of a case in relation to them must be subjective and qualitative, and articulated in general terms only. For the judicial aphorism "each case turns on its own facts," read "each case is a special case." The present study's data base of judges' more or less conscious thoughts as they apply legislation and appellate principles in individual cases can be used to indicate the extent to which this process is deliberative or is accessible to consciousness. From an examination of the content and pattern of these thoughts, and with the aid of the theoretical literature on intuition, it is possible to offer an interpretation of the nature of the judges' intuition, whether it represents an implicit understanding awaiting transfer to the deliberative realm, or masks an absence of thought or something else. The point of this analysis is to investigate whether a more deliberative approach is required for skilled judicial sentencing; until this question is resolved, an informed consideration of what, if any, policy development and guidance are required for better sentencing practice is difficult.

From the foregoing it will be apparent that the present project involves the application of behavioral science (psychological) methods to a legal problem, sentencing, with due consideration being given to the law, legal thought and the sentencing system. Psychology has been applied to the legal system from a number of perspectives; this study is in the decision-making tradition, of which notable examples are Pennington and Hastie's (1993) study of juror decision making and Greenberg and Ruback's (1992) work on victim decision making. In this approach the research task is not directly to discover those factors which influence the decision; rather the problem is to model the decision process – its structure and content. This perspective can be contrasted with the more traditional correlational and factorial approaches, illustrated in the study of sentencing by the work of Ebbesen and Konečni (1981) and Kapardis and Farrington (1981), respectively.

Now that the goals of the study have been stated and the matters of importance relevant to the attainment of these goals have been aired, the detailed reporting of the study can begin. The various theoretical and empirical analyses and policy matters are covered throughout the book. In the remainder of this chapter four topics are addressed: the contribution of the study in the context of sentencing reform; the nature of sentencing policy and the sentencing decision; studies of judicial sentencing and sentencing guidelines in regard to the multiple offender; and sentencing law and policy matters as applying to the multiple offender, including the attempts by Thomas (1979) and Ashworth (1983, 1992a) to discern a decision strategy in appellate judgments of the Court of Appeal in England. (In the second and third sections some matters, but not those specifically related to the nature of intuition or to the multiple offender, have been canvassed comprehensively in Lovegrove, 1989, and, accordingly, although updated are treated here in outline only.)

Chapter 2 presents Lovegrove's (1989) decision model describing the determination of quantum of sentence for single and multiple counts of the same kind. Its presentation here is a priority, because it was used by the author to elaborate, combine and inform with precision the part-strategies formulated by Ashworth (1983, 1992a) and Thomas (1979), and in this way is the conceptual foundation of the detailed and comprehensive decision model underpinning the present empirical exploration of sentencing in cases where the multiple counts differ in kind; this latter model is set out in Chapter 3.

The next step was to derive predictions from the author's decision model and to formulate, as a means of testing the model, a series of approximately forty sentencing problems relating to critical aspects of the decision process. This is described in Chapter 4. The case or cases comprising a problem were presented in the form of skeleton descriptions. For example, in one of the problems one case comprised an armed robbery for which the appropriate sentence was four-and-a-half years and a three-year arson, and the second case a four-and-a-half year burglary and a three-year arson. (In each case the assumption was to be made that the offender had a serious relevant criminal record and little if anything by way of mitigation.) The judges' task was to determine an effective sentence for each case. The point of this problem, of course, was to investigate whether the seriousness of the legal category of the principal offence is a relevant factor in the decision regarding the degree of cumulation of the sentence for the secondary offence.

The subjects were eight County Court judges, all of whom were regarded as experienced in the criminal jurisdiction. The problems were presented to the judges individually in two sessions. In the first session each of the judges was required to determine sentences for the cases and provide a record of his thinking (verbal protocol); in the second session the author explained how the hypothesized decision model applied to each problem and the judge was asked to comment on its validity (reflective report). Details concerning the method are set out and justified in Chapter 5.

In the following chapter the quantitative and qualitative responses of the judges to the sentencing problems are presented and analyzed.

A discussion of the fate of the author's model at the hands of the data introduces the next chapter – Chapter 7. The model was not supported; however, the outline of an alternative decision model for the sentencing of the multiple offender could be discerned in the judges' responses, although only two of the judges could be regarded as having more than a vague and fragmentary understanding of this sentencing problem. The next section of this chapter sets out the comprising principles of what is called the alternative decision model and discusses the limitations of this model. Finally, the records of the judges' protocols and reflective reports, together with the relevant theoretical literature, are used to assess the extent to which their thought is marked by deliberation and to interpret the nature of their intuition. The principles of the alternative decision model form the draft written policy statements of a sentencing guideline for the multiple offender.

Following this analysis it was necessary to validate and quantify the alternative model. In respect of validation, the question was whether the judges in determining effective sentences for multiple-count cases combined the sentences they had considered appropriate for the comprising counts in accordance with this model. In respect of quantification, the task was to find and quantify an algebraic model, one consistent with the decision model and providing a good fit to the data showing the relationship between the effective and component sentences. This model forms the numerical decision aid by which means in multiple-count cases effective sentences can be generated from the sentences considered appropriate to the comprising counts and in accordance with the written policy statements. A prototypal numerical guideline was developed for the judge who was best able to give quantitative effect to his stated policy. Four of the eight judges participated in this part of this study. The data base comprised the sentences they imposed for approximately forty fictitious cases, comprising armed robberies and burglaries, presented as comprehensive summary descriptions, and varying in terms of the number and the seriousness of the comprising counts. The judges individually did them in three parts, and worked on them in their own time. The method details, including the basis of the construction of the fictitious cases, are set out and justified in Chapter 8; here, there is also an evaluation of the external validity of sentences imposed for fictitious cases. In Chapter 9 the notion of requisite modelling is elaborated and, then, the judges' sentencing data for the fictitious cases are presented and analyzed in accordance with it.

In the final chapter the two decision structures – the one based on Lovegrove's (1989) decision model, the other based on the alternative decision model from the present study – are linked to form the armature of judicial sentencing; it is a tentative framework and incomplete, particularly in respect of offender characteristics. This chapter closes with a discussion on how the armature is to be used as a decision framework for guidance in sentencing, in the light of the possible roles of intuition and deliberation in judicial decision making.

The study in the context of sentencing reform

A useful framework for assessing the scope and the potential contribution of the present study is provided by Ashworth's (1995) overview of what he considers to be the matters of importance to be resolved by the sentencing scholar.

(1) Sentencing theory. Under this point come debates about the purposes of sentencing. Should it be desert based, or perhaps desert modified by rehabilitation, or something else? And if desert based, what should be the indices of offence seriousness, and how is sanction severity to be graded? Moreover, what is to be made of more recent proposals: for example, that severity be judged in regard to equality of impact?

(2) Application of principle. It is one thing to have an agreed-upon policy, it is another thing to ensure that it is applied in a principled fashion. Where there are multiple goals, there must be rules covering the circumstances – type and facts of the offence and characteristics of the offender – in which one has priority over the other or controlling how one modifies the other. There is also the problem of how best to give effect to the aim(s) of sentence in the circumstances of the case.

(3) Structuring judicial discretion. There are four aspects to this topic – the source, style, and scope of the guidance and the extent to which the framework is binding. The guidance can come from the legislature, a body such as a sentencing commission, or the appellate judges; its content can be expressed in words or numbers; it can take the form of general principles covering major areas or be detailed and all encompassing; and

it may be binding or be for information only, offering, for example, statistical data on current practice. Indeed, in respect of each of these aspects, the guidance may incorporate more than one approach; so, for example, the legislature may set out a broad principled framework, on which the appellate court elaborates.

(4) Implementation of the system. Of concern here is that the sentencing system as reformed is user-friendly and that it is resilient to the potentially adaptive behavior of judges and other criminal justice professionals, such as prosecutors. The principles and rules must be coherent and understood by those who are to apply them; they are at risk of being circumvented where the judges and prosecutors are uncomfortable with them or are answerable to a disenchanted public.

(5) Research. Two categories of research are significant. First, research into the sentencing process and, specifically, how judges apply sentencing law and policy to a set of case facts in order to determine sentence; the research may or may not take account of the personal characteristics of the judge. Secondly, there is the research needed to inform policy matters associated with the preceding points; for example, the effectiveness of sanctions as deterrents.

Where does the present study stand and what does it have to offer with respect to these matters? Each one is now considered in turn.

The principle of proportionality between offence seriousness and punishment severity is well established in common law in Australian jurisdictions (Fox, 1988) and in England (Thomas, 1979). It is grounded in the idea of just deserts. At the time of this study proportionality was regarded by the courts as a limiting principle: the proportionate sentence could be reduced to achieve a penal goal, for example rehabilitation, but not exceeded, for example for the purposes of incapacitation. While the position is now somewhat more complex in Victoria (see Fox, 1993) and in England (see Ashworth, 1992b; Thomas, 1992), the recent legislative developments leave proportionality unscathed as a direct or indirect touchstone of what is appropriate by way of sentence. Since the present study is concerned with how judges attempt to make the severity of punishment appropriate to the seriousness of the offending, it requires for relevance that desert be the primary aim of sentencing. Were, say, rehabilitation the main aim, a very different set of case facts would be relevant, the combination of these facts would take a different form, and numbers would play little if any part in the decision. Nevertheless, as intimated earlier, this work does not merely accept the status quo, it attempts theoretical development: that part of the armature offering a principled limit to the cumulation of sentence in multiple-count cases being a theoretical formulation rather than an empirical discovery. In respect of theory, limitations of this study include the non-coverage of non-custodial options and of possible differences in the impact of imprisonment across individuals.

As stated in the introduction, this study is concerned with identifying the extent to which judges have developed working rules for the purpose of giving effect to sentencing law and policy in actual cases. The specific target here is what is considered by judges to comprise offence seriousness in multiple-count cases and how they scale these factors and relate this assessment to an appropriate quantum of punishment. Where relevant implicit and explicit rules are identified, the task is to document them. The present study proceeds on the assumption that there should be such rules and, what is more controversial, that there should be a numerical aid giving effect to them. A finding that in judicial thought such rules are few and disparate would enhance not diminish the importance of the work, since it proposes a method designed to facilitate the formulation and representation of an agreed on, comprehensive and detailed set of rules. The present study is agnostic in regard to the appropriateness of what rules there are; it requires for significance simply that knowing what is facilitates discussion of what ought to be. Since the present study addresses the determination of proportionate sentences according to desert, the other component of the principled applica- tion of policy – the selection and mix of penal goals – is not dealt with here. This is something which could be added, as long as desert was primary.

The present project is an exercise in behavioral science and law. Although sentencing is a criminological topic, the present work should not be regarded as a criminological study, because the analysis is restricted to problems directly related to greater precision being introduced into the sentencing judgment and does not canvass broader issues associated with the development and imple- mentation of schemes for structuring the judicial sentencing discretion. While there would be several imperatives for a system of guidance based on the present analysis, it would leave open most matters relating to its source, style, scope and degree to which it was binding. Clearly, the form of guidance envisaged here is too detailed to be set out in legislation, and, in any case, because of this detail would require a level of expertise in sentencing not found in legislatures; but it could be devised by judges or a specially constituted body, such as a sentencing commission. Style is, of course, settled: written policy statements (words) and a related numerical decision aid (numbers). In view of the complexity of the guidance, in regard to both content and development, there would be little point to it unless it covered more rather than less of the sentencing decision. Nevertheless, in a highly individualized system of justice, as in England and Australia, it would not be appropriate to attempt to make it all-embracing, since it would not be practicable to cover the rare or possible to anticipate the novel. Finally, the nature of the guidance carries no requirement regarding whether it should be treated as binding or informative.

The immediately preceding matters, as well as being of significance *per se*, also relate to the implementation of the system and, particularly, whether the system of structuring discretion would promote justice and would be resistant to circumvention by the judiciary and prosecution. Again, these potential problems are criminological and outside the scope of the present study, which is limited to discovering and representing what sentencing policy is and to devising a means of formulating what it ought to be.

In regard to research, this is a study of how judges determine sentence. Now, because it is concerned with the structuring of the sentencing discretion, the variables are necessarily exclusively legal. Of course, a full understanding of judicial sentencing behavior would require factors tapping motivations and attitudes, an area beyond the scope of the present study, as is, for the reasons given earlier, research needed to inform matters relating to policy, the nature of the guidance and its implementation.

The nature of sentencing policy and the sentencing decision

The introductory discussion foreshadowed possible value in the development of sentencing guidelines, comprising comprehensive written policy statements and a numerical decision aid. This section justifies these goals.

Sentencing policy
The impetus for this and the first investigation (Lovegrove, 1989) was the author's unease over the current state of the art of sentencing and, in particular, the apparent vagueness and paucity of the principles comprising current sentencing policy and the rules governing the application of this policy. Indeed, for diagnostic purposes, the description of sentencing as subjective, qualitative and intuitive seems reasonable. Two undesirable consequences follow from this. First, it is often difficult or impossible to ascertain what particular aspects of a case are taken into account and how they affect the determination of sentence. Accordingly, debates about the proper content of sentencing policy are restricted: it is difficult to ascertain, except in the most general terms, what legal, jurisprudential and social-policy considerations underlie sentencing policy, and whether sentencing decisions are fair, soundly based, and reflect community values; moreover, there is a consequent stunting

of the development of a principled and sound sentencing policy. Secondly, a vague statement of sentencing policy must result in the inconsistent application of that policy. On matters on which there is no guidance or imprecise guidance, it falls to the individual judge to formulate policy and the rules for applying policy, and to the extent that sentencing lies with the individual judge, it will be to some extent idiosyncratic and may not always be well thought out. In such an important area of public policy this state of affairs is not acceptable. Under these circumstances, the judges' discretionary powers must be regarded as not sufficiently structured (see Davis, 1969). It follows that an aim of the present investigation, then, should be to ascertain empirically the current nature and content of sentencing policy and to apply relevant concepts and methods for the purpose of giving it a more objective, quantitative and deliberative character. This may not only require an express statement of the explicit and implicit working rules developed and now used by judges to give effect to the broad sentencing provisions and principles but also require judges to develop additional and more detailed explicit rules. Of course, there would be an unacceptable consequence associated with a fully structured sentencing policy: namely, that the opportunity for individualization and innovation in sentencing would be removed; in regard to the former, it would be impossible to cover every potentially relevant matter, and concerning the latter, allowance must always be made for new insights by sentencers and new developments in the treatment of offenders.

The Court of Criminal Appeal in Victoria has expressed its view of the nature of the sentencing judgment clearly and unequivocally. Three judgments in particular strike at the heart of the matter and support the preceding conclusions about the nature of sentencing policy. Adam and Crockett, JJ. made the following observation in *Williscroft and others* (1975:300):

> Now, ultimately every sentence imposed represents the sentencing judge's instinctive synthesis of all the various aspects involved in the punitive process ... it is profitless ... to attempt to allot to the various considerations their proper part in the assessment of the particular punishments presently under examination ...
>
> We are aware that such a conclusion [the decision of the appellate court in this case] rests upon what is essentially a subjective judgment largely intuitively reached by an appellate judge as to what punishment is appropriate.

And Young, C.J., Kaye and McGarvie, JJ. in *McCormack and others* (1981:111) asserted:

> The perils of seeking to make a logical progression from the sentence in one case to the sentence in another are well illustrated by Crisp, J. in *Wise v. R.*, (1965) Tas. S.R. 196, at pp. 200–201. He said: "Sentencing is an art and not a science. By that I mean that if in any given case it were possible to arrive at the exact measure of the

punishment to be awarded by the application of logical rules which proceeded with mathematical inevitability to a determinate conclusion, then indeed the judge's responsibility would be a different one from that which we know."

And this is the position today, expressly reaffirmed by Young, C.J., Crockett and Nathan, JJ. in *Young and others* (1990). The significance of this decision is that the sentencing judge in the course of determining sentence had relied on a structured approach; it appears that the judge sought first to determine "proportionate" sentences for each of the counts, on the basis of the facts of each offence, and then to reduce each of these sentences to arrive at "appropriate" sentences, having regard to matters personal to the offender. Indeed, the Court of Criminal Appeal in its judgment stated that the appeal raised important matters regarding the way in which courts should approach the sentencing task. In his report to the Court of Criminal Appeal the sentencing judge had said: "I have found that approach helpful in that it requires the sentencer to go about the sentencing task in a more orderly way and helps to ensure that all relevant matters are considered" (p. 952). However, the Court was not persuaded; in the judgment, the Court quoted the notion of instinctive synthesis with approval, and rejected decision processes connoted by the terms "rigid formulae," "staged or structured," "other formalised steps" and "objective facts," before concluding:

> It is sufficient for us to observe that we can find no warrant in authority or justification or advantage from a practical point of view in the adoption of an artificial process for arriving at an appropriate sentence or any process which unnecessarily limits further the discretion of a sentencing judge. We think that the adoption of such a process is calculated to lead to error and injustice. (pp. 960–961)

(See, also, the judgment of the Victorian Court of Criminal Appeal in *O'Brien*, 1991.)

To those taking a contrary view, what specifically are the undesirable characteristics of the traditional intuitive sentencing judgment? Simply, decisions regarding the selection, classification and the aggregation of information about a case are, to an unnecessary degree, unarticulated, subjective and qualitative. In selection, the relevance of certain factors is left open; the offender's employment status may be an example. For classification, the relative seriousness of instances of particular case factors is unclear; for example, the relative seriousness of the violence associated with a particular rape in relation to the range of violence shown in the commission of this legal category of offence. Regarding aggregation, the relative importance or weight of the various material factors and their lines of influence are largely untouched; for example, the importance of organization compared with violence, and how seriousness cumulates across factors. Judgments relating to these three matters are largely personal to the sentencer, and the possibility of quantifying the latter two aspects is not normally entertained. It will be seen in the last section in this chapter, "The multiple offender as a sentencing problem," that the conclusions drawn in this critical appraisal of sentencing policy considered generally also apply to that aspect of policy of concern in the present investigation, namely, the sentencing of the multiple offender.

This picture of the sentencing process apparently accurately describes the traditional sentencing judgment as it is to be found in other common-law countries such as England (see Ashworth, 1992a) and Canada (see Canadian Sentencing Commission, 1987).

About two decades ago in England there was a significant development in the nature of appellate sentencing judgments; it was the introduction of the guideline judgment by the Court of Appeal (Criminal Division). The relevance of this innovation to the present discussion is that these judgments offer a more structured approach to the description of sentencing policy in that they are more deliberative, quantitative and objective than the traditional judgments. Indeed, the Court has expressly stated that it is "aiming at uniformity of approach" (see the judgment in *Bibi*, 1980:361). Guideline judgments are delivered from time to time, take various forms and cover a range of matters including general policy, and recommended and forbidden patterns of reasoning (Ashworth, 1984). In comparison with the traditional sentencing judgment, some are similarly general, while others are quite specific (see Ashworth, 1984; and Harvey and Pease, 1987). In these judgments, the Court has for a significant number of legal offence categories covered one or more of the following matters: listed the relevant factors; indicated the relative serious-ness of several levels of at least one of the more important factors; considered the relative importance of two or more factors; and set out the ranges of sentence appropriate to particular patterns of offending. For one of the more detailed judgments see *Aramah* (1982) (for revisions, see *Aroyewumi and others*, 1995). Nevertheless, it can be reasonably concluded that in the guideline judgments taken as a whole, there is much room for improvement in the scope and detail of their coverage of the selection, classification and, especially, the aggregation of case facts. Indeed, the Court has recognized the inherent limitation of a legal analysis in respect of the aggregation of case facts, raising the point in *Gould and others* (1983) that it is difficult to give a precise indication of the appropriate sentence for a particular offence in advance because there are so many possible combinations of circumstances in the commission of an offence. See, also, the judgment in *Mussell and others* (1990), and Ashworth's (1992b) comment on it regarding the need for guidelines in view of the difficulty of comparing the seriousness of cases where the variation between them is in terms of numerous factual circumstances.

In view of the preceding discussion, the qualitative data from the present study – the judges' protocols and reflective reports – would be expected to reveal that the judges could not articulate a detailed and comprehensive account of how they apply the general provisions and principles relating to the sentencing of the multiple offender, but at best could articulate with varying clarity only unintegrated part-strategies, there being considerable disparity of response. Such a pattern and content in the verbal record would be consistent with thought characterized largely by intuition.

Now what would be expected to be the nature of this intuition? The psychological literature is of some help in this regard, distinguishing two forms of possible relevance. The notions of thought encapsulated by the two share common elements, but the difference is sufficient to warrant separate consideration. According to one view of intuition, the underlying thought processes, however rapid, are not consciously experienced; the decision makers have a ready apprehension of the problem, know immediately what course of action to take, but cannot explain their understanding or decision and do not reach these by inference (see, for example, Blattberg and Hoch, 1990; and Bunn, 1984). A second view of intuition is to be found in Kahneman and Tversky (1982); to these authors intuitive judgments are reasoned, but not characterized by structure, analytic methods or deliberate calculation. The first form appears to correspond to von Winterfeldt and Edwards's (1986) Intuition - I and the latter to their Intuition - R. But their expression of Intuition - R is sufficiently different to warrant presentation here: the answer or judgment is an approximation, there is no pretence of precision, it is reached with mental effort but without mental computational aids. Two of Abernathy and Hamm's (1995) descriptions of intuition, one as pattern recognition – the apparent instantaneous recognition in qualitative terms of a pattern of significance and with the knowledge of how correctly to respond to its appearance – and another as functional reasoning – a more or less immediate appreciation in quantitative terms of how the assessment about a situation changes as a function of variation in one or more of the comprising elements – parallel this distinction and further expand the two notions.

Pronouncements and reasoning of the appellate courts on the determination of quanta of sentence in regard to various combinations of patterns of offending and circumstances of offenders throw some light on the category into which judicial intuition would be expected to fall.

In the recent judgment of the Victorian Court of Criminal Appeal in *Scadden* (1993:7), Phillips, C.J. said:

This Court has often said that the question of whether a sentence is manifestly, as distinct from arguably, inadequate does not ordinarily admit of a great deal of argument. Upon inspection of it and identification of the relevant circumstances, it either appears to be manifestly inadequate or it does not.

An apparently similar sentiment was expressed in the Court of Appeal (Criminal Division) in England. In response to a 1985 editorial suggestion from the *Criminal Law Review* that the Court give guidance on the application of a particular statutory provision dealing with the degree of offence seriousness above which a non-custodial sentence cannot be justified, Lawton, L.J. rejoindered that the editor perhaps did not understand that judges can recognize an elephant without necessarily first referring to a definition of one (see Ashworth, 1994). These views appear to favor a "pattern recognition" interpretation of intuition.

However, the style of the reasoning in some appellate sentencing judgments suggests that judicial intuition has a significant component more in accordance with the "calculative" interpretation of intuition. Nevertheless, the determination of sentence generally appears at its most deliberative to involve the explicit listing of aggravating and mitigating factors in association with what amounts to little more than a descriptive calculus of addition, subtraction and cancellation of the effects of these factors. This approach applies both to the determination of whether custody is appropriate and the deserved length of imprisonment in a particular case as well as to the comparison of sentences across cases for the purposes of uniformity. The nature of this calculus is well illustrated in the judgment of the Victorian Court of Criminal Appeal in *Coltman* (1993:5); Phillips, C.J. said:

> The task of the sentencing Judge in this matter was one of considerable difficulty. It involved, in large part, arriving at a balance between the gravity of the applicant's crime on the one hand and the weight of a number of mitigating factors on the other. Plainly enough, the applicant's offence was a bad one. It was committed on a family in their own home; the premises were indeed somewhat isolated; it was committed at night; and the method used, namely terror, would not be felt the less because the applicant appeared uncertain and confused.
>
> In my opinion, the true mitigating factors in this matter lie almost entirely outside the offence itself. It is said it was amateurish, but the applicant procured a gun and effectively disguised himself. His selection of the Woods' house is not without significance. It is true, though, as the Judge found, that no great deal of premeditation was involved. Outside the offence the mitigating factors are, in my opinion, substantial. They are: the applicant's youth (he was, at the time of the offence, only eighteen years and six months); the absence of prior convictions; his early plea of guilty; his co-operation with the police; his efforts at rehabilitation before sentence – and other matters, such as his saving money to repay the debt and his letter of apology, which indicate remorse. (pp. 5–6)

It is clear enough, I think, that the Judge formed a serious view of the applicant's offence. It was plainly open to him to do so. It is also clear that his Honour regarded some mitigating factors, principally the applicant's youth, as, in effect, removing the offence from one warranting a sentence of imprisonment to one warranting detention in a Youth Training Centre. Having taken that step, the Judge, it seems to me, was unprepared to go further, and he imposed the maximum youth training sentence available. In my view, his Honour, in the particular circumstances of this case, erred in regarding his discretion as so constrained. The gravity of the applicant's crime demanded a custodial sentence, but the mitigating factors were such that not only did they make detention in a Youth Training Centre appropriate, but, in my opinion, they also made a sentence less than the maximum appropriate. (pp. 6–7)

Further evidence for the view of intuition as weakly calculative is to be found in the test the Victorian Court of Criminal Appeal applies to determine whether a sentence is in error, which includes, *inter alia*, the appropriateness of the factors taken into account and the weight given to them (see *Williscroft and others*, 1975).

The sentencing decision

The author's second concern over the state of the art of sentencing has its origin in the complexity of the sentencing decision. In a sentencing system involving multiple penal goals and a high degree of individualization, the sentencing judge has to synthesize intuitively a large number of offence and offender factors to determine what is appropriate by way of type and level of sentence for a particular case. It takes little imagination to understand that the typical case, requiring as it does the selection, weighting and aggregation of a large number of aggravating and mitigating circumstances, would exceed the quite limited capability possessed by humans, even experts, of processing information. And when a judge's capacity for information processing is overloaded, then certain factors will inadvertently be omitted, or included, or not given the weight the judge thinks is being given to them and, accordingly, sentencing decisions will be characterized by inconsistency and error. Indeed, Diamond (1981) has provided empirical evidence of the deleterious effects of complexity on sentencing decisions. In view of this, a second purpose of this investigation, then, should be to lay the conceptual and empirical foundation for an information system designed to assist the judge in classifying, weighting and aggregating case facts material to sentence. Of course, a framework providing guidance on the combined effect on sentence of more than the important and common case factors and relationships would be unwieldy. And discretion must reside with the sentencing judge to make allowance for the less significant and the new, as justice would require in individual cases. In view of the need to preserve individualization and innovation in sentencing, the role of the system of guidance must be circumscribed, namely, to reduce the degree to which judges must exercise their discretion intuitively and in the absence of a detailed policy applying to the circumstances of the case.

Studies of sentencing and sentencing guidelines for the multiple offender

The above review has pointed to the need for a detailed understanding of how judges apply the few broad principles of sentencing policy in particular cases and the desirability of there being a more detailed policy and a decision aid of some sort to assist judges in aggregating information about the manifold aspects of a case as they determine what is appropriate by way of sentence. The purpose of this section is to review in relation to the sentencing of multiple offenders the steps taken in these two directions.

Studies of the sentencing decision

Unfortunately, this part must necessarily be brief. In psychology and criminology there are a number of significant attempts to describe in a conceptual model incorporating legally relevant factors how sentences are determined in individual cases; for example, Hogarth (1971) and Hood and Sparks (1970). However, in these studies the dependent variable of sentence is not differentiated; to the author's knowledge none of the studies in this category analyzes separately the determination of the sentences appropriate to the counts comprising a case and the sentence appropriate to the case considered in its totality. And in behavioral science the number of empirical studies of the relationship between case fact and sentence in terms of legal factors is legion, mainly comprising archival studies – for example, Ebbesen and Konečni (1981), Moxon (1988), and Polk and Tait (1988) – but also including a small number of subjective analyses of decision making – for example, Lawrence (1988) and Palys and Divorski (1984). However, studies in this category have not always recognized multiple offending as part of the sentencing decision, and when they have studied this aspect of the problem, their treatment of the identification and definition of potentially relevant legal variables, let alone the way the various elements are combined, has been so narrow and general as to throw little light on the decision process; for example, the whole of this part of the decision is commonly represented by the number of multiple counts, no regard being had to other potentially relevant legal aspects, such as the seriousness of the principal and other counts and the seriousness and nature of the legal offence categories of which they are instances. Moreover, in the archival analyses, the aspect of policy covering the combination of factors is left uncritically to be described according to a standard statistical model; and while the subjective studies often treat combination as a part of sentencing policy it is handled qualitatively. Finally, again with exceptions generally among the subjective analyses, studies of the sentencing decision implicitly assume uniformity and present an averaged approach rather than attempting to portray diversity.

Sentencing guidelines for multiple offenders

There are a number of guideline schemes for the sentencing of multiple offenders; some remain as proposals, others have been implemented, and they vary in terms of the nature and precision of the guidance. The present discussion is confined to those schemes providing numerical guidance.

In England the Advisory Council on the Penal System (1978) saw the need to prevent an untrammelled approach to the sentencing of multiple offenders in which cumulative sentences for cases comprising multiple counts of minor or intermediate seriousness reach levels appropriate to serious acts of criminality. In this regard the Council proposed that the total sentence should not exceed the statutory maximum for the principal offence unless the criterion for exceeding the maximum is satisfied.

The disadvantage of this approach is that it is based on a limiting principle; it provides no guidance as to what is appropriate by way of a total sentence within this limit in cases comprising multiple counts. Moreover, where the statutory maxima for most of the offence categories are well above the levels of sentence typically imposed for single instances of these categories – and this is the case in most if not all common-law jurisdictions, see Sentencing Task Force (1989) – this type of principle would prevent only the worst and, indeed, obvious excesses. It should be noted, however, that this latter criticism does not apply to the Council's proposals, since it also recommended that maximum penalties for the various offence categories be fixed at the level below which 90 percent of prison sentences had been set by the courts in the recent past for individual instances of each of the offence categories. Clearly, this figure of 90 percent must be regarded as somewhat arbitrary. As a complement to this rigorous confining of the sentencing discretion at its upper reaches, perhaps because of it, the Council proposed that there should be provision for the courts to pass sentences of imprisonment exceeding the new maxima when this course was necessary to protect the public against serious harm. And it was noted that a case comprising a number of grave offences would almost certainly qualify for a sentence exceeding what in the absence of these exceptional circumstances would be the maximum sentence, i.e., the maximum sentence for the legal category of the most serious of the counts; yet for this type of case the Council offered no precise limiting principle.

The Canadian Sentencing Commission (1987), too, saw the necessity of confining the courts' sentencing discretion in the sentencing of multiple offenders. The Commission proposed that the total sentence should not exceed whatever is the lesser of the sum of the statutory maxima for the comprising offences or the statutory maximum for the principal offence enhanced by one third.

Like the Advisory Council on the Penal System (1978) the Commission also sought to make the maximum penalty structure reflect, *inter alia*, current sentencing practice to a greater degree. The outcome of this process would be a general lowering of the maximum penalties for offences. As well, the Commission similarly recommended there be provision for exceptional sentences: a maximum of a 50 percent enhancement on the maximum penalty for an offender who committed a serious personal injury offence carrying a high maximum penalty and who constituted a threat to public safety; but the total sentence for multiple offences could not be used in conjunction with this enhanced sentence for one offence. In view of the similarity of these two sets of proposals, the thrust of the evaluation of the Advisory Council on the Penal System's (1978) scheme can be applied to the Commission's approach, the main points being that it is based on a somewhat arbitrarily defined limiting principle and provides no guidance as to what is appropriate by way of a total sentence within these limits.

Hogarth (1986a, 1986b) in British Columbia, Canada, proposed a multi-faceted information system as an aid for sentencing judges. This brief exposition and critique of Hogarth's approach is confined to those aspects bearing on the quantification of the relationship between case fact and sentence.

The purpose of the system is to record the ranges of sentence for various combinations of offence and offender characteristics of cases determined in the jurisdiction. These material factors are identified on the basis of a legal analysis of sentencing law and policy and of its interpretation by individual judges. There is a separate classification of case factors for each legal offence category (or at least each group of closely related legal offence categories), although some factors are common, and the scheme comprises the more common material case factors and their associated categories. A large data base of recent cases is required, each case being filed according to its place in the classificatory scheme. The system is computer-based. The sentencer enters the case description in terms of the classificatory scheme, and the output is the sentences that have been imposed in the jurisdiction for cases with that particular combination of offence and offender characteristics.

The Judicial Commission of New South Wales is developing its Sentencing Information System along the lines proposed by Hogarth (Chan, 1991; Potas, 1990;[1] Weatherburn, Crettenden, Bray and Poletti, 1988). In relation to the problem of sentencing the multiple offender, this system has but one factor: it is the number of counts of the principal offence, for which there are two categories, namely, one and more than one count of the principal offence, although in certain types of case comprising multiple counts of the same kind (e.g., multiple thefts) there is provision for one important element of the offence to be cumulated (e.g., the value of the property). However, the output is limited to sentences for the principal count in cases where the sentences for the comprising counts were all made concurrent; total seriousness cannot be cumulated by way of the individual seriousness of the comprising counts and, more importantly in regard to the present study, the seriousness of a series of disparate counts (e.g., theft and burglary) cannot be cumulated.

Clearly, this delineation of offence factors does not adequately cover all of the considerations potentially relevant to the sentencing of the multiple offender. This problem arises from an inherent weakness in the system – it has a thirst for cases. As the number of factors and associated categories increases, so there is a dramatic increase in the number of cells – offence–offender combinations – in the guidelines. Clearly, unless for each offence classification there was a multitude of cases in the data base, many of the cells, particularly those representing the less common combinations, would have few if any cases; yet reliable guidance requires that each cell be well represented. This is its fatal flaw, particularly in a jurisdiction like Victoria, where in the higher courts, even for the more common offences, there are not large numbers of instances of the various offences before the courts in any one year. And this problem cannot be solved by incorporating cases from the distant past, because the effects of changes in sentencing policy and legislation on practice would be unknown. The effect of this is that the guidance cannot be based on more than a small number of the more common case factors and categories; it cannot be detailed. The problem arises because there is no rule covering how the various case facts are combined to determine an overall assessment of the case. With an aggregation rule it would not be necessary to have cells for the various offence–offender patterns in order to represent the relationship between the quantum of sentence and the facts of the case. What is required, then, is an understanding of how judges approach this aspect of the determination of sentence.

The second problem concerns the use of the guidance by judges in actual

[1]   Also, personal communication, 1993.

cases. It will be recalled that a decision aid must of necessity be limited to showing the combined effect on sentence of the more important and common case factors and relationships, its function being to provide a reference point against which judges can then exercise their discretion in allowing for the effects on sentence of less significant and novel considerations. In Hogarth's scheme it would be difficult for judges validly to estimate the effects on sentence of the unique elements in relation to the common case characteristics because the various combinations of the case characteristics are not systematically related by a logic, covering the importance of the various case factors and the rules for combining the information about the case, consistent with the judges' approach to the determining of an appropriate sentence. (The decision errors associated with this shortcoming would be exacerbated to the extent that the sentences in these guidelines were not the product of a common judicial policy applied reliably.) Two critical pieces of information are required here for the intelligent and accurate application of this guidance: (1) how the factors included in the system have been weighted and combined in the determination of the sentences in each of the cells; (2) the extent to which the sentences comprising each cell have been influenced by case factors not included in the guidelines. For a solution to this problem, as for the first, what is needed is a conceptual framework faithful to the structure of judicial thought as the basis of the system of guidance.

The third problem of Hogarth's approach becomes apparent in the light of considerations relating to sentencing policy. Clearly, this system of guidance can provide no more than consistency of sentence and then only in terms of coarse distinctions between cases and averages across disparate judges. A danger associated with an approach based on consistency of sentence is that the effects on sentence of material factors not included in the guidelines may be overlooked; moreover, it provides no means of moving towards the goal expressly established by the Court of Appeal (Criminal Division) in England in the judgment in *Bibi* (1980) when Lord Lane, C.J. called for uniformity of approach, which can be satisfied only by a detailed and comprehensive statement of sentencing policy.

The United States Sentencing Commission (1987a, 1987b, 1994) has developed and implemented numerical guidelines providing detailed guidance on what is appropriate by way of quantum of sentence in individual cases. This necessarily brief description of them does not do their complexity justice, but is sufficient for the purposes of this present discussion.

The guidelines are presented in the form of a two-dimensional grid, one dimension representing the seriousness of the legal category of the offence and incorporating the circumstances of the actual offence, and the other dimension covering the offender's criminal history. The guidelines provide for discriminations within and between offence categories. There is specific guidance for offences in regard to their base severity levels together with their associated aggravating offence-specific characteristics. For example, burglary of a residence is a category and one of the specific factors is whether the commission of the offence involved more than minimal planning. Offence seriousness is further differentiated according to aggravating and mitigating non-offence-specific factors, such as the offender's role in the offence. The seriousness of each offence's base level is quantified by a score. Also, the seriousness of each of the offence-specific and non-offence-specific factors is quantified by a score, and the scores for the factors applicable in a particular case are incorporated as adjustments to the base-level score to determine a score for the seriousness of the offence characteristics of the case. At this point the case can be placed in one of the forty-three levels on the dimension representing offence seriousness. The criminal history score is also measured in terms of several aspects, one being whether the present offence was committed while the offender was under sentence. In the grid there are six levels on the dimension representing the seriousness of the offender's criminal history. Each cell in the table shows whether a sentence of imprisonment is appropriate and, if it is, the length (presented as a range of 25 percent on the lower limit, except for the short presumptive sentences). The guidelines also permit departures by the sentencing judge in terms of factors in the guidelines as well as factors not mentioned. In the development of these guidelines regard was had primarily to past sentencing practice, although modifications were introduced on the basis of policy considerations by the Commission.

One of the non-offence-specific factors relates to multiple counts. It is the Commission's handling of this particular aspect of the sentencing decision which is, of course, of concern in the present study. Again, this necessarily brief description oversimplifies the Commission's approach. The Commission has developed rules for calculating a level (score) on the dimension of offence seriousness and accounting for the counts on which the offender has been found guilty. One general principle to which the rules give effect is that there be an increment in the penalty for each significant additional instance of criminal conduct. The most serious offence is used as the starting point, the other counts determining the quantum increase in the offence level. A second general principle is that the additional punishments cumulate by way of decreasing gains as the number of extra counts increases. The guidelines cover multiple counts relating to single and separate transactions, but only the latter are of interest and, hence, outlined here. There are three steps. First, counts in a multiple-count presentment are considered in one of two ways: (1) offences in which the guidelines determine the offence score primarily on the amount of money or quantity of the substance involved; for example, theft and drug trafficking; (2) offences relating to non-fungible harms; for example, robbery and burglary. The second step has two parts, the appropriateness of each being dependent on the preceding distinction. (1) In regard to counts in the first of the above two categories, closely related counts are grouped (e.g., a series of thefts or a larceny and a fraud) and an offence level is determined for each of these groups of counts; the level for each group is the score calculated using the aggregated quantity of the most important factor. For example, for a series of thefts, the guideline for theft is applied and the figure used for the value of the theft is the total of the amount taken in each of the counts; and where the offences are different but sufficiently similar to be grouped under this rule (e.g., a larceny and a fraud), the offence guideline that produces the highest offence level is used. (2) In regard to counts in the second of the above two categories, an offence level is determined for each of the counts. In the third step, the combined offence level is calculated, using as the base the offence level of the group or count with the highest score and increasing that level according to the (offence) seriousness of the additional count(s). Seriousness is measured in units, where:

(1) each additional count or group that is as equally serious as the base or is from one to four levels less serious than the base is worth one unit;
(2) each additional count or group that is five to eight levels less serious than the base is worth one-half unit;
(3) each additional count or group that is nine or more levels less serious than the base is ignored for the purposes of this calculation; and
(4) the base is equal to one unit.

The additional seriousness is equal to the sum of the units for these counts and is converted to offence levels according to the following scale:

No. of units	Increase in base offence level
$1\frac{1}{2}$	1
2	2
$2\frac{1}{2}$–3	3
$3\frac{1}{2}$–5	4
>5	5

There are two potential problems associated with the United States Sentencing Commission's guidelines. The first concerns the level of detail in the guidelines, the second the extent to which the empirical analyses permitted past sentencing practice to be reflected in the guidelines.

The Commission initially sought to describe case characteristics in a significantly greater level of detail than is to be found in its final product. However, the Commission abandoned this attempt at developing what it described as a pure real offence system on several grounds, two of which are relevant to the present discussion: (1) it would have had to decide precisely what factors are relevant to sentence and how the courts aggregate this information; (2) it found no practical way of representing the relationship between case fact and sentence for the potentially very large number of relevant case factors. In regard to the former, the analyses of the sets of archival data, either by systematic inspection of simple relationships in the data or by standard multivariate techniques applied to complex data sets, did not provide the required information (this point is elaborated in the discussion of the second problem); and in respect of the latter, the proposed mathematical solution was so complex as to be impracticable. For these reasons, the Commission accepted that it would have to be satisfied with a guidelines system in which there was a less than ideal number of distinctions within and across case characteristics and a simpler representation of the relationship between case fact and sentence. Accordingly, for the multiple offender there will be cases where the guidelines oversimplify the cumulation of seriousness. The following instances illustrate the general problem acknowledged by the Commission. In representing the seriousness of a group of closely related counts, the quantity of the most important offence factor is aggregated across counts; a problem would arise, for example, where there were differences between these counts in regard to the seriousness of the other material offence factors. And the Commission gave examples of circumstances under which the formula for determining the combined offence level may produce adjustments for the additional counts that are inadequate or excessive; for example, for a number of minor offences not grouped together the calculated increase in the sentence may be excessive. In respect of the sentencing of multiple offenders, Breyer (1992), a former Commissioner, recognized that the Commission's solution falls well short of capturing the complexity of this sentencing problem and that, accordingly, frequent departures from the guidelines may be required. The Commission takes the view that its guidelines will not always sufficiently provide for the degree of individuation necessary for just sentencing and, as a consequence, accords judges discretion within and outside the guidelines. An opinion and a finding are of relevance here to point out the resulting dilemma. Robinson (1986), then a Commissioner, in his dissenting opinion on the Revised Draft of the Commission's proposed guidelines, expressed the view that they represented in effect a failed attempt at capturing the complexity of the sentencing process; the guidelines were characterized by overwhelming complexity and yet failed to overcome the necessity for the sentencing judge to retain a considerable discretion – the source of disparity and the reason for the sentencing system's need of guidelines. And experience has shown that appellate courts have favored the view that where the Commission has adopted a rule or policy the matter must be regarded as having been adequately covered; accordingly, the grounds for departures appear to be exceedingly limited (see Tonry, 1992).

Now to the second matter, concerning the extent to which the empirical analyses permitted past practice to be reflected in the guidelines. This is a fair question to ask about the Commission's research program, because it was expressly stated by the Commission that in the first stage of the development of the guidelines it was appropriate that heavy reliance be placed on past practice and, indeed, departures from the status quo incorporated in the guidelines in this initial phase be made where possible as reasoned and conscious modifications to current practice. Ideally, then, the Commission required an empirical strategy that would provide it with an accurate, detailed and comprehensive picture of current practice – the case factors, and their associated categories, underlying the determination of sentence; the importance attached to these factors in this decision; and the rules for aggregating this information in determining what is appropriate by way of quantum of sentence for the possible combinations of these factors. To get information on these three matters, the Commission ran simple and multivariate statistical analyses on various sets and subsets of archival data, including conviction and pre-sentence reports and information held by the prison and parole authorities; these data were supplemented by analyses of the policies of relevant bodies and officers in the justice system. The Commission's estimates – to use its own term – of current practice were based on what appeared to be to some extent an intuitive synthesis of the results of its analyses of the various data sets, and were restricted to the more significant offence factors, their principal categories, and their relative importance. The Commission resiled from modelling the component of policy covering the rules for aggregating the elements of a case on the grounds that there is not a consistency of approach between judges in their decision making and the complexity of the nature of this aspect of the determination of sentence. The Commission's reference to the analysis and description of current practice in relation to multiple counts illustrates the position: the guidelines are not based on a detailed empirical analysis, rather they simply conform to the observation that sentence length increased, though at a decreasing rate, with the number of offences or the total harm. It seems reasonable to conclude that the types of analysis adopted by the Commission were not capable of providing it with an accurate, detailed and comprehensive description of current policy and practice.

In summary, the task of developing an appropriate and adequate decision aid for judges in their determination of what is appropriate by way of quantum of sentence for a particular set of case facts remains a problem to be solved. Attempts have foundered because there has been a failure to develop means of ascertaining and representing current sentencing policy and practice, especially in relation to the aggregation of information about cases, in sufficient detail and in a way consistent with the structure of judicial thought.

The multiple offender as a sentencing problem

This section sets out sentencing law, policy, and legal considerations and justifications relating to how judges should attempt to determine the effective (maximum) sentence of imprisonment for a case comprising multiple counts where each offence is properly regarded as a separate transaction. In this type of case the counts may be of the same kind or the counts may belong to more than one legal offence category. This sentencing problem would arise, for example, where the offender is to be sentenced on a presentment comprising one count of armed robbery and two counts of burglary, and the offences relate to separate incidents. The purpose of this discussion is to seek clues from the law about the approach judges should adopt in this type of case, the purpose of this being to develop a model of this aspect of judicial decision making. A model constructed on this basis will be what may be termed an ideal model of decision making, i.e., how judges should determine effective sentences in the light of sentencing policy. It would seem intuitively clear that a model of ideal judicial decision making is the appropriate basis for under-standing current policy and developing a system of guidance. There may be, of course, significant discordance between ideal and actual decision processes, since the latter are partly the product of distorting influences, such as information overload arising from the complexity of cases.

In Victoria, Australia, the court when sentencing offenders convicted of multiple counts, properly considered as separate transactions, imposes a sentence for each one of the counts, together with an effective (maximum) sentence and, for effective sentences of twelve months' imprisonment or more, it may and almost invariably does set a minimum term. The effective sentence is not normally the sum of the individual sentences; although the court may order that these sentences be served cumulatively, it typically makes orders of partial concurrence between the individual sentences so that the effective sentence is less than the sum of the individual sentences, full concurrence not normally being considered appropriate for separate serious offences. The sentence for each count should properly reflect the gravity of that particular count. Moreover, the effective sentence should be of a degree of severity appropriate to the seriousness of the criminal conduct viewed as a whole; this is what Thomas (1979) has called the totality principle. The High Court of Australia has in decisions referred to the totality principle with approval (see *Griffiths*, 1989; and *Mill*, 1988).

Generally, orders of partial concurrence are necessary to give effect to the requirement of appropriateness of sentence in respect of both the individual counts and the case; this is because the sum of a series of appropriate individual sentences would normally result in an inappropriately harsh effective sentence, while with full concurrence the appropriate sentence of only one of the counts can contribute to the total with the effect that the effective sentence would be in most instances unduly lenient.

The Victorian Court of Criminal Appeal in its judgment in *Tutchell* (1979:252) gave some indication of the way in which courts should approach the determination of sentence for multiple offenders. McInerney, Menhennitt and McGarvie, JJ. said:

> One of the first decisions in a case such as this is whether to impose sentences of imprisonment or non-custodial sentences ... An important consideration in making this decision is the seriousness of the ten offences considered separately and in the aggregate. If imprisonment is decided to be the appropriate form of sentence, the judge would then impose a sentence on each count. In considering the orders of concurrency to be made and the effective sentence to result from those orders, the judge would consider the individual offences and sentences and also the offences and sentences in the aggregate. Similarly in deciding on the minimum period to be served before becoming eligible for parole the judge would consider the individual offences and sentences and also consider them as a whole. At each of the stages of deciding whether to impose custodial sentences or not, what concurrency orders are to be made, and what minimum sentence is to be imposed, the weighting given to each offence is most important.

The totality principle not only applies to single presentments comprising multiple counts; it also may apply to multiple sentences arising from more than one presentment. What is required for the totality principle to be invoked is that the temporal proximity between the offender's serving of the sentences is such that the offender may be regarded as being currently subject to more than one sentence; for example, when an offender is sentenced on a second presentment while serving a term of imprisonment for sentences relating to an earlier presentment. (For more information on Victorian law relating to the sentencing of the multiple offender, see Fox and Freiberg, 1985; and Fox, 1993.)

In England, the courts in determining whether a custodial sentence is appropriate for an offender convicted of a series of offences were restricted by statute in 1992 to assessing the seriousness of the offence characteristics of the case in terms of the most serious offence or combination of the most serious two offences, although reference could be made to circumstances surrounding the other offences to the extent that they disclosed aggravating aspects of the two offences. In 1993 an amendment removed this restriction, so that the courts in determining seriousness could have regard to all the offences for which the offender is being sentenced. Now, as before, where the threshold of seriousness for custody is passed, the determination of what is appropriate by way of sentence for the case is to be based on the seriousness of all the comprising counts considered together, according to the totality principle. A matter worthy of comment is that in England the device of partial concurrency is not available, the effect of this being that the courts, in applying the totality principle to a case comprising multiple counts, are often not able to fix sentences for these counts which are better than a crude reflection of their individual gravity and, as a consequence, not truly appropriate sentences. (See, generally, Ashworth, 1992a, 1992b; Ashworth and Gibson, 1994; Judicial Studies Board, 1993; and Thomas, 1992.)

The question of how the court should determine the appropriate effective sentence in a case comprising multiple counts remains. The law provides no answer and little direction regarding the path to the solution. Thomas (1979) has made a systematic analysis of the practice of the English Court of Appeal (Criminal Division) in a search for the principles underlying its decisions on sentence. As a part of the results of his analysis Thomas set out a decision framework which appeared to him to capture the approach adopted by the courts for this sentencing problem. He expressed the principle in three different forms:

- the aggregate sentence must not be "... substantially above the normal level of sentences for the most serious of the individual offences ..." (p. 57);
- "...the aggregate sentence should not be longer than the upper limit of the normal bracket of sentences for the category of cases in which the most serious offence committed by the offender would be placed" (p. 59);
- the aggregate sentence may be "... longer than the sentence which would be passed for the most serious offence if it stood alone ..." but must bear "... some recognizable relationship to the gravity of that offence" (p. 59).

The meanings of the first and the third forms of the principle are clear and obviously equivalent. The interpretation of the second is obscure and requires an understanding of Thomas's framework for tariff sentencing; this is explained in the next chapter. Thomas, in presenting his analysis, makes no distinction between cases comprising multiple counts belonging to the same or different statutory offence categories.

To the matter of deciding whether the sum of the individual appropriate sentences exceeds the quantum of sentence appropriate to the overall seriousness of the offender's current criminality, Thomas's (1979) analysis of appellate judgments offers partial guidance: the sum of the individual sentences may be excessive if its severity is appropriate to an offence belonging to a significantly more serious class of crime. Where this occurs, there has been insufficient constraint on cumulation. The idea, illustrated in Ashworth's (1992a) terms, is that no number of counts of a minor offence (e.g., a middle-range intentional damage to property – exclusive of arson) nor a moderate number of offences of medium seriousness (say, middle-range burglaries) could amount to the heinousness of one count of a serious offence (perhaps a middle-range rape). The point of the preceding decision framework of Thomas (1979) is to prevent an untrammelled cumulation of sentence in multiple-count cases.

There is, according to Thomas (1979), a second guiding consideration associated with the totality principle: it is that the sentence must not crush the offender in respect of his or her prospects of returning to the community a reformed person. Considered in terms of its general application to cases, its potential as a relevant factor increases with the sum of the sentences for the comprising individual counts. Whether, and how, it is applied in individual cases is tied to the presence of mitigating characteristics unique to the offender, such as youth. (See, also, Fox and Freiberg, 1985.) Since the present study does not deal with offender characteristics, the application of this second element of the totality principle by judges to individual cases is not analyzed further in this discussion.

From Thomas's (1979) analysis it has been possible to adumbrate a framework for the decision governing the fixing of effective sentences; but Thomas does not cover the interrelationship between the seriousness/sentences associated with individual counts and the overall seriousness of the case and the effective sentence appropriate to it. Accordingly, it offers some guidance to the sentencing judge, but only to the extent that rough indications could be made available for the various legal offence categories from statistical data describing sentencing practice (e.g., the quantum of sentence appropriate to the most serious of the multiple counts). However, this guidance is obviously coarsely calibrated, because the scheme offers no rational basis for making gradations and setting limits in relation to the framework. While the conceptual basis of this scheme can be regarded as helpful, but certainly not adequate, for the purpose of guidance in cases comprising multiple counts for which a sentence of imprisonment would be appropriate for each of the counts considered alone, it does not cover cases in which each of the comprising counts standing alone would not be sufficiently serious to warrant a term of imprisonment.

In his review of relevant judgments of the English Court of Appeal (Criminal Division), Ashworth (1992a) offers some insight into how gradations should be made within the framework describing the sentencing of multiple offenders and the justification for this approach. Ashworth sets out the Court's approach by way of an illustration of a case comprising multiple counts of car theft, each one of similar gravity and, in the light of the offender's circumstances, warranting a term of imprisonment of one year. The proposed effective sentences are fictitious but said by him to be consistent with the principle followed by the Court; the effective sentence for 2, 3, 5, 10 and 20 counts is set at 18, 22, 25, 30 and 36 months, respectively. The principle is that each additional count adds a quantum of sentence to the running effective sentence, but each increase is less than the preceding one. Clearly, Ashworth's example can be taken as no more than illustrating the way in which the effective sentence relates to the sentences for the individual counts, and not to the way in which the Court constructs a sentence by way of actual concurrency orders; indeed, in a jurisdiction where the device of partial concurrency is not available, the construction of an effective sentence in the judgment cannot mirror the principle. A justification for the determination of effective sentences according to a principle of decreasing gains in the quanta of sentence for additional multiple counts is that it allows a sentencer at once to give effect to the import of the totality principle – proportionality between sentence severity and the seriousness of different classes of crime – and to ensure that the additional seriousness associated with multiple counts of a particular class of crime is punished (see, also, Ashworth, 1983).

As a result of this analysis it has been possible to sketch a tentative outline for a decision model describing the sentencing of multiple offenders in cases comprising separate transactions. Nevertheless, the analysis is riddled with conceptual blank spaces; the structure of the model must be developed; it is so spare in its current state that it could not be used to determine with any degree of precision the overall seriousness of a case comprising multiple counts and the quantum of sentence appropriate to this seriousness. Nevertheless, this derived outline does give some indication of the form a decision model for the sentencing of multiple offenders should take in order for it be consistent with these legal analyses. With this background it is now necessary to take the development of the model further and to inform the framework with the precision necessary to develop consistency of approach and a system of numerical guidance. This analysis first turns to multiple offences of the same kind; this problem has been investigated previously (Lovegrove, 1989) and it is necessary to re-present this solution and to interpret it in the light of the present discussion. Then the analysis turns to the subject of the present book – cases comprising multiple counts from separate statutory offence categories.

A sentencing decision model: single and multiple similar counts

Lovegrove (1989) developed a decision model describing how judges determine what is appropriate by way of sentence for a case comprising a single count, or multiple counts belonging to the same legal offence category (e.g., multiple burglaries) and properly regarded as separate transactions. The purpose of the model was to provide the basis for a numerical formula for calculating the overall seriousness of a case described in terms of several common offence factors and, then, relating this result to the appropriate quantum of sentence. The product of this work was a numerical guideline. In the achieving of this aim, it was necessary to develop a conceptual scheme representing a solution to what Ashworth (1983) identified as the problem of integrating the seriousness of two or more offences of one kind into a coherent system of proportionality principally related to the seriousness of single offences or classes of offence. So that the model was faithful to the structure of judicial thought it was based on an analysis of sentencing policy – policy dealing with the determination of sentence for particular legal categories of offence. This aspect of sentencing policy, also, is characterized by generality and incompleteness; yet a quantitative analysis demanded precision. Accordingly, it was necessary to develop the model further, and this was achieved by formulating sentencing exercises for the purpose of facilitating judicial input on matters of detail. This study is described in summary by way of introduction to the present research, since it provides the foundation for the solution to the present problem, namely, developing a decision model describing how judges determine what is appropriate by way of sentence for a case comprising multiple counts, properly regarded as separate transactions and belonging to different legal offence categories.

Now to the author's model of judicial decision making for the sentencing of cases comprising single counts and multiple counts from the same offence category; offence characteristics relating to sentence are covered but not the circumstances of offenders. The model is a representation of decision making in the light of current sentencing policy and practice; it is a model of ideal decision making, because it takes account of neither judicial prejudices, the illogicalities and limitations of human information processing, nor judicial ignorance of sentencing policy. Its progenitor is the English legal academic David Thomas's account of the nature and structure of the judicial determination of sentence, based on his analysis of judgments of the Court of Appeal (Criminal Division) in England; this analysis appears to be the only substantial attempt to offer an account of the legal considerations that do or should more or less consciously exercise the minds of judges as they apply sentencing policy in individual cases. Accordingly, Thomas's (1979) work was used as a point of departure for the present analysis.

According to Thomas, the judge must first decide whether the sentence ought to emphasize the seriousness of the offence or whether the rehabilitation prospects of the offender should be the salient determinant of sentence. (Thomas used the terms "tariff sentence" and "individualized measure" to denote these respective approaches.) This is the primary sentencing decision, and normally turns on the seriousness of the offence and the strength of the offender's rehabilitation prospects. In practice, a tariff sentence is usually an amalgam of the aims of retribution, deterrence and denunciation. When a tariff sentence is determined to be appropriate, the judge's task is to fix a term of imprisonment so that it is proportional to the culpability of the offender: this is dependent upon the seriousness of the circumstances of the offence and, normally, any factors acting by way of mitigation to reduce the offender's culpability. And where a judge opts for an individualized measure, it is a matter of selecting from among the non-custodial sentences the disposition most likely to maximize the offender's chances of rehabilitation. These are the secondary decisions. Nevertheless, it would appear that two qualifications must be made in order to apply this analysis to Victorian sentencing practice. First, a non-custodial sanction may be imposed on the grounds of proportionality. Secondly, there may be considerable overlap between the tariff and the individualized approaches, such that not infrequently regard to an offender's rehabilitation may moderate the quantum of imprisonment which would have otherwise been deemed appropriate on the grounds of culpability but not be seen as justifying a non-custodial option.

In the determination of sentences, then, there are two types of decision making. One type is quantitative, where the sentencer must develop and refer to an implicit scale of seriousness based upon the relevant offence and offender characteristics of the case. This scale is used in part to determine whether a tariff sentence is appropriate and, if it is, it acts as a basis for the judge's fixing of the type and quantum of sentence. The second type of decision involves qualitative assessments in which case characteristics, either singly or in combination, are used as indicators of the appropriateness of a tariff sentence or an individualized measure and, if the latter, the measure most appropriate to the offender's rehabilitative needs. In illustrating the development of the decision model, the present discussion is confined to the scaling of seriousness and the proportionality between seriousness and quantum of imprisonment in the determination of a tariff sentence.

Thomas defined the tariff as a framework to which a sentencer can refer in order to determine what factors in a particular case are relevant and the weight that should be attached to each of them. He proposed that judges follow three steps to determine the quantum of sentence.

(1) Defining the range. The assumption behind the tariff is that within a legal category of offence, such as burglary, a variety of factual situations relating to the offence will recur, and that for each set of factual situations (category of cases) there are upper and lower limits within which the sentence is presumed to fall (normal bracket of sentences) in the absence of exceptional circumstances relating to the offence and without regard to mitigating circumstances relating to the offender. (The terms in parentheses are taken from the second form of Thomas's, 1979, statement of the totality principle; see Chapter 1.)

(2) Fixing the ceiling. Typically, the judge's task is to relate the facts of the offence to one of the established patterns for that type of offence and then to locate the established range of sentence for that particular set of facts. The "ceiling" sentence for any particular offence is determined by adding (or subtracting) the effects of aggravating (or extenuating) factors in relation to the sentence range for the group in which the particular offence is most appropriately placed.

(3) Reducing the sentence to allow for the effects of mitigating factors.

For technical reasons, however, patterns of offending are not satisfactory as units of analysis. Indeed, Thomas found that he could not delineate patterns of offending for his analysis of burglary; one reason for this was that burglary covers such a wide range of factual situations. Rather, he merely characterized burglary according to one or more case factors in an unsystematic fashion and, accordingly, failed to provide a logical structure in which combinations of case characteristics are systematically and precisely related to sentence. One way of overcoming this problem would be to classify offences not according to groups, but in relation to a set of dimensions and defining levels (e.g., a dimension of financial loss, the levels being specified by monetary values). Indeed, the use of dimensions and levels seems implicit in judicial thinking. For one can discern from Thomas's descriptions of various patterns of offending that many of the defining characteristics (e.g., violence) or their contrasts (no violence) recur across groups.

The present illustration of the development of the model of decision making is limited to the determination of the "ceiling" tariff sentence for all possible combinations of the offence characteristics incorporated in the guidelines, and is particularized in relation to cases of burglary of a dwelling for financial gain.

A set of dimensions (and defining levels) which it seemed would comprehensively describe offences of burglary was identified and defined. Source material for this analysis was provided principally by legal analyses of sentencing judgments in England (Thomas, 1979, 1982, as updated), Canada (Ruby, 1980), and in several Australian states (Daunton-Fear, 1977, 1980; Newton, 1979), as well as case factors which were found in the data collected for an archival study of sentencing decisions in the higher courts in Victoria (Lovegrove, 1989). On the basis of this review it was decided that cases of burglary could be comprehensively described according to the following general dimensions: the total value of the money and property stolen (*total value of the theft*), the number of counts of burglary (*counts of burglary*), the degree of organization characterizing the count(s) (*organization*), and the amount of violence and property damage associated with the counts (*violence to the victims*). Fox and Freiberg's (1985) analysis of appellate sentencing judgments in Victoria confirmed the validity of these four offence factors as determinants of the seriousness of burglary.

The advantage of the dimensional solution is that Thomas's (1979) framework is no longer restricted to the varieties of offending within a legal offence category but can be applied to the range of seriousness associated with the legal category. This point is taken up later in this chapter.

The first element of the sentencing decision – the identification of the material offence factors – could be determined satisfactorily on the basis of the legal literature, since there is an extensive quality literature on this topic and it is not marked by significant contention. However, the other elements of the sentencing decision – the classification of case facts in relation to these factors, the weighting of the case factors, the rules for combining the case factors, and the appropriate types and levels of sentence for the various combinations of case factors – have not been adequately specified. For example, consider the matter of weighting the four offence characteristics of burglary. The only guidance which could be discerned from the appellate court judgments was that extreme forms of each of these offence characteristics have been mentioned where the courts have stressed the gravity of particular cases. Fortunately, there is a formal and well-established method for eliciting and handling this information, known as multi-attribute utility measurement (MAUM). MAUM is both an approach to the study of how individuals make decisions as well as a set of techniques for analyzing and investigating decision making (see, for example, Bunn, 1984; Edwards and Newman, 1982; Keeney, 1977; Keeney and Raiffa, 1976; von Winterfeldt and Edwards, 1986; and Watson and Buede, 1987).

How does MAUM characterize decision making and how does it apply in the present context? First, there is the decision – here it is the assessment of the seriousness of offences of burglary. (It ought to be noted that MAUM procedures cannot be applied directly to the study of sentencing, since determining what is appropriate by way of sentence for an element of a case is meaningless. Moreover, not all cases for which non-custodial sentences are imposed are equally serious.) Secondly, there are the criteria (offence attributes) upon which the overall seriousness of the offence characteristics of a case is to be based – the offence characteristics identified are *violence to the victims, organization, counts of burglary* and *total value of the theft*. Thirdly, it is necessary to develop a seriousness scale for each attribute to show how seriousness varies with changes in the objective values (e.g., the number of counts) along each attribute. At this point an offence of burglary is represented by four assessments of seriousness – one for each attribute. Fourthly, there is the determination of the relative weight of each of the attributes in the overall assessment. Finally, MAUM offers a number of formal models specifying how the single-attribute seriousness assessments may be combined, taking account of the weights, to provide an overall assessment of the seriousness of the offence characteristics of the case; for each model there is a set of assumptions to be satisfied for its validity. It will be immediately obvious that MAUM's characterization of the structure of a decision is isomorphic with Thomas's (1979) model of the judicial determination of offence seriousness for a tariff sentence, as that model has been modified here.

In the light of this background, this discussion now considers the classification of case facts in relation to the four material offence factors. This is achieved by developing scales of relative seriousness for each of the offence factors in relation to objective, case-specific facts. First, it is necessary to identify the content of each factor. For example, for the factor *total value of the theft* the content is amounts of money representing the value of the cash and merchandise stolen. Then, a range is established for the factor; the levels marking the extremes should represent maximum and minimum plausible

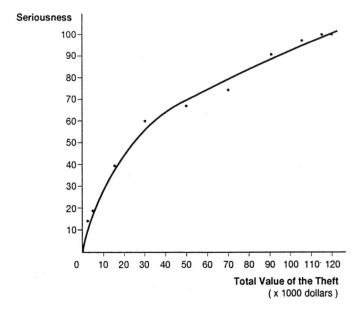

Figure 2.1 Seriousness scale for _Total Value of the Theft_

values, and may be based on the estimates of experts or actual case data. The content and values were based on Lovegrove's (1989) previously mentioned archival study of sentencing for a sample of cases of burglary determined in the higher courts in Victoria. The upper limit on this factor was accordingly set at $120,000; this is about the value of the total amount of the theft in the case which was most extreme on this factor. The lower limit was set at $100.

The range and content for each of the three other offence factors were determined similarly. For example, the objective scale value marking the lowest level of seriousness on _violence to the victims_ was "victim not at home," and the highest level was "assault of victim – offender initiated" (illustrated in this study as: the home-owner returned home to find a burglar in the house; before the offender ran off, he threatened to strike the victim with a metal object and then bound his hands and feet).

A group of seven judges of the County Court, all experienced in the criminal jurisdiction, participated in a study to investigate the feasibility of judges making input into the model of the determination of what is appropriate by way of sentence. This was done by means of a series of sentencing exercises. The first exercise involved each judge individually in developing a seriousness scale for each of the four offence factors. In this task a number of objectively

Scale value	Case-factor level
100	assault of victim – offender initiated
95	assault of victim – victim in pursuit
90	
80	
70	
65	threat of assault of victim – offender initiated
60	threat of assault of victim – victim in pursuit
50	
40	victim at home – offender left when seen by victim
30	on victim's return, offender decamped – running past victim
20	victim at home – offender avoided confrontation
10	
0	victim not at home

Figure 2.2 Seriousness scale for *Violence to the Victims*

defined levels was presented for each of the offence factors – the levels for *total value of the theft* were $2,000, $5,000, $15,000, $30,000, $50,000, $70,000, $90,000, $105,000 and $115,000 – and each judge was required to rate the relative seriousness of these levels on a 0–100 interval scale and in relation to the two extreme levels – $100 and $120,000. The seriousness scale for *total value of the theft* of one of the judges is shown in Figure 2.1. This figure is the numerical representation of this element of sentencing policy for this particular judge. Figure 2.2 shows the same judge's seriousness scale for *violence to the victims*. (Since these are interval scales, the zero point on the dimension does not connote that there is no seriousness associated with a level lying at this point; the numbers, therefore, are measures of relative seriousness.)

In the second exercise, judges quantified the relative weights (contributions) of the four factors in the determination of the overall seriousness of an offence. Relative weight may vary across offence factors. Operationally, this means that the increase in perceived seriousness from the least serious (usually

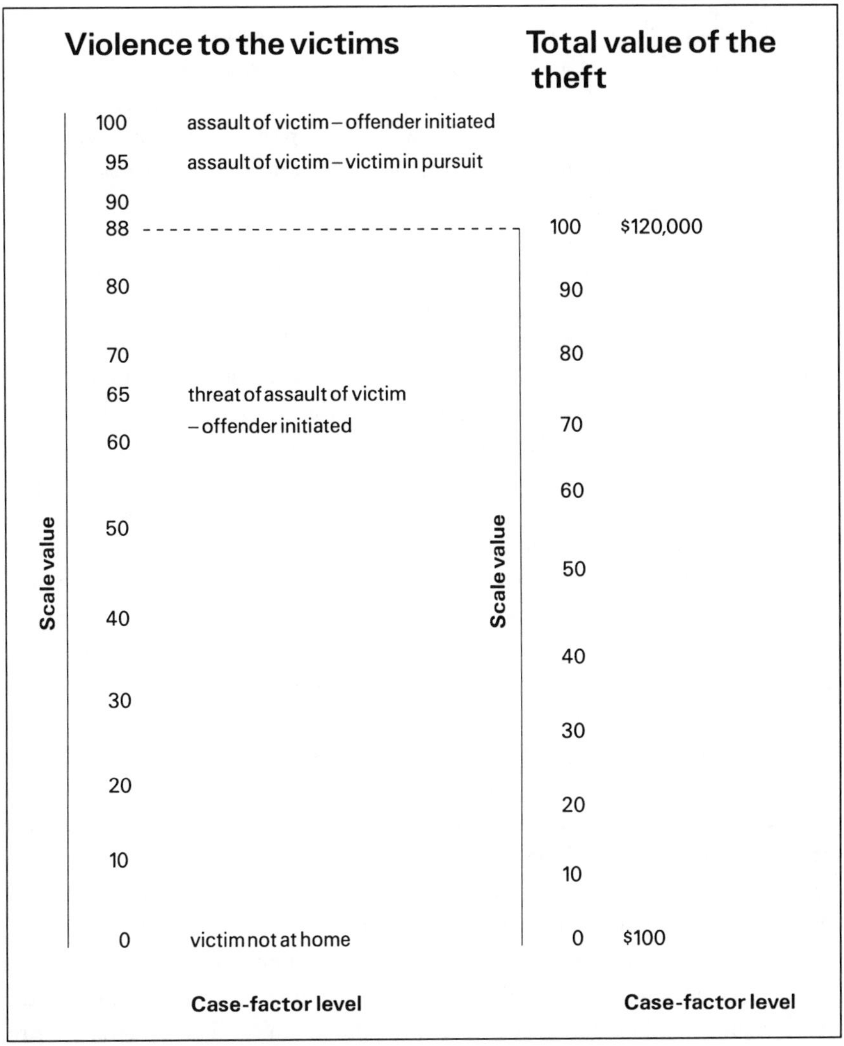

Violence to the victims	Total value of the theft
100 assault of victim – offender initiated	
95 assault of victim – victim in pursuit	
90	
88 - ┐	100 $120,000
80	90
70	80
65 threat of assault of victim	
60 – offender initiated	70
	60
50	
	50
40	
	40
30	
	30
20	
	20
10	
	10
0 victim not at home	0 $100
Case-factor level	Case-factor level

Scale value (Violence to the victims) · Scale value (Total value of the theft)

Figure 2.3 Relative weight of *Violence to the Victims* in relation to *Total Value of the Theft*

assigned a seriousness value of 0) to the most serious (usually assigned a seriousness value of 100) objective level of a factor may vary across the offence factors comprising offence seriousness. The reason for this is that the values of "0" and "100" may represent different degrees of seriousness across the factors, arising from differences in importance and range. In this exercise each judge's task was to determine, for each of the possible pairs of offence factors, the factor with the potential to make the greater contribution and then to establish the level on this factor at which the difference in seriousness between this level of seriousness and its least serious level is equal to the difference in seriousness between the most serious and least serious levels on the other factor. Figure 2.3 shows the way in which the previously mentioned judge viewed the relative weights of *total value of the theft* and *violence to the victims*. This figure is the numerical representation of this element of sentencing policy for this particular judge: it shows that *total value of the theft* has the potential to make .88 of the contribution of *violence to the victims* to the assessment of the overall seriousness of the offence characteristics.

In order to determine the overall seriousness of the offence characteristics of a burglary the assessments of seriousness on each of the component offence factors must be aggregated, having regard to the factor weights. This in turn raises the matter of the nature of the composition rule. Now, Thomas (1979) on the basis of his analysis of the judgments of the English Court of Appeal (Criminal Division) has identified the line of reasoning which judges appear to attempt to follow in order to quantify offence seriousness on the basis of the facts of the offence. From his discussion it appears that judges arrive at a quantum judgment by adding (or subtracting), as it were, points for aggravating (or extenuating) circumstances surrounding the offence. Moreover, one may deduce implicitly that the determination of offence seriousness should be neither super- nor sub-additive: the overall assessment of seriousness, then, should not be greater or less than the sum of the components, because Thomas expressly provides for interaction only between certain combinations of mitigating factors. In the light of this discussion, the simplest veridical composition rule describing the judicial determination of the quantum of seriousness of an offence is described by a weighted additive value function: this rule states that to determine the overall seriousness of an offence the single-attribute seriousness assessments on each offence factor are multiplied by the appropriate factor weight and then these multiples are summed; in this joint value function the relative weights add to unity. The equation representing this rule is the formal statement of this element of sentencing policy.

Once the judge's sentencing policy in respect of seriousness scales and relative weights had been ascertained for the two other offence factors – *counts of burglary* and *organization* – it then would be possible to determine, according to that policy, the relative overall seriousness of offences of burglary for all possible combinations of levels on these four major constituent offence factors.

Consider a case of multiple burglary in which the total value of the theft is $50,000, in one count there is an offender-initiated assault on the victim, and the case comprises sixteen counts. From Figures 2.1, 2.2 and 2.5 it follows that for this judge the seriousness ratings on *total value of the theft, violence to the victims* and *counts of burglary* are 69, 100 and 58, respectively. Assume the relative seriousness of the case in regard to *organization* is 100. Assume, also, the judge rated the relative weights of the four factors *counts of burglary, violence to the victims, total value of the theft* and *organization* in the proportions 31, 25, 22 and 22, respectively (note, 22 is .88 of 25). Accordingly, this judge's assessment of the relative seriousness of the offence characteristics of this case of burglary on a 0–100 scale is 80 (58 × .31 + 100 × .25 + 69 × .22 + 100 × .22).

The analysis to this point has dealt with the scaling of offence seriousness; the product is a decision model describing how judges determine the overall seriousness of the offence characteristics of a case of burglary.

The final element of the sentencing decision is the determination of the types and quanta of sentence appropriate to the various combinations of these four offence characteristics. To determine the relationship between case seriousness and sentence, the judges' final exercise consisted of a set of forty-one cases of burglary of a dwelling, for which they were asked to fix appropriate effective sentences. Each of the cases represented a different pattern of offending based on the levels comprising the preceding four offence factors, and were distributed across the range of overall offence seriousness. (The descriptions of the offence characteristics were presented in the form of comprehensive summary descriptions, as in the present study.) So that the judges could fix a sentence for each case, it was necessary to incorporate offender characteristics (prior convictions and personal mitigation) with the offence characteristics; these were presented in a similar degree of detail. (An illustrative case taken from the present study is presented in Appendix 1.) Since the focus of the study was tariff sentencing in respect of offence factors, the offender characteristics had to be related to the offence characteristics so that judges would have no alternative but to attempt to make the sentence proportional to the seriousness of the case (rather than impose a sentence for which the main or substantial aim was rehabilitation) and would not be able to make allowance for mitigation. From Thomas's (1979) analysis of the principles of sentencing it follows that these conditions would be satisfied where the offender had an extensive record of relevant prior convictions and very little credit available by way of a plea in mitigation. Since the point of interest here was the judges' fixing of sentence in relation to offence seriousness, the offender characteristics were held constant. (Again, Lovegrove's, 1989, previously mentioned archival burglary study was used as a basis for the content of the criminal history and plea in mitigation, and for determining realistic upper and lower limits, respectively, for these two offender characteristics.)

A score quantifying the overall seriousness of the offence characteristics was calculated for each of the cases, on the basis of each judge's seriousness scales

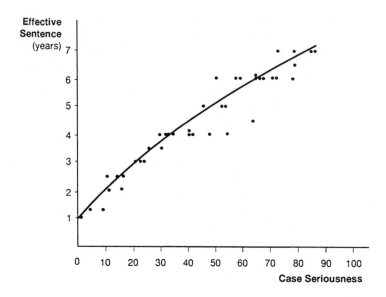

Figure 2.4 Relationship between Effective Sentence and Case Seriousness

and relative weights for the four constituent offence factors, and these scores were plotted in relation to the corresponding sentences imposed by the judge for this set of cases. The analysis was made separately for each of the judges. The results are shown in Figure 2.4, again for the previously mentioned judge, and represent that element of sentencing policy covering the relationship between the overall seriousness of the case characteristics and the appropriate quantum of sentence. The line of best fit marks the proportionality between case seriousness and effective sentence and shows the upper limit or ceiling of the quantum of sentence appropriate to the overall offence seriousness for all possible combinations of levels on the four offence factors incorporated in the analysis. In the preceding example, the "ceiling" sentence for the overall case seriousness associated with that particular combination of offence facts (i.e., 80) is about 6 years 10 months.

In Figure 2.4 each dot represents a case; if all the dots fell in a uniform line, although not necessarily in a straight line, then that would be consistent with the interpretation that the judge was aware of his sentencing policy, it was internally consistent, and he could apply it reliably, i.e., his understanding of the determination of sentence was coherent. Of course, lack of correspondence between seriousness and sentence could be due to the invalidity of the MAUM model or its procedures for eliciting responses. An analysis of the relationship between case seriousness aggregated from the component assessments and effective sentence, based on a weight-sensitive sample of cases, found a high degree of correspondence for each of the judges (Lovegrove, 1989).

The preceding decision model offers a framework in sufficient detail to provide a numerical formula for calculating the total seriousness of a case, described in terms of several common offence factors, and comprising a single count, or multiple counts belonging to the same legal offence category and properly regarded as separate transactions. It is now possible to examine the nature of the underlying decision strategy.

Perhaps at this point it is helpful to explain the nature of each of the offence factors. *Total value of the theft* is measured in dollars and defined as the sum of the value of the money and goods stolen in the counts comprising the case. *Counts of burglary* is the number of counts of burglary on the presentment. *Violence to the victims* scales the actual violence experienced by a victim in a single count of burglary and, in cases comprising multiple counts of burglary, the violence associated with the case is defined as the degree of violence associated with the most violent of the counts. *Organization* is described in terms of a series of elements, each one indicative of planning and sophistication of approach in the conduct of the count(s) (e.g., using a car stolen for the purpose of the burglary), with seriousness being proportional to the number of elements characterizing a count; where there are multiple counts the organization associated with a case is defined as the level of organization associated with the most serious of the counts; as defined, it relates to the level of organization characteristic of the case.

In the light of this clarification it is possible to deduce, from the approach assumed in the decision model, the more or less conscious thought process crossing the minds of judges as they construe the relative seriousness of a case of burglary: this is an O-planned series of burglaries in which the offender broke into homes on C occasions, netted T dollars, and was prepared to inflict V violence on a victim to make good an escape. This is what can be described as a global strategy to sentencing the multiple offender: it is a process for determining the seriousness of the offender's criminal conduct viewed as a whole, an assessment which a sentencer must make to give effect to the totality principle. (Of course, this does not relieve the sentencer of the task of determining the seriousness of each count since, in addition to the effective sentence, an appropriate sentence must be set for each of the constituent counts.)

The comments of the seven County Court judges who took part in these sentencing exercises provide additional support for the validity of the concept of a global approach to the determination of overall case seriousness. Five of the seven judges said that this was their strategy. Nevertheless, one of these five judges thought that the global approach in sentencing is not easy to follow in those cases in which one of the counts is much more serious than the other counts. However, this judge took the view that this circumstance did not apply to the cases in the exercise, because it could be reasonably assumed that where the offender had resorted to the assumed highest level of violence in one of the counts he had a propensity to resort to this level of violence in all of the counts, but that this propensity could not have been assumed if the highest level set on *violence to the victims* had been more extreme.

One judge disavowed the global approach, believing that the proper course is to impose an appropriate sentence for each count and then determine orders of concurrency and partial concurrency so that the effective sentence is not crushing. Then there was another judge who clearly favored this latter view but thought that the overall seriousness of the case may unconsciously influence his determination of the effective sentence.

There is another piece of evidence arising from the scaling exercises described above and relevant to the present argument. For validity the concept of the global approach requires that the factor of *counts of burglary* is considered as relevant to the determination of overall case seriousness. In this regard it should be noted that six of the seven judges agreed that it was a relevant offence factor and had no difficulty in developing a seriousness scale for it. And the dissenting judge – the first-mentioned judge in the preceding paragraph – agreed that generally cases with multiple counts would attract more severe sentences; indeed, an analysis of this judge's sentencing practices in the exercise, as shown by the relationship between case seriousness, aggregated from the component assessments, and effective sentence, revealed that the factor of *counts of burglary* was in fact weighted heavily by him.

In appreciating the role of this factor in the global approach it is instructive to consider the seriousness scale for *counts of burglary* of the judge whose responses to the sentencing exercises have been presented in this chapter; it is shown in Figure 2.5. Its shape is similar to the curves produced by the other judges and approximates a line of decreasing returns; each additional count adds a quantum of seriousness to the total, but each increase is less than the preceding one. This would favor an outcome in which for additional counts there were corresponding decrements in the additional quanta of sentence.

What then is the solution offered by Lovegrove's (1989) model to what Ashworth (1983) identified as the problem of integrating the seriousness of two or more offences of one kind into a coherent system of proportionality principally related to the seriousness of single offences or classes of offence? The solution is illustrated for the offence characteristics of multiple-count cases of the legal offence category of burglary.

Seriousness

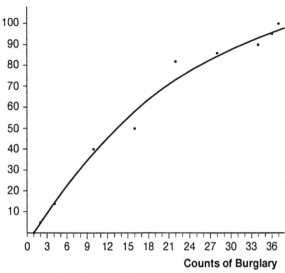

Figure 2.5 Seriousness scale for *Counts of Burglary*

One key to the solution is in the way the factors describing case seriousness are defined.

(1) The seriousness of a case of multiple offending is not defined as the sum of the seriousness of each of its comprising counts. Rather, it is described in terms of a common set of dimensions together providing a global measure of the seriousness of the criminal conduct viewed as a whole; the seriousness of a multiple-count case is decomposed in regard to these dimensions. Now, the seriousness of a multiple-count case would be less when defined globally than when treated as the sum of the seriousness of each of its comprising counts.

(2) Since for burglary, by definition, each of the four factors covers the normal variation in seriousness of the characteristic it describes and together the factors comprehensively describe the variation in the offence characteristics of this type of case, it permits the creation of a dimension defining the possible range of seriousness of the offending covered by the legal category of burglary.

(3) Three of the four component dimensions – organization, violence and the amount stolen – relate to the possible variation in the circumstances of individual counts. Accordingly, the aggregation of the seriousness associated with these three factors for a particular multiple-count case can be used to define the total seriousness of what is a composite principal (most serious) offence. (The term "composite" is used because violence is measured according to the most serious count of violence.) The appropriate sentence for the principal offence provides the reference point against which to judge the appropriateness of the additional quantum of sentence for the multiple counts.

(4) The fourth component – number of counts – relates to the possible variation in the seriousness associated with the additional counts. The aggregation of seriousness in respect of this and the above three components for a particular case equals the seriousness of the offence characteristics of the offender's course of criminality viewed as a whole. This factor of counts of burglary is weighted in relation to each of the three other offence factors to determine its potential contribution to the seriousness of the criminal conduct viewed as a whole. In this way the quantum of seriousness that can be added by these additional counts to the seriousness of the principal offence is limited and, accordingly, this has the potential to ensure that the effective sentence bears a recognizable relationship to the sentence for the principal offence.

The relative weight of the component relating to the number of multiple counts can be treated as operationalizing Thomas's (1979) vague concept of "recognizable relationship" and informing it with precision. And the sentence appropriate to the seriousness of 100 on the dimension defining the possible range of seriousness of the offending covered by the legal category of burglary represents Thomas's "upper limit of the normal bracket of sentences." (See Chapter 1.)

Viewed in this light, the second form of Thomas's (1979) statement of the totality principle can be reworded as: the effective sentence should not be above the upper limit of the range of the sentences imposed for the legal offence category to which the most serious of the multiple counts belongs. Now, since this range of sentences includes cases in which there are multiple counts of the offence, there is no conflict between the meanings of this statement and Thomas's first and third forms of the totality principle, rather they are supplementary (see Chapter 1).

The second key to this solution to the Ashworth problem is the construing of total seriousness in terms of components aggregated according to a formal decision model for which there is a sound and explicit axiomatic basis. This provides for a rational and coherent relationship between the seriousness of the principal offence and the overall seriousness of the offences comprising the case, since the dimension representing the number of multiple counts can be weighted systematically in terms of the (three) dimensions defining the circumstances of individual counts.

Is this solution in any way incoherent? The answer is yes. Somewhat. The main potential problem relates to the weighting of the dimension covering the number of counts. It is no more than generally a good approximation of the extent to which the quantum of seriousness associated with the additional counts of burglary may appropriately add to the seriousness of the principal offence. Its value would be, of course, almost always to some extent an underestimate of the correct quantum; and the quantum of seriousness associated with the composite principal offence, *mutatis mutandis*, correspondingly an overestimate. In a particular case, the degree to which the quantum of seriousness measured by the dimension of the number of counts was less than the seriousness associated with those counts would be at its greatest where a large amount of money was stolen in one or more of the secondary counts while the value of the theft in the principal count was not high; where this latter value was high there would be less of a problem, since seriousness is related to value by way of decreasing returns (see Figure 2.1). To the extent that this was a problem in a particular case so the derived quantum of sentence covering the seriousness of these additional counts would be inadequate. This problem arises because the seriousness associated with the additional counts relates not only to the dimension of *counts of burglary* but also to the *total value of the theft*. There is no such difficulty in this respect for *violence to the victims* and *organization* since the seriousness associated with these dimensions is the same for one as for multiple counts.

Nevertheless, there are two potential problems in relation to the factors of violence and organization, and they too concern the validity of the global definition of case seriousness. Two circumstances can be envisaged where it would not be tenable. One would arise where there was a particularly violent incident in one of the counts and it arose under unusual circumstances such that it could not be assumed that the offender had a propensity to resort to this level of violence in order to carry out this type of offence. A second would occur where the counts comprising the case varied markedly in the level of the sophistication behind their planning and execution, and for this reason it could not be assumed that the offender's business was organized in a characteristic way. These two sets of circumstances would be expected to occur only rarely.

This solution for multiple counts of the same kind is the foundation for the decision model for the sentencing of the multiple offender whose offences belong to a variety of legal offence categories. To this matter we now turn.

CHAPTER THREE

A sentencing decision model: multiple disparate counts

The purpose of this chapter is to develop a model describing how judges determine quantum of sentence for a case comprising multiple counts belonging to different offence categories (e.g., armed robbery and burglary) and properly regarded as separate transactions. Again, it is to be what has been described in this study as an ideal model of decision making. The present analysis begins by exploring how the previous decision model, covering offences of the same kind, provides a foundation for the decision model relating to offences of a different kind; it continues with a statement of the proposed model, described in terms of sixteen principles.

One critical element in the just-described solution to the problem of determining the overall seriousness of a series of offences of the same kind is the viewing of seriousness as an aggregation of the seriousness associated with dimensions describing aspects of the seriousness of a case viewed as a whole: for burglary these four dimensions are the characteristic level of organization of the offences, the level of violence in the most violent of the offences, the number of offences, and the total amount stolen. This decision structure is compatible with the totality principle, requiring, as it does, the sentencer to fix a sentence proportional to the offender's course of criminal conduct viewed as a whole. This global notion of case seriousness is similarly appropriate for cases comprising multiple counts from different offence categories, since the totality principle applies in that sort of case as well. However, it can readily be demonstrated that the way in which the global approach was operationalized for multiple offences of a similar kind is not appropriate when the counts are of a different kind.

First, in a case comprising a series of similar offences, such as multiple burglaries, committed over a period of time but linked as part of a course of conduct, the seriousness associated with the planning and execution of the plan can be viewed as a characteristic level of organization and as covering the series of counts. This view of these aspects of offence seriousness is manifest in the words one may well expect to hear from a sentencer in describing a crime: "a series of six well-planned burglaries." Accordingly, these aspects of seriousness can be captured by the dimensions of organization, defined in terms of the typical level characterizing each offence, and the number of counts of burglary. However, the seriousness of a series of offences comprising separate transactions and belonging to different legal offence categories – for example, a burglary of a dwelling and, some time later, an armed robbery of a bank – cannot be captured by the notion of a characteristic level of planning and *modus operandi* repeated on a number of occasions. For there is no common organization to be repeated – the organization for an armed robbery takes a very different form than for a burglary. Simply, it cannot be viewed as a course of conduct with a common strategy. In the two types of offence the relative levels of organization may be similar; both the burglary and the armed robbery may be regarded as well-planned instances of these two offences, but that is another matter, since in respect of comparative seriousness they may be very different. Consequently, seriousness cannot be based on a single dimension of organization in conjunction with a dimension covering the number of counts.

Also, Lovegrove (1989) argued that as part of the move to greater uniformity of approach in sentencing, the offence factors must be defined in concrete, case-specific terms; for example, for organization, the use of a stolen getaway vehicle in an armed robbery as one of a number of components, rather than a dimension ranging from well planned to poorly planned. Now, since many of the elements characterizing a well-planned offence in one legal category have no relevance to other offence categories, there can be no common dimension of organization. The same point could be made for the case factor of violence.

Another point is that offence factors material to seriousness vary across legal offence categories; for example, violence and amount stolen are required to define the seriousness of rape and theft, respectively, but the converse does not hold. Moreover, one would not expect that material offence factors, common to more than one legal offence category, would be regarded as having the same relative importance in the determination of offence seriousness across the various offence categories.

The consequence of this is that the overall seriousness of a series of offences from different legal offence categories cannot be treated by way of the aggregation of the seriousness associated with dimensions describing aspects of the seriousness of the case viewed as a whole. Nevertheless, it will be recalled that in Chapter 2 there was a second operationalization of the global notion of case seriousness, namely, the idea of scaling the overall seriousness of a case on a dimension representing the possible range of seriousness of the offending associated with a particular legal offence category, partitioned into a composite component available to the seriousness of the offence characteristics used to define the circumstances surrounding the commission of the individual counts (for burglary: worst violence, characteristic organization, and total value of the theft) and a component available to the seriousness associated with the number of multiple counts of that offence (number of counts). And Thomas's (1979) "recognizable relationship" between the seriousness of the principal offence and the overall seriousness of the offences comprising the case was quantified by weighting the dimension representing the number of multiple counts in terms of the dimensions defining the circumstances of the individual counts. There appears to be no conceptual or practical reason why this second aspect of the solution to the problem of integrating the seriousness of multiple counts of a similar kind cannot be applied to cases comprising counts of a different kind.

The reference point for determining overall case seriousness where the multiple offences are of a different kind is, according to principle, the seriousness of the principal offence. Now, the seriousness of the principal offence is simply the sum of the seriousness associated with each of its component offence characteristics (for burglary: violence, organization, and value of the theft), and this aspect of the case would be scaled on the composite component available to the seriousness of the (three) offence characteristics used to define individual counts on the dimension representing the possible range of seriousness of the legal category to which the principal offence belonged. This is how the offence characteristics of a case comprising one count would be scaled on this dimension and, accordingly, it can be used without modification to scale the seriousness of the principal offence in a case comprising offences belonging to different legal offence categories. (This, of course, requires the assumption that offences belonging to the various legal offence categories can be decomposed according to a set of components describing the commission of an offence, such as violence, organization, etc. The author has shown this assumption to be tenable for burglary in this study, and for armed robbery in another study (Lovegrove, 1988) and there would appear to be no reason why it would not hold for most if not all of the other offences in the criminal calendar.)

Now consider the component available to the seriousness associated with the number of multiple counts of the principal offence on the dimension representing the possible range of seriousness of the legal category to which that offence belongs. When the principal offence is of the same legal category as the multiple offences this component sets the limit on the extent to which the seriousness of the additional (lesser) offences may add to the seriousness of the principal offence. There is a good argument to be made that it should also fulfil this function when the additional offences are in a different category from that to which the principal offence belongs. The point is perhaps best made with a concrete example in terms of the judge's responses to the sentencing exercises described in the previous chapter. The component made available to the seriousness associated with thirty-seven multiple counts of burglary was 31 on the 0–100 seriousness scale of the dimension representing the possible range of seriousness of this offence category. (The assumed upper limit of the offence factor of *counts of burglary* was thirty-seven counts and the judge determined its relative weight to be 31.) It would follow from the approach to multiple offending proposed here that the overall seriousness (and, hence, effective sentence) of a case comprising a burglary of a particular level of seriousness as the principal offence in association with thirty-six less serious counts from one or more legal offence categories, but not belonging to the offence category of burglary, could not be more than the overall seriousness of a second case comprising an identical principal offence of burglary in association with thirty-six similarly less serious counts but of burglary. This would appear to be an intuitively reasonable outcome. Ashworth (1992a) has asked rhetorically why the most serious of a group of offences, separated in time and of a different legal character, should be used as a benchmark for the total sentence, why the total sentence should be limited by the "upper limit of the normal bracket of sentences" for the principal offence. Perhaps the preceding analysis at least informs the working rule with some rationality.

It should be noted parenthetically that it is necessary to specify the number of counts here since the component of seriousness available to the number of multiple counts is governed by its weight and this, in turn, is partly a function of its assumed range, which in the sentencing exercises was taken to be one to thirty-seven counts. It does not follow that the upper limit is arbitrary: it should be remembered that it represented a level above which on the basis of empirical experience few cases would be expected to fall. Nevertheless, the specification of the number of counts for this purpose does not require precision; Figure 2.5 clearly shows that in the upper reaches of this dimension substantial changes in the number of counts have little impact on seriousness.

This, then, is the framework for the solution to the problem of integrating the seriousness of two or more offences of a different kind into a system of proportionality principally related to the seriousness of single offences or classes of offence, as required by the totality principle. It falls short of coherence in one respect, the source of this perturbation lying in the way in which the global approach to the sentencing of cases comprising multiple offences of the same kind was operationalized. The problem arises from the use of the component available to the seriousness associated with the number of multiple counts of the principal offence as a means of setting the limit on the extent to which the seriousness of the additional (lesser) counts may add to the seriousness of the principal offence. The point was made in the previous chapter that this component underestimates the additional seriousness associated with these counts because they add to the seriousness of the principal offence not only through this component but also through the dimension representing the total value of the theft. It follows that the limit on cumulation defined by this component of multiple counts must be less than the correct value. This error would remain when this component was used to govern the extent to which offences of a different kind may add to the seriousness of the principal offence.

So far the proposed solution to the problem of sentencing cases comprising multiple counts differing in kind provides a framework for the decision and a rationale for setting the limit on the extent to which the seriousness of the additional (lesser) offences may add to the seriousness of the principal offence. How the seriousness of the additional counts is actually added in order to determine the effective sentence is the subject of the next section.

One word on the development of the decision model as it is now to be presented. The author attempted to identify all possible implications for a decision strategy of Thomas's (1979) and Ashworth's (1983, 1992a) legal analyses, this step including matters not directly covered by them, and then to formulate a model so that it was consistent with the implied strategy. Since the model produced by this process is comprehensive and detailed and these two legal analyses are relatively narrow and general, the product was necessarily largely of the author's imagination. The model's main ties with reality are these two academic interpretations of sentencing policy and the rules of algebra. Its development was also shaped by what might be called thought-validity, amounting to little more than systematic face validity of the model as it stood, in which effective sentences were calculated for various combinations of offence seriousness to investigate whether the result was absurd and remodelling was required.

Principles governing the addition of sentences for offences from different statutory categories

(1) The seriousness of the instant principal offence and the range of seriousness for the legal category to which it belongs determine the extent

to which the sentences for the secondary and subsequent offences cumulate on the sentence for the principal offence.

(2) The principal offence is the offence with the highest sentence (effective sentence where there are multiple counts of one offence type) and, if two or more offences satisfy this criterion, then (1) the offence belonging to the legal category for which judges have imposed the most severe sentences for the worst instances of those offence types, and (2) the offence belonging to the legal category with the highest number of counts, are introduced in order as the criteria. The principal offence may include multiple counts within a common legal offence category, as may the non-principal offences. Counts common to a particular legal offence category are considered together as the principal offence, secondary offence, etc., as appropriate.

(3) The quanta of sentence for the secondary and subsequent offences are added to the principal offence.

(4) The addition of the sentences for the principal and subsequent offences to determine the effective sentence for the case is based upon the seriousness of these offences.

(5) The legal category of the principal offence is used to build a framework for considering the addition of the sentences for the subsequent offences to the sentence for the principal offence. The framework is in the form of a dimension representing the possible range of seriousness of the offending associated with this legal category and is partitioned into a component available to the seriousness of the offence characteristics defining the circumstances surrounding the commission of the individual counts (e.g., for armed robbery the offence factors might be worst violence, characteristic organization, total value of the theft) and a component available to seriousness associated with the number of multiple counts of the (principal) offence. The relative size of the partition representing the component of counts is determined directly by the weight assigned to the offence factor of counts for this legal offence category. Of course, only the most serious offence provided for in the framework would fully cover both components. In the context of the present study, the zero point on this scale is the level of seriousness of a case in which the instant principal offence may be regarded as trivial in terms of the offence characteristics defining a particular offence in that legal offence category and it has been committed by an offender who has a very serious record of relevant prior convictions and negligible mitigation (see Chapter 2).

(6) The seriousness of the instant principal offence or, where there are multiple counts of the principal offence, the most serious count of the principal offence incorporating the circumstances surrounding the commission of the other counts comprising the principal offence, is fully allotted to the component available to the seriousness of the offence characteristics, commencing at the zero point on the dimension representing the possible range of seriousness of the legal category of the principal offence. And where there are multiple counts of this offence, the seriousness associated with the number of these counts is fully allotted to the component available to the seriousness of multiple counts on the same dimension, commencing at the least serious point on this component.

(7) The seriousness of each of the subsequent offences is defined by its quantum of sentence (this sentence includes a quantum due to associated multiple counts, where there are such counts), and is independent of the seriousness of its legal offence category, but it is quantified in terms of seriousness for addition to the principal offence according to the scale relating the dimension of seriousness to quantum of sentence for the legal category of the principal offence, at that point on the scale at which the addition is made (if the point of addition is at a level of seriousness not warranting a term of imprisonment, then the quantification is made at that point at which a term of imprisonment becomes appropriate). The seriousness of all subsequent offences is quantified as a term of imprisonment for the purposes of transformation.

(8) The addition of the secondary and subsequent offences is made separately and in turn, priority being determined according to greater seriousness as it is defined for the selection of the principal offence.

(9) In adding the seriousness due to the secondary offence to the seriousness of the principal offence there is always partial concurrence. Where the seriousness of the offence characteristics associated with the instant principal offence is negligible relative to the component available to offence characteristics on the dimension representing the seriousness of its legal offence category (i.e., the instant principal offence may be regarded as trivial in terms of the offence characteristics defining particular offences in that legal category), then the seriousness added is a substantial proportion of the seriousness due to the secondary offence. Where the seriousness of the offence characteristics of the instant principal offence covers the whole of the component available to offence characteristics on the dimension representing the seriousness of its legal offence category (i.e., the instant principal offence is as serious as envisioned, in terms of the offence characteristics defining particular offences), then the seriousness added is only a small proportion of the

seriousness due to the secondary offence. Within these limits the seriousness added to the principal offence, for a given level of seriousness of the
secondary offence, is in a monotonically decreasing relationship with the
seriousness of the principal offence.

(10) Notwithstanding the preceding point, the degree to which the seriousness
of the secondary offence may add to the sentence for the principal
offence is limited by the component of seriousness available to the
number of multiple counts on the dimension representing the seriousness
of the legal offence category of which the instant principal offence is a
member minus the seriousness due to the number of multiple counts of
the instant principal offence. Where the seriousness associated with
multiple counts of the instant principal offence is zero (i.e., the principal
offence comprises one count), then the whole of the proportion of the
seriousness due to the secondary offence and to be added to the principal
offence, as calculated under the previous point, is actually added or as
much of the proportion as falls within the available limit. Where the
seriousness arising from multiple counts of the instant principal offence
covers the whole of the component available to multiple counts on the
dimension representing the seriousness of its legal offence category, then
little or none of the proportion of the seriousness due to the secondary
offence and to be added to the principal offence is actually added. Within
these limits the seriousness actually added to the principal offence, for a
given proportion of the seriousness of the secondary offence, is in a
monotonically decreasing relationship with the quantum of seriousness
due to the number of multiple counts of the instant principal offence; the
available limit acts as a cut-off. (Where the total number of counts in a
case exceeds to a significant extent the number of counts assumed for the
purposes of the weighting of the component covering the number of
counts, it may be appropriate to exceed this limit.)

(11) The overall seriousness of the principal and secondary offences is equal
to the seriousness of the principal offence (including the component of
seriousness due to the number of multiple counts of the principal offence,
where there are such counts) plus the seriousness calculated under the
preceding point. The scale relating the dimension of seriousness to
quantum of sentence for the legal category of the principal offence is then
used to determine directly the quantum of sentence appropriate to the
overall seriousness. This is the effective sentence for the case.

(12) Consequent upon the above principles, the effective sentence for the case
must always be less than the sentence which would result from the simple
addition of the (effective) sentence for the principal offence and the

sentence for the secondary offence. This difference is the part of the quantum of the sentence for the secondary offence which is made concurrent with the sentence for the principal offence.

(13) Tertiary offences are in turn added to the principal offence in the same manner as the secondary offence, with the exception that the component of seriousness available to the number of multiple counts on the dimension representing the seriousness of the legal offence category of which the principal offence is a member is reduced by the seriousness associated with the quantum of sentence actually added to the principal offence and arising from the secondary offence (as well as the seriousness arising from multiple counts of the instant principal offence, where there are such counts).

(14) A secondary offence (which may include multiple counts) is regarded as having a minimum level of seriousness defined as a term of imprisonment. This measure of seriousness is calculated in two steps. First, the seriousness of this offence is determined from the scale showing the relationship between counts and seriousness for the secondary offence and is equal to the seriousness of two counts (the seriousness level of one count is zero), modified by the weight of the component of counts for the legal category to which the secondary offence belongs (see Chapter 2). Secondly, the scale showing the relationship between offence seriousness and sentence for the secondary offence is used to determine directly the term of imprisonment appropriate to this degree of seriousness, at that point on the scale at which a term of imprisonment becomes appropriate. This sentence defines the minimum seriousness of the secondary offence. Tertiary offences are treated in the same way as secondary offences.

(15) The seriousness of a secondary (or tertiary, etc.) offence which would warrant a non-custodial sentence if it stood alone is equal to, not more or less than, its minimum level of seriousness. Where the effective sentence for the principal and secondary offences, calculated according to this set of principles, is a term of imprisonment, then the sentence actually imposed for the secondary offence is the sentence defining its minimum level of seriousness. However, where the overall seriousness for the multiple offences does not warrant a term of imprisonment, then a term of imprisonment is not appropriate for the secondary offence.

(16) This analysis is limited to offences belonging to a legal category of offence for which there is a statutory provision for a term of imprisonment as a maximum penalty.

The justification for all but one of these principles is that they are consistent with the decision framework developed by the author and the relevant legal principles distilled by Thomas (1979) and Ashworth (1983, 1992a). The use of the word consistent should not be taken to imply that this is the only way in which this framework and these principles could have been elaborated. Not at all. The scope and level of detail of these progenitors are comparatively limited and for this reason different but equally consistent sets of working rules could have been envisioned.

The one principle whose justification is not implicit in this background analysis relates to the definition of the principal offence (Principle 2), and is justified in this way. If it is accepted that the quantum of sentence marks the seriousness of a particular offence independently of the legal category to which it belongs, then it is appropriate that the offence with the highest (effective) sentence should be regarded as principal in the context of the present analysis. An illustration will reinforce the point. Consider an offender convicted of four counts of burglary and an armed robbery, the five counts relating to separate incidents, and appropriately sentenced to an effective sentence of four years' imprisonment for the burglaries and to two years for the armed robbery. Is not the offender more appropriately regarded as a burglar than an armed robber and, as a consequence, should not the effective sentence for these five counts fall within the range appropriate to a burglar with multiple offences? Now, if the sentences for the offences from different legal categories do not differ, then there seems little alternative but to regard the offence belonging to the more serious legal category as principal. This raises the problem of how the relative seriousness of the various legal offence categories should be determined. Since these criteria defining the principal offence are to be a part of a model of judicial decision making and, indeed, the quanta of sentence appropriate to the various levels of overall seriousness are to be taken directly from the views of judges, then it follows that judicial practice offers a more appropriate measure of the relative seriousness of the various legal offence categories than does the statutory maxima, which for many offences do not accord with judicial practice (see Sentencing Task Force, 1989). Finally, other criteria being equal, as the number of counts of a particular offence on the presentment increases, so this favors the view of the offender as a person whose offending is characterized by this type of offence and, accordingly, the range of seriousness of its legal offence category as properly setting a limit on the effective sentence appropriate to the case.

Now to the testing of this decision model for the sentencing of the multiple offender.

Testing the decision model for multiple disparate counts

The structure of the model describing the way in which judges attempt to determine, according to current sentencing policy, the effective sentence for a case involving multiple offences from different legal offence categories, each offence properly regarded as a separate transaction, and once appropriate sentences have been fixed for the multiple offences, is defined by the sixteen principles set out in the previous chapter. The next step is to derive testable propositions or general predictions from these principles and to formulate a set of sentencing problems for the purpose of testing the model by way of these propositions. This is the task of the present chapter. In the first section testable propositions are stated and related to the model; following this, there is the presentation of the problems used to test these propositions; in the final section, the problems are grouped according to the proposition for which they serve as a validity test.

It is noted in parenthesis that a sample of judges was required to determine effective sentences for the cases comprising the sentencing problems; at the same time the judges provided verbal protocols (immediate retrospective reports) of their thinking. In a second session the author explained how the decision model applied to each of the problems and the judges were asked to comment on its validity (reflective retrospective reports). These aspects of the method, addressed in detail in the following chapter, are foreshadowed here to facilitate the reader's understanding of parts of the present discussion.

When considering the testing of the model, it must be borne in mind that some of the sixteen principles comprising the model are not open to direct test. A qualitative statement of a model requires some principles whose function is no more than to set the scene. This type of statement is necessarily couched in general terms and is not directly linked to the operation of the model, and for these reasons does not generate specific predictions. Principle 1 is an instance of this; it no more than directs attention to the pivotal role of the principal offence in the determination of effective sentences for multiple offenders. Moreover, in a model some of the elements are highly abstract. It is through these unifying concepts that order is brought to apparent disorder. Because these principles are intangible they are not amenable to direct test but they do have derivable consequences and it is these predictions which are tested. Principle 5 illustrates this type of principle: it introduces the concept of a framework for the addition of sentences, which framework takes the form of a dimension representing the range of seriousness of the legal category of the principal offence. It follows then that the principles describing the model are used to derive predictions – predictions as to how a judge would answer each of the sentencing problems if he were consistent with the model – and it is the accuracy of these predictions upon which the test of the model's validity is founded. Some individual principles give rise to more than one prediction and some of the predictions require more than one of the principles for their derivation. Of course, some of the principles do translate directly to a prediction; for example, the first part of Principle 7, that the seriousness of a secondary or subsequent offence is defined by its quantum of sentence and is independent of its legal offence category.

Against this background it is now appropriate to identify those aspects of the decision model capable of being related to sentencing problems and to express them in the form of testable propositions or general predictions. These general predictions are set out below together with the number(s) of the principle(s) in the formal statement of the decision model from which they are derived.

(1) In each case a principal offence is selected to provide the foundation sentence upon which the effective sentence is built – the appropriate sentences for the secondary and subsequent offences are added with a degree of cumulation to the sentence for the principal offence (3).

(2) There is a monotonically decreasing relationship between the quantum of sentence for the main count of the principal offence and the degree of cumulation of the sentence for a secondary offence (1, 9).

(3) There is a monotonically increasing relationship between the seriousness of the legal category of the principal offence and the degree of cumulation of the sentence for a secondary offence (it is assumed that the more serious the legal category of an offence the greater the range of sentence available for the possible variation in the offence characteristics of that offence) (1, 5, 9).

(4) The seriousness of a secondary offence is defined by its quantum of sentence and is independent of the seriousness of its legal offence category (7).

(5) Where the multiple secondary counts to be added to the principal offence belong to the same legal offence category they are considered together as a secondary offence and are not added separately to the principal offence (2, 7).

(6) Where a secondary offence comprises multiple counts its effective sentence defines the seriousness of these counts considered together for the purpose of cumulation (7).

(7) Where there are multiple counts of the principal offence the degree of cumulation of the sentence for a secondary offence is determined first by reference to the sentence for the main count of the principal offence (see the second proposition) and then the quantum of sentence cumulative upon this sentence and arising from the extra counts of the principal offence (see the following proposition) (5, 6, 10).

(8) There is a monotonically decreasing relationship between the quantum of sentence cumulative upon the sentence for the main count of the principal offence and arising from extra counts of the principal offence and the degree of cumulation of the sentence for a secondary offence (5, 6, 10).

(9) Multiple secondary offences belonging to separate legal offence categories are added to the principal offence in turn, first the sentence for the secondary offence, then the tertiary offence, cumulation being by way of decreasing gains (8, 10).

(10) Where a case comprises multiple secondary offences cumulation of the sentences for these counts is made in regard to a notional limiting quantum of sentence above which extra counts would have a negligible additional effect on what would be the running effective sentence for the counts considered up to that point; the limiting quantum of cumulation is the same whether the multiple secondary counts belong to the legal category of the principal offence or are equally or less serious offences belonging to a different legal category; the limiting quantum of cumulation for the multiple secondary counts is independent of the quantum of sentence appropriate to the principal offence; and, the limiting quantum of cumulation is defined as the component available to multiple counts of the principal offence on the dimension representing the seriousness of the legal category of the principal offence, and its value varies across legal categories of the principal offence (1, 5, 6, 10).

(11) Where there is a secondary offence the degree of cumulation of the sentence for a tertiary offence is determined first by reference to the sentence for the main count of the principal offence (see the second proposition) and then the quantum of sentence cumulative upon this sentence and arising from the secondary offence (see the following proposition) (5, 6, 10, 13).

(12) There is a monotonically decreasing relationship between the quantum of sentence cumulative upon the sentence for the main count of the principal offence and arising from a secondary offence and the degree of cumulation of the sentence for a tertiary offence (5, 6, 10, 13).

(13) An offence of a level of seriousness warranting a non-custodial sentence if it stood alone would as a secondary offence and for the purposes of cumulation be regarded as having a minimum level of seriousness defined as a very short term of imprisonment, a term independent of the seriousness of the instant offence (7, 14, 15). (It should be noted that for this prediction a suspended sentence of imprisonment is not regarded as a sentence of imprisonment.)

(14) The principal offence is the offence with the highest effective sentence and, if two or more offences satisfy this criterion, then (1) the offence belonging to the most serious legal offence category, and (2) the offence belonging to the legal offence category with the highest number of counts, are introduced in order as the criteria. The principal offence may include multiple counts within a common legal offence category (2).

Having identified those aspects of the decision model capable of being tested and having expressed them in the form of general predictions, this discussion now turns to the formulation of sentencing problems which can be used to test these general predictions.

Formulation of the sentencing problems

Most of the sentencing problems use the legal offence categories of armed robbery and burglary (ss.75A and 76 of the *Crimes Act* 1958 (Vic.)), with armed robbery as the principal offence and burglary as secondary. The reason for this is that the author had already conducted in Victoria large archival studies of judges' sentencing practices in regard to these two offences (Lovegrove, 1983, 1988, 1989) and, for burglary of a dwelling for financial gain, he had also investigated judges' decision making in a series of sentencing exercises (Lovegrove, 1989) described in Chapter 2; this body of data and the experience gained from conducting this research could be drawn upon to assist in the task of formulating realistic sentencing problems. An offence from another legal offence category was used only when it was required to test adequately the decision model.

There was good reason for validating the model in regard to armed robbery and burglary in addition to the author's familiarity with the patterns of offending and judges' sentencing practices for these two offences. First, these two respective legal offence categories represent significantly different levels of intrinsic offence seriousness and, consequently, it was easy to formulate instances of these two offences where the armed robbery was clearly the principal offence and the burglary was secondary. Secondly, it was considered realistic that an offender might commit these two offences as separate transactions and be charged for both of them at the one time, and on a plea of guilty that the offender might well be sentenced for these offences at the one hearing. Thirdly, long sentences are regarded by the courts as appropriate to very serious instances of both armed robbery and burglary; this made for a more sensitive test of the predictions derived from the model, since at higher levels of sentence similar percentage differences represent greater absolute differences in the quanta of sentence. (For the data relating to the first and third points, see Attorney-General's Department – Victoria, 1987, 1988, 1989, 1990.)

In this study variation within the offence categories is in regard to the circumstances relating to the offence. It was important in formulating these problems, then, that the facts relating to the offender not only did not vary across cases but also took the form of a very serious record of relevant prior convictions together with little by way of personal mitigation (e.g., youth, stable employment history, minor role in the offence, remorse). Under these conditions the quanta of sentence for the cases could be assumed to be proportional to the seriousness of the offence, since there is not the opportunity for sentences to be reduced to make allowance for mitigating offender factors or for weight to be given to the offender's rehabilitation prospects. It follows, therefore, that variations in the quanta of sentence for offences belonging to the same legal offence category reflect differences between these offences in the seriousness levels of the offence characteristics defining that type of offence (e.g., for a series of burglaries, differences in the amounts of money stolen, etc.). Three sentencing principles are of import here: (1) a tariff sentence – a sentence in which the quantum of sentence is made proportional to case seriousness – is imposed where an individual's rehabilitation prospects do not appear to be favorable; now, where there is little available to an offender by way of personal mitigation and a serious relevant criminal history, then the offender's rehabilitation prospects would not appear favorable; (2) case seriousness is equal to the seriousness of the offence characteristics minus the extenuating effects of good character and other personal mitigating factors; and (3) prior convictions do not aggravate case seriousness beyond the level set by the overall seriousness of the offence characteristics. (See Lovegrove, 1989.) It was decided, nevertheless, that the mitigating personal characteristics should include a plea of guilty but with no evidence of contrition; by this means details about the offence, particularly regarding the organization, which would otherwise not generally come to light, could be realistically presented in the information about the circumstances of the offence and yet the credit for the guilty plea by way of mitigation would be minimal. This decision was taken particularly with an eye to the third sentencing exercise, in which the fictitious cases were presented in the form of comprehensive summary descriptions. The preceding facts relating to the offender are, unless stated to the contrary, to be assumed in the following analysis.

In regard to the counts comprising the cases in the sentencing problems, there was the task of setting sentences appropriate to the levels of seriousness required for the valid testing of the propositions. Where the sentence for a count was required to be appropriate to the lower or the upper level of seriousness for a single count or the upper level for a series of multiple counts on the dimension representing the possible range of seriousness for the offence category to which the count belonged then the task of setting its quantum was left to the judge. In the other instances, the vast majority, where a sentence within these limits was required, the author determined its value in advance of the administration of the problems. In these latter instances, it was thought possible to be able to fix sentences whose appropriateness would not be invalidated by individual differences between the judges in their preferred severity levels. For this task the author drew on information in the sentencing statistics for the higher criminal courts from the preceding four years (Attorney-General's Department – Victoria, 1987, 1988, 1989, 1990) and data from his previously mentioned studies of armed robbery and burglary.

The official statistics provided data on what the realistic upper limits of the ranges of (maximum) sentence were at that time for the offences of armed robbery and burglary. For armed robbery, twelve years' and six years' imprisonment seemed appropriate to extremely serious and moderately serious single counts, respectively; in respect of custodial sentences, instances falling at the former level of seriousness were infrequent, and single counts warranting at least six years were in a clear minority but not uncommon. For burglary, sentences for roughly comparable levels of relative seriousness would be six years and a value approaching two years. In the light of this, of those sentences fixed by the author, the highest sentence set for a single count of armed robbery or burglary was nine and four-and-a-half years, respectively.

These figures represent a compromise between two competing sets of considerations. As it was noted earlier, long sentences make for a more sensitive test of the predictions. Against this, it was realized that most of the judges would have little or no experience of cases warranting particularly long sentences and, for this reason, might not exercise their discretion with assurance at this level of case severity; moreover, for some judges, very high sentences might fall outside what they consider to be the ranges of sentence appropriate to these particular categories of offence.

In regard to the lower end of the scale for these two offences, there was the matter of the type and quantum of sentence considered by the courts to be appropriate to a trivial single count of armed robbery or burglary. On the basis of a group of Victorian judges' responses to the previously described sentencing exercises involving fictitious cases of house burglary (Lovegrove, 1989, and see Figure 2.4), it was expected that the quantum of sentence appropriate to a trivial burglary would lie on the scale of sanction severity near the boundary between a non-custodial sentence and a term of imprisonment, and would be regarded by most judges to be a short prison term (say, six months). (The use of the term "scale of sanction severity" should not be taken as implying that such a scale has been formally set out in legislation or sentencing policy; it has not. Rather, the term merely recognizes that non-custodial sentences vary in severity and that judges may make use of this variation as a means of making sentence proportional to the severity of a case in tariff sentencing. Indeed, Freiberg and Fox, 1986, claim that in Victoria there is a default but implicit hierarchy of non-custodial sanctions. This is not to deny that these sanctions are also used in terms of their appropriateness as individualized measures.) In view of this conclusion for burglary it was expected that the quantum of sentence appropriate to a trivial armed robbery would be a term of imprisonment at the lower end of what may be regarded as a moderate period of custody, say, a term of two years; this was also based on the fact that a substantially greater proportion of armed robbers are imprisoned and for longer periods of time. It follows that where a non-custodial sentence was fixed by the author for a count of armed robbery it would almost certainly require the assumption that there was for the offender in addition to the plea of guilty a degree of personal mitigation (e.g., the offender played a minor role in the offence); this assumption might be required for some judges for burglary also.

It was necessary to select four other offences and levels of sentence for them in order to test how sentences are aggregated according to the totality principle. The offences selected were rape, indecent assault, arson and intentional damage to property (ss.45(1), 44(1), 197(1) and 197(1) of the *Crimes*

Act 1958 (Vic.), respectively; s.197(6) of the same Act provides that s.197(1) can be charged as arson if it is committed by fire). Again reference was made to the previously mentioned official sentencing statistics. They showed that a rape for which a custodial sentence of five years was appropriate could be regarded as a moderately serious instance of this legal category, sentences of this magnitude being in a clear minority of custodial sentences but not uncommon. For a single instance of the offence of indecent assault, four years' imprisonment seemed to be appropriate only to an extremely serious case. In respect of arson, sentences approaching three years' custody could be regarded as appropriate to moderately serious counts, such sentences being a clear minority of custodial sentences but not uncommon. For the offence of intentional damage to property, for which arson was not charged, a sentence of one year in prison seemed appropriate to a moderately serious count of this offence, sentences above this level being a clear minority of custodial sentences but not uncommon; however, the vast majority of sentences for this offence category were non-custodial.

Finally, there is the matter of the sentences appropriate to trivial instances of counts representing these four legal offence categories. Again, taking the legal category of burglary as the standard, it was expected that the quantum of sentence appropriate to a rape at the bottom end of the scale for this offence category would be a term of imprisonment at the lower end of what may be regarded as a moderate period of custody, say, a term of two years. On a similar basis, it was expected that the type and quantum of sentence appropriate to trivial instances of indecent assault, arson and intentional damage to property would be, respectively, a non-custodial sanction at a level of severity on the sanction scale just below a term of imprisonment, a short custodial term of, say, not more than twelve months, and a non-custodial sanction of a level of severity on the sanction scale well below a term of imprisonment.

The reasons for selecting these four offences and for the levels of sentence set for them in the sentencing problems are more easily explained or readily apparent in the context of the various problems as tests of particular propositions and, accordingly, are introduced there, in the following section.

In the light of this background material the problems formulated to test the first thirteen general predictions derived from the decision model are presented in Table 4.1, and the problems for the fourteenth proposition, relating to the definition of the principal offence, follow in Table 4.2. A readily intelligible notation was developed as a means of setting out each of the problems; in this form the problems could be presented more easily and with greater clarity in the administration of the tasks to the judges. The cases in the

Table 4.1 *Sentencing problems for Propositions 1–13*

Problem number	Case description	Problem number	Case description
1	$1AR_9 + 1B_{4.5}$	14	$1AR_0 + 1B_0 + 1IA_0 + 1IDP_0$
	$1AR_{4.5} + 1B_{4.5}$		
2	$1AR_{4.5} + 1A_3$	15	$1AR_9 + 1B_0$
	$1B_{4.5} + 1A_3$		$1AR_9$
3	$1AR_9 + 1B_{4.5}$	16	$1AR_9 + 1IDP_0$
	$1AR_9 + 1R_{4.5}$		$1AR_9 + 1IDP_-$
4	$1AR_9 + 1B_4$	17	$1AR_9 + 8B_{(3.5+1)}$
	$1AR_9 + 1IA_4$		$1AR_9 + 1B_{4.5}$
5	$1AR_{4.5} + 1B_3$	21(1)	$1AR_L + 1B_1$
	$1AR_3 + 1B_{4.5}$	21(2)	$1AR_L + 1B_2$
6	$1AR_9 + \ldots + 1AR_{4.5} + \ldots + 1AR_{4.5} + \ldots$	21(3)	$1AR_M + 1B_2$
	$1AR_9 + \ldots + 1R_{4.5} + \ldots + 1B_{4.5} + \ldots$	21(4)	$1AR_M + 1B_{4.5}$
7	$1AR_9 + \ldots + 1R_{4.5} + \ldots + 1B_{4.5} + \ldots$	21(5)	$1AR_H + 1B_2$
	$1AR_{4.5} + \ldots + 1R_{4.5} + \ldots + 1B_{4.5} + \ldots$	21(6)	$1AR_H + 1B_{4.5}$
8	$3AR_{(6+3)} + 1B_{4.5}$	22(1)	$1AR_H + 1B_2 + 1A_1$
	$1AR_9 + 1B_{4.5}$	22(2)	$1AR_H + 1B_2 + 1A_2$
9	$3AR_{(9+3)} + 1B_3$	22(3)	$1AR_H + 1B_{4.5} + 1A_1$
	$1AR_9 + 1B_3 + 1A_3$	22(4)	$1AR_H + 1B_{4.5} + 1A_2$
10	$8AR_{(9+5)} + 1B_{4.5}$	23(1)	$xAR_{(H+M)} + 1B_2$
	$2AR_{(9+2)} + 1B_{4.5}$	23(2)	$xAR_{(H+M)} + 1B_{4.5}$
11	$1AR_H + \ldots + 1B_3 + \ldots + 1A_3 + \ldots$	23(3)	$xAR_{(H+H)} + 1B_2$
	$1B_H + \ldots + 1AR_3 + \ldots + 1A_3 + \ldots$	23(4)	$xAR_{(H+H)} + 1B_{4.5}$
12	$1AR_9 + 1B_4$		
	$1AR_9 + 1B_2 + 1A_2$		
13	$1AR_9 + 1B_{4.5} + 1A_3$		
	$1AR_9 + 1B_3 + 1A_3$		

Table 4.2 *Sentencing problems for Proposition 14*[a]

Problem number	Case descriptions		Problem number	Case descriptions	
30(1)	$1AR_9$	$1B_{4.5}$	30(6)	$2AR_{(2.5+2)}$	$1B_{4.5}$
30(2)	$1AR_{4.5}$	$1B_{4.5}$	30(7)	$1AR_9$	$8B_{(4.5+1)}$
30(3)	$1AR_3$	$1B_{4.5}$	30(8)	$1AR_{5.5}$	$8B_{(4.5+1)}$
30(4)	$3AR_{(3+3)}$	$1B_3$	30(9)	$1AR_{4.5}$	$8B_{(4.5+1)}$
30(5)	$3AR_{(3+3)}$	$1B_{4.5}$	30(10)	$1AR_3$	$8B_{(4.5+1)}$

Note: [a] In each problem there are two offences, and the judge is required to select the one which is principal.

problems comprise counts of armed robbery (AR), burglary (B), arson (A), rape (R), indecent assault (IA) and intentional damage to property (IDP). In Problem 1 there are two cases; in the first case the appropriate sentences are nine and four-and-a-half years, and in the second both are four-and-a-half years; the judge's task is to determine an effective sentence in each case. In Problem 6 both cases comprise an unspecified number of counts; in the first case the counts are all armed robberies, and in the second they represent a variety of legal offence categories; the question in each case is whether there is an (effective) sentence acting as a limit after which the addition of extra counts would have little if any cumulative effect and, if there is, the quantum of this sentence. In Problem 8 the first case comprises three counts of armed robbery and one count of burglary; the sentence appropriate to the main count of armed robbery is six years and the additional two counts of armed robbery together add three years to the sentence for the first count, these sentences being partially concurrent, with the result that the effective sentence for the three counts of armed robbery is nine years. The figure of two for the additional number of counts appropriate to a sentence of three years for the component relating to multiple counts was estimated by the author. In Problem 11 it was left to the judge to determine sentences appropriate to the upper levels of seriousness for single counts of armed robbery and burglary. Problem 14 comprises an unspecified number of counts, each belonging to a different legal offence category, and the sentence appropriate to each count if it stood alone is of a level of severity on the sanction scale just below a term of imprisonment. It should be noted that in this problem a suspended sentence of imprisonment is not regarded as a sentence of imprisonment. In Problem 16 in the second case the sentence appropriate to the count of intentional damage to property is of a level of severity on the sanction scale well below a term of imprisonment. In Problem 21(3) the quantum set for the armed robbery was midway between the values fixed by the judge for AR_H and AR_L. Finally, in Problem 23(1) it was left to the judge to assume an appropriate number of counts of the principal offence.

It will be noticed that where it was not inappropriate problems comprised pairs of cases. This was a device to address an insidious problem springing from an apparent characteristic of the way in which judges differentiate levels of seriousness in terms of quanta of sentence, and if it is a real effect then it would render the precision of a quantitative analysis illusory. On the basis of an analysis of sentencing statistics showing the distribution of prison sentences in England (Fitzmaurice and Pease, 1982) it would appear that judges make fine discriminations in seriousness between cases requiring short terms of imprisonment but only coarse discriminations between cases for which medium to long terms of imprisonment are appropriate. The import of this apparent characteristic of judicial sentencing for the present study is that many of the predictions derived from the model involve quanta of sentence of medium and high severity and, consequentially, cases for which judges may calibrate seriousness in units no finer than six to twelve months. Now, such a scale would not be sensitive enough to test the model rigorously. To circumvent this problem, judges, when imposing effective sentences for two cases as part of the one problem, were instructed to fix different sentences if in their view the difference in seriousness between the two cases was not negligible.

A comment should also be made on the fact that each problem was presented at only one level of seriousness and across the cases there was only one category of offence as principal. Now, ideally, there should have been variation in regard to these two offence characteristics. This would have reduced the hazard of conclusions being drawn which were perhaps specific to a particular combination of levels of sentence severity and principal offence. However, the use of more than one level and offence would have placed significantly greater demands on judicial time, an imposition considered unwarranted in view of the fact that the model was speculative and untested and the method untried and its validity an open question.

The relationship between the propositions and the sentencing problems testing their validity

This discussion is now in a position to link each of the general predictions to the particular problem(s) used to test its validity.

The analysis of the data is not organized around a separate and serial consideration of each of the problems. The reason for this is that most of the general predictions are tested by more than one problem and, accordingly, the significance of the judges' answers in regard to the validity of the various aspects of the model can be more clearly considered by the organizing of the analysis around the propositions rather than the problems.

The problems were formulated, of course, to test the general predictions. Analytic rigor would be favored if each problem tested one general prediction and only one prediction. This ideal, however, is not possible when the model is comprehensive and the decision complex; in this circumstance multiple aspects of the decision model simultaneously bear upon any one problem, even a relatively simple problem. Take Problem 1, which was designed to test the second general prediction: $1AR_9 + 1B_{4.5}$; $1AR_{4.5} + 1B_{4.5}$. The validity of this problem as a test of this prediction was predicated on the assumptions that armed robbery is the principal offence and that the sentence for the secondary offence cumulates upon the sentence for the principal offence. Now, since the truth of these assumptions appeared to be reasonable in view of personal experience and evidence (e.g., the ranges of sentence imposed in actual cases for these two offence categories), this problem was regarded as a direct test of the second general prediction. A problem directly tests a prediction when one element of the model relates to the problem and there are no other relevant aspects of decision making contemplated by the model and reasonably regarded as contentious. In a direct test the predictions regarding the quanta of sentence provide a rigorous test of the hypothesis. And in respect of the immediate retrospective report of a judge, if express reference was not made to the aspect of the model under test or there was not implicit recognition of it in the report, then the significance of that particular element for decision making would come under serious question; however, it could mean that the element was established and stable in the judge's thinking, albeit intuitive and unconscious rather than deliberative and in full awareness. Simply, where a solution turned on one matter, it would be expected that the matter would be reflected in a protocol. Moreover, in this type of problem the author should be able to convey to the judge concisely and unambiguously the decision principle which according to the model governs that problem, and so the presentation of the principles for the reflective retrospective reports should be facilitated.

Most of the problems can be considered as direct tests, but not all. Problems 8, 9 and 12 each involve more than one element of the model and these other aspects of decision making contemplated by the model cannot reasonably be regarded as not contentious, and the propositions relating to the former two require of the judges relatively complex mental arithmetic to calculate the proportion of the secondary offence made cumulative. For example, it can be seen from Table 4.3 that, for Problem 8, the second, seventh and eighth general predictions are all of critical import; and the three are open to question. Accordingly, it would not be clear from a negative result whether one or all of these three elements were inconsistent with judicial decision making. There is a second problem: it is that the solution does not follow directly from the application of principle; the reason for this is that the application of the propositions involves conflicting influences across the two cases – in the first case relative to the second, one requiring greater cumulation (see the second prediction) and the other leading to less cumulation (see the eighth prediction) – and in order to determine the overall result the judge is required, in effect, to make mental calculations. As a consequence it would not be clear from a negative result whether one or more of the relevant propositions were invalid or the judge's answer was due to a miscalculation, perhaps arising from information overload. On the same ground a positive result offers no more than tenuous support for the general predictions. Accordingly, quanta of sentence are not appropriately considered in an indirect test. And because of the complex interactions between the hypothesized principles determining what is appropriate by way of sentence, the omission by a judge of a reference in the protocol to any one of the three relevant propositions could not be taken as hard evidence of its invalidity. Nevertheless, a reference in the protocol to an element of the model could be treated as offering support for or against its significance. The conceptual complexity of this type of problem similarly militates against the author's conveying to the judge concisely and unambiguously the decision principles which according to the model govern the problem, and so the reflective retrospective reports too are a tenuous test of the model; in view of these circumstances it would not be prudent to give much weight to a judge's simple statement of agreement or disagreement with the approach outlined by the author, since from an unelaborated response there could be no confidence that the judge had even an intuitive understanding of the problem. For these reasons, problems in which multiple and contentious aspects of the model bear upon the solution are appropriately regarded as indirect tests of the model.

Problems may also provide no more than indirect tests of a general prediction where the proposition relates to a case but according to the model the answer to the problem does not turn on it. For example, consider Problem 6 in relation to the fourth proposition: the predicted equality of sentence for the two cases comprising this problem (see the tenth proposition) does not turn on whether the seriousness of a secondary offence is independent of the seriousness of its legal offence category, but the presence of the offence of rape in the second case may prompt a judge to comment on its relative contribution to the effective sentence of the case. Now, because the hypothesized solution to the problem does not turn on this element, a judge's failure to refer to it would not lead to its validity being questioned; however, an incidental yet express avowal or disavowal of it in the verbal protocol or reflective retrospective report could be taken as support or rejection, respectively, of the validity of this element of the model, but again a general statement of agreement or disagreement in the reflective report would not be informative; and, of course, quanta of sentence are not relevant to an indirect test of a proposition under these circumstances.

Some of the general predictions, namely, the first, fifth, seventh, ninth and eleventh, do not have direct quantitative implications, but describe how according to the model judges would be expected to structure their reasoning

Table 4.3 *Relationship between Propositions 1–13 and the sentencing problems as direct and indirect tests*

Proposition number	Problem number(s) – direct test	Problem number(s) – indirect test
1	1–7, 10–11, 13–17	8, 9, 12, 30(1–10)
2	1,[21(1–6)][a]	7, 8
3	2, 5	11
4	[3, 4][a]	6
5	17	
6	17	
7	10	8, 9
8	10,[21(5–6), 23(1–4)][a]	8, 9
9	13	6, 7, 9, 11, 12
10	6, 7, 11	
11	13	9, 12
12	13,[22(1–4)][a]	12
13	14, 15, 16	

Note: [a] The responses to the problems in brackets are considered together.

as a means of reaching a solution to the problem. The fact that a prediction does not have quantitative implications should not be taken *per se* to render it incapable of direct test. Something as fundamental as a judge's approach to a sentencing problem should be reflected in a verbal protocol and the relevant propositions should be capable of being conveyed concisely and unambiguously by the author to the judge for the reflective retrospective reports. Again, not much weight was given to simple statements of agreement or disagreement in the reflective reports, since there could be no certainty that reference was being made to the decision process rather than just to the outcome (i.e., the effective sentence[s]).

Table 4.3 sets out for each of Propositions 1–13 the problem(s) regarded as the direct/indirect test(s) of its validity. Each general prediction and problem is identified by the same number by which it was labelled earlier in this chapter. It is appropriate at this point to explain and justify how the offences of rape, indecent assault, arson and intentional damage to property complement armed robbery and burglary in the testing of the general predictions. In Problem 2 a third offence was required and arson was chosen because it did not seem to be obviously an intrinsically more serious crime than burglary, a view confirmed by judges' sentencing practices as reflected in the official sentencing statistics; consequently, it was expected that the judges would not regard this offence as principal to the burglary; in addition, it appeared that in conjunction with either armed robbery or burglary it would not introduce special connotations regarding the type of offender or the nature of the offending. In Problem 3 rape was used because it is clearly an intrinsically more serious crime than burglary and was not expected to be regarded by the judges as principal to armed robbery. Again, this conclusion is consistent with the official sentencing statistics. Problem 3 tests whether the seriousness of the secondary offence is defined by its quantum of sentence and is independent of the seriousness of its legal offence category. Now, the offence of rape differs from burglary in a number of respects: it belongs to a more serious legal offence category – as required by the nature of the problem; but it is a different type of offence – sexual compared to property; and it shares with armed robbery an element of violence and confrontation, but unlike burglary does not have a property element in common with armed robbery. These latter two differences between rape and burglary confound the test. To counter this, Problem 4, comprising a case with the offence of indecent assault, was introduced as a control; the official sentencing statistics suggest that it does not belong to a significantly more serious legal offence category than burglary, and yet it is similar to rape in terms of its relationship to burglary and armed robbery. The aim of Problem 16 was to test whether for the purposes of cumulation the seriousness of a secondary offence, for which a non-custodial sanction would be appropriate if it stood alone, is independent of the seriousness of the instant offence. In respect of this, the relevant characteristic of intentional damage to property is that it would be expected that the sentence appropriate to a trivial instance of this offence would be a non-custodial sanction at a level of severity on the sanction scale well below a term of imprisonment.

To this point in the analysis, the propositions, viewed as predictions, relate to their respective problems in general terms only. When the data bearing on these problems are analyzed (see Chapter 6) it is in terms of predictions specific to each of the problems used to test a proposition and derived from that proposition.

In regard to the testing of the validity of the model, it must be borne in mind that an important aspect of the model has been ignored. It is fundamental to the model that the determination of cumulation is made in terms of seriousness rather than sentence. The present omission here of this aspect of the model does not preclude the valid testing of the general structure of the model; indeed it would have been time-wasting to descend to this level of detail until the structure of the model had been confirmed. In view of this, for some of the problems, the analysis requires the assumption that the relationship between the dimension of seriousness and the quantum of sentence for the legal category of the principal offence does not depart significantly from linearity, an apparently reasonable assumption in the light of the data in Figure 2.4.

CHAPTER FIVE

The techniques of data collection

In the previous chapter the model describing how judges reach sentencing decisions in cases comprising multiple disparate and separate counts was used to derive hypotheses so that it was possible to test this model by means of a series of sentencing problems. This chapter describes how the data were collected for this purpose. Three sets of data were used, each set generated by a different technique, although the sentencing problems provided a common framework within which these three techniques were applied. The three techniques were: (1) sentences imposed by a sample of judges for the cases in the sentencing problems, to investigate which aspects of the model were consistent with the judges' sentencing behavior and which were not; (2) verbal protocols based on immediate retrospective reports and providing direct, detailed and accurate information on the content and sequence of the judges' thoughts as they worked through the sentencing problems; and (3) reflective retrospective reports in which the judges were asked to comment on whether the various elements of the model were accepted by them as valid descriptions of the method to be adopted when sentencing the multiple offender. For these three techniques of data collection, the judges in the sample were tested individually.

Each of the three techniques is now described, justified, and its place in the testing of the model explained, in turn. Following this, the procedural details relating to the administration of these techniques are described.

Techniques: description and justification

Sentences for the sentencing problems

The judges' first task was to impose effective sentences for each of the cases in the sentencing problems and these responses were compared with the pattern of responses predicted on the basis of the proposed decision model as a test of its validity. The reader will recall from the previous chapter that each sentencing problem consists of one or two cases; each case is fictitious and presented in the form of a skeleton description.

This, of course, immediately raises the question of why judges' responses to fictitious sentencing exercises were used as a basis for understanding how judges determine appropriate sentences in multiple-count cases. It will be apparent from the previous chapter setting out the problems that the validation required a relatively large number of cases and each case had to meet a tight specification in respect of case characteristics and appropriate sentences; moreover, the judges' responses had to be analyzed individually so that expected individual differences in the approaches adopted by the judges could be monitored. Clearly, it would not have been possible to find in the archival records a set of cases whose offence characteristics satisfied these exacting requirements for one judge let alone a small sample of judges, and not to mention the problems of matching cases on offender characteristics and other extraneous variables such as time periods.

There is a second potential advantage associated with the use of fictitious cases. What is required for an ideal model is an understanding of how judges would determine sentence where they were free from the potentially distorting influences of confounding factors such as information overload due to the complexity of cases, and factors that may be legally immaterial and yet emotionally and personally compelling (e.g., sympathy for distressed relatives of the offender). The advantage of fictitious cases in this context is that they do not carry this artifactual baggage.

The preceding discussion offers reasons why the technique of fictitious cases was used in this study as a means of obtaining information about how judges determine sentence. This having been done, it is now appropriate to explain why for the sentencing problems information about the cases was not presented to the judges by way of comprehensive summary descriptions of the relevant offence and offender characteristics, but rather in the form of skeleton descriptions. These comprised the legal categories of offence to which the constituent offences belong, the number of counts of each of the offences, the sentence appropriate to each of the offence categories, together with the information that it was to be assumed that the offender had a very serious record of relevant prior convictions together with little if anything by way of personal mitigation; for each case in the exercise, then, it fell to individual judges to envisage a description of the offence and offender characteristics satisfying the given outline of the case, at least in a sufficient degree of detail to enable them to arrive at a sentence. The reason for adopting this form of presentation for the problems relates directly to the aim of the study, namely, how judges aggregate two or more appropriate sentences for offences comprising a case. It was important, therefore, that where for the validation it was necessary to ascertain what judges determine as the appropriate effective sentence for a case comprising, say, two offences for which the individual appropriate sentences are twelve years and four years, that the judges were in fact aggregating sentences of twelve and four years. Now, this could not have been assumed if the cases had been presented in the form of comprehensive summary descriptions of the facts of the offences comprising the case and the characteristics of the offender. The untenability of this assumption is shown dramatically in Lovegrove's (1989) study: there a sample of judges meeting the same defining characteristics as the one used in this study imposed sentences for a set of fictitious cases of house burglary presented in the form of comprehensive summary descriptions of the circumstances of the offence(s) and the characteristics of the offender. One of the findings was that the judges' sentences for the same cases varied widely. For example, for the case deemed by each judge to be the most serious (the judges did not all agree on which of the cases in the set was the most serious) the effective sentences varied from a low of 45 months to a high of 108 months for the sample of seven judges, and for the next most extreme pair of judges the range was 108 to 54 months. Clearly, the between-judge variation in regard to what is appropriate by way of sentence based on a description of the circumstances of a case is too great for the purpose served by the sentencing problems.

Lovegrove (1989) discussed and empirically affirmed the validity of the technique of fictitious cases as a means of studying judicial decision making in sentencing (see Chapter 8). However, one of the conditions which held in that study – presentation of the cases in the form of comprehensive summary descriptions – did not apply here. Thus the conclusion from that study upon which the soundness of the fictitious procedure was supported cannot be applied to the present sentencing exercise without further comment. It is possible that the requirement on a judge to envisage a description of the case characteristics satisfying the given outline of a case may render a judge's responses of doubtful value as a basis for studying ideal decision making, since judges might adopt a different method of determining effective sentences under these conditions from that which they would follow when cases were presented as comprehensive summary descriptions. This was not thought likely to be a problem, however, since the judges were all experienced in the criminal jurisdiction and it is easy to accept that they could readily envisage appropriate patterns of offending normally associated with the quanta of sentence to be assumed for the offences comprising the cases. Moreover, the skeletal descriptions included a description, albeit a very brief outline, of the circumstances of the offender, and this was expected to facilitate the judges' considering appropriate patterns of offending associated with the offences comprising the cases. Then again, it might be thought that greater mental effort would be required of the judges in their determining of sentences for cases presented in skeletal form and that this effort would be so great as to exceed their information-processing capability and would thereby induce distortions in their characteristic modes of reasoning. If the view outlined in the previous point is accurate, then information overload could not be regarded as a problem here. A second potentially unwanted impact of the skeletal description of cases arises from the fact that an appropriate sentence is given for each comprising count (or series of multiple counts belonging to a particular legal offence category). Clearly, this favors an analytic approach to the determination of effective sentences and would perhaps incline some judges against what may be their natural tendency to adopt a global approach in which an effective sentence is determined, somewhat intuitively, first and then sentences are fixed for the comprising counts to accord with this. Nevertheless, in considering the validity of this study in relation to its aim of developing a model of ideal decision making, it must be remembered that the effective sentence for a case, however determined, should be appropriate to the combined seriousness of the comprising counts and this is dependent on the quantum of sentence appropriate to each of those comprising counts.

Verbal protocols

The sentencing problems provide a rigorous test of the decision-making model in the sense that the predictions are precise and the judges' responses in the form of quanta of sentence can be shown unambiguously to be either consistent with the various aspects of the model and so in support of it or inconsistent with the model and thereby demonstrating that at least some aspects of it require modification. Now, although this approach offers precision, this is not sufficient; several limitations attend the analysis.

First, consider the outcome in which all aspects of the model are found to be consistent with the judges' decisions. Such a finding would not rule out the possibility that there are other aspects of judicial decision making associated with the sentencing of the multiple offender but not contemplated by the model. This circumstance arises because the exercise is theory-dependent: only problems which test the validity of one or more features of the model's structure were included in the analysis; clearly, it is not possible logically and systematically to formulate problems testing unanticipated aspects of decision making. Now, the more adventurous the model-builder and the more plentiful the legal clues, then the less cause there should be for concern over the insufficiency of the exercise as a test of the structure of the decision process under study. Fortunately, the present model can be reasonably regarded as quite complex in that it is not limited to a few elements. This was made possible because legal analyses by academic lawyers of sentencing judgments and the author's own observations provided a rich set of clues about the possible structure of the model. Moreover, since the model is quantitative, the algebra governing the relationships between the various elements also played its part in ensuring that the model was more rather than less developed. And the author, being aware of this limitation in the process of model development, strove to wring the legal data as hard as possible so as to extract the last clue and to incorporate as many of these clues in the model as his imagination would allow. At this point an error of commission was to be preferred to an error of omission, since experimentation provides for the detection of the former but not the latter. While this device minimized the likelihood of an outcome in which all or most aspects of the model were found to be consistent with the judges' decisions and yet significant aspects of judicial decision making in the sentencing of multiple offenders were overlooked, clearly, this approach was not immune to this error.

There is another limitation associated with an outcome where all aspects of the model are found to be consistent with the judges' decisions. It is that it offers no insight into the nature of the judges' more or less conscious thoughts preceding the decision. One possibility concerning this process is that judges draw upon the totality principle – the principle upon which the model is based – and consciously and correctly apply it to particular problems in the form of related rules, these rules being used in conjunction with their knowledge of the values of relevant parameters such as the quantum of sentence appropriate to a single count of armed robbery falling at the upper limit of seriousness of this offence category. In reaching their decisions in this way, judges would be thinking in the same way as one, say, applies the rules of arithmetic to multiply two numbers. An alternative possibility is that judges know from experience what are acceptable effective sentences for particular combinations of individual sentences associated with particular combinations of legal offence categories, and reach a decision solely and directly on the basis of this knowledge, in a process analogous to one's learning the multiples of common numbers. Now, as long as what they considered to be the appropriate effective sentences were originally determined through the application of the correct legal principle, then the judges' answers would be consistent with the model, even though in reaching their decisions they did not refer to principle nor were even conscious of the principle underlying the accepted tariffs. And so the use of predicted numerical outcomes alone in the sentencing problems as a means of testing the decision model would not have provided information about the decision makers' conscious thought processes. Yet an appreciation of how judges consciously approach the task of sentencing the multiple offender and their level of understanding of the rules associated with the totality principle is necessary in order to understand current sentencing policy and may well be invaluable when determining how a system of numerical guidance is to be applied.

Secondly, consider the outcome in which one or more aspects of the model are found to be inconsistent with the judges' decisions. When the data base comprises no more than confirmed or unconfirmed numerical predictions the problem is that there are no available clues about the appropriate structure of the model in regard to the unconfirmed aspects. There are a number of possibilities. One is that the element is not a necessary part of the judges' decision or that the element is a part of the decision but takes a different form. A second alternative is that the aspect of the model under test marks a gap or fuzzy point in the judges' decision making, i.e., an aspect which has never been covered by an explicit and coherent principle or, indeed, consistent practice, and yet about which judges should form a view in the course of reaching a decision. The third possibility relates to method. It may be that the failure of the judges' behavior to confirm the model's predictions is an artifact of the method: the body of principle which the judges were attempting to apply is consistent with those underpinning the model, but their application of it was distorted by factors peculiar to the sentencing exercise but not characteristic of the sentencing task confronting them in court. Fourthly, the task of sentencing the multiple offender may exceed the judges' capacities to process information; if this is so, decision making would be sub-optimal and for this reason there would be inconsistency between the model's predictions and the judges' decisions. The culprit here is not of methodological origin, but is a potential source of influence on judges as they sentence offenders in court as well as in a sentencing exercise.

Clearly, a data base of confirmed and unconfirmed numerical predictions leaves much to be desired as a basis for understanding the application of current sentencing policy and for developing a system of numerical guidance. What is required is the direct observation of the judges' thought processes during the course of their decision making. The observations must have a high temporal density so that the trace of the judges' thinking can be as complete as possible. Fortunately, there was a well-developed body of theory and an associated method which could be applied to this problem. Ericsson and Simon (1984) developed a theory on verbal thinking-aloud protocols as data, and the culmination of their work is a proposed set of readily applied techniques for obtaining verbal protocols. (See, also, Svenson, 1989, particularly regarding methodological considerations in process studies of judgment.)

Ericsson and Simon (1984) claim that two forms of verbal protocols can be regarded as providing direct, detailed and accurate information on the content and sequence of individuals' thoughts as they attempt to solve problems, namely, concurrent verbal reports and immediate retrospective verbal reports. This information may be treated as a data base for the purpose of developing or testing theories about how the individuals under study reach particular decisions or solve given problems, i.e., what information is processed and how it is processed by decision makers.

Concurrent verbal reports are generated when subjects are given a problem to solve and are asked to report what they are thinking (i.e., to think aloud) as they attempt to solve the problem. There are two conditions under which verbal reports are acknowledged by Ericsson and Simon (1984) to contain serious gaps as a record of the subjects' decision processes. One of these circumstances is where the subjects find the problem cognitively too demanding; the second of the circumstances arises where the task has been well practised by the subjects. Moreover, it appears that mediating steps leading directly to a solution are often not verbalized.

Immediate retrospective reports are generated when subjects are given a problem to solve and, immediately upon completing it, are asked to report orally everything that they can remember about the sequence and content of their thoughts as they attempted to solve the problem. In most respects immediate retrospective reports have the same characteristics as concurrent verbal reports; nevertheless, at least under some circumstances there may be differences (see Ericsson and Simon, 1984): these reports may omit significant information actually heeded by the subjects, where they took a relatively long time to reach a solution; and reports for a particular problem may contain information not actually heeded by the subjects during its solution, but heeded at some earlier time, especially where the problem was one of a series of similar problems. If the subjects are not able to remember the sequence and content of their thoughts as they solved the problem or are not prepared to make an attempt to remember the details, then they might respond to the instruction by reporting as a memory what is in fact a set of inferences based on personal supposition about how they may have solved the problem.

There appeared to be no reason to believe that if judges were asked to provide immediate retrospective reports of their attempts to solve the sentencing problems then they would not be of good quality in terms of completeness and accuracy. The judges in the present sample were volunteers and no doubt would want to appear competent; for these reasons they could be assumed to be well motivated. While each of the sentencing problems appeared to have a sufficient number of parameters and individuality to be cognitively demanding, there was no reason to believe that any of them would exceed the cognitive capacity of experienced judges. Furthermore, the problems, just as the real-life sentencing cases they represented, could scarcely be regarded as routine or repetitious and for this reason not requiring thoughtful and separate attention. Finally, the judges were expected to reach a decision on each problem in a relatively short time. After considering the various relevant factors, it was decided on balance that data on the judges' thought processes as they attempted to solve the sentencing problems might be of a higher quality in immediate retrospective reports than concurrent verbal reports. Reasons have just been given for the conclusion that immediate retrospective reports would be expected to be of a high quality. Two considerations relating to concurrent verbal reports favored the conclusion that they might produce data of a somewhat lower quality under the conditions of the present study. First, judges are not accustomed to thinking aloud and there was the possibility that they may have found the experience disquieting and distracting. Secondly, although the sentencing problems were not expected to exceed the judges' cognitive capacities it was thought they might nevertheless place comparatively heavy demands on their short-term memories. Under these circumstances, it seemed to be foolish to require the judges to think aloud, thereby placing upon them an even greater cognitive load.

There is a voluminous literature covering theory and method in relation to this technique (see White, 1988). The relevant matters concerning method have been raised already. Some of the theoretical issues require discussion. Doubts have been raised over whether concurrent verbal reports and immediate retrospective reports obtained under ideal conditions can be regarded as providing direct, detailed and accurate information on the content and sequence of subjects' thoughts as they attempt to reach a solution to a given problem. Nisbett and Wilson (1977) can perhaps be regarded as the best-known protagonists of one of these concerns. Decision makers, these two researchers have argued, have negligible access by means of introspection to the higher-order cognitive processes actually determining their decisions. Accordingly, when individuals are asked to give an account of the actual cognitive factors responsible for their decisions their reports are based on personal speculation about the more plausible causes of their decisions. This leads to the conclusion that decision makers' reports about the basis of their decisions will be accurate only when the actual causes are the causes seen by them as plausible causes or the actual determinants are the cognitive processes heeded by them in the course of their solving of the problem. (These conditions would hold when decision makers consciously apply known rules to solve a problem; see Smith and Miller, 1978.) However, Nisbett and Wilson do recognize that individuals in the course of solving a problem are aware at any particular time of what thoughts are the focus of their attention. Now, Ericsson and Simon (1984) seize on this concession by Nisbett and Wilson as a basis for their counter-argument: the data appropriate to a valid protocol analysis are not the subjects' inferences about the factors underlying their decisions, but are the information heeded by them as they attempt to solve the problem; rather, it is the researcher who draws the inferences about the nature of the underlying decision process on the basis of the material in the subjects' focal attention during the course of the decision making.

Is this rebuttal definitive? Payne, Braunstein and Carroll (1978), prompted by the conclusions of Nisbett and Wilson (1977), questioned the validity of verbal protocols when strong norms apply to a behavior or decision. This point must raise doubts about the validity of verbal protocols (concurrent verbal and immediate retrospective reports) when the decisions are made by experts, and a part of the decision makers' expertise is a knowledge of the principles established by their profession as being applicable to these decisions. Now, the appellate courts have formulated an approach, albeit an incomplete and general one, known as the totality principle, an approach applying to the problems in the sentencing exercise. And so the conditions hold under which properly obtained verbal protocols may reveal information heeded by the decision makers and plausibly determinative and yet the information on which their decisions were based may not have been in their awareness or, even if it was in their awareness, may have been camouflaged by or indistinguishable from the information heeded but not determinative. In order to explain how this outcome might arise, it is necessary to recall the two previously stated alternative views of the judges' possible conscious thought processes preceding a decision. The first view is that judges consciously apply rules relating to the totality principle – the principle upon which the model is based – in conjunction with their knowledge of the values of relevant parameters such as the quantum of sentence appropriate to a single serious count of armed robbery; the second view is that judges know from experience what are the acceptable effective sentences for particular combinations of individual sentences and legal offence categories. Consider the contents of the verbal protocols produced by each of these strategies. In the former case the information heeded by the judge would comprise references to legal principle and tariffs; in the latter case the protocols would cover tariffs only. Now, would not the inferences made by the experimenter about the determinants of the judges' decisions on the basis of the protocols be problematic if the effect of the instruction to think aloud were to cause the judges to apply rules relating to the totality principle, though they would not otherwise have thought about them, while they still solved the problems simply and solely by drawing upon their knowledge of the appropriate tariffs? Such verbal reports would provide an accurate record of the information actually heeded by the judges but could not be regarded as a sound basis upon which researchers could draw valid inferences about the cognitive processes underlying the judges' decisions.

What is the import of these deliberations for the interpretation of verbal protocols obtained from the judges in this study? In considering the significance of this discussion it is helpful to recall the purposes intended to be served by the verbal reports as an adjunct to the data base of confirmed and unconfirmed numerical predictions from the sentencing problems. These were to obtain information about aspects of the judges' decision making not contemplated by the model, to determine whether judges view this task as a problem involving the application of principle and the extent to which they are capable of applying an appropriate body of principle to the sentencing problems, to propose alternative hypotheses where predictions have failed, to identify gaps in policy, and to have some chance of detecting unwanted methodological influences and information overload. In this context it matters not that a possible effect of the instruction to think aloud is that it might have encouraged the judges to adopt a principled approach in relation to these problems when they would not otherwise have done so. The principle applied by these judges might be based on their knowledge of sentencing policy or just speculation – what seemed to them to be a reasonable method and not inconsistent with their understanding of policy. Again, for the validity of the present analysis it matters not. The important point is that there is no reason to believe that the information in the protocols would not be a record of the judges' actual thoughts; there are no grounds for supposing that the protocols would be a record of the judges' inferences about what they were thinking. Moreover, it matters not that under these circumstances the judges' consideration of principle might not have determined their decisions, since the information heeded by the judges as they worked toward a solution to a problem is not being used to draw inferences about how they actually reached a decision. This approach could be taken because the aim of the research is to build a model describing how judges should ideally aggregate sentences in cases comprising multiple offences from different legal offence categories; it follows that the purpose of obtaining the protocol data is to draw inferences about how the judges understand and attempt to apply this aspect of sentencing policy. There is nothing in the preceding discussion suggesting that properly obtained immediate retrospective reports would not provide valid data for this purpose.

Reflective retrospective reports

In order to explain the significance of a set of data comprising the judges' reflective retrospective reports about the validity of the decision model as applied to the sentencing problems, it is important that the role of the sentencing judge be understood. The sentencing principles enunciated or discovered in appellate court judgments are invariably couched in general terms and do not address the majority of the matters which arise in the determination of sentence in particular cases. Accordingly, it falls to the judges sentencing in the first instance to fill in the gaps and give detail to the policy; these judges may make policy consciously and explicitly in arriving at their decisions, or they may determine sentence intuitively; in the latter instance, policy may not be in their awareness, but be implicit, merely a consequence of their having determined a sentence. (This detailed aspect of policy is perhaps more appropriately regarded as a set of working rules, rather than being described by the more elevated notion of "principles.") The consequence of this position is that the policies of judges sentencing in the first instance must at some point be used as a data base upon which inferences regarding the structure of a model of judicial decision making are made. The verbal protocols and the reflective retrospective reports were seen as the means to this end.

Now, there is a critical limitation associated with immediate retrospective reports as a means of testing the model. Consider judges who have an established and stable yet intuitive understanding of the determination of sentence and, for this reason, cannot verbalize their deliberations. Such judges may offer little content in their protocols or, though providing a substantial protocol, their strategy may not be apparent. Reflective retrospective reports were thought to be a possible means of addressing this problem. Accordingly, the validity of the decision model was also tested by the author's describing to each judge how the model applied to each problem and simply asking whether he accepted this as the correct approach to the determination of sentence. The judges' answers are the reflective retrospective reports. This approach requires the view that what is correct by way of sentencing policy is what judges say, explicitly and in full awareness, it is, and only that to which they give their assent. Again, it must be remembered that the model, since it was intended as a basis for understanding current policy and developing a system of numerical guidance, attempts to describe how judges should determine sentences for multiple offenders. If the purpose of the model had been to describe how judges actually sentence in this type of case, then the technique of asking the judges whether they approved of the principles underlying the model would not have been an appropriate procedure for validating the model. Ericsson and Simon (1984) have analyzed the deficiencies of this type of report as a source of information about how decision makers actually reach decisions: these accounts are incomplete and inaccurate. The reports are incomplete because some of the information heeded does not enter the decision makers' long-term memory or cannot be retrieved from it. The reports are inaccurate because to a significant extent the information conveyed is a composite of the decision makers' knowledge about how the judgment should be made as well as their inferences and abstractions based on incomplete recollections about how they did arrive at particular decisions. Of course, the testing of model validity by means of these reflective reports cannot be regarded as definitive. It requires the assumption that the judges understood and were aware of the full implications of the author's statements of the various elements of the model as reflected in the sentencing problems.

To test the validity of the model the judges were shown individually how the relevant principle(s) or working rule(s) of the model applied to each problem. They were asked to comment on whether the aspect of the model, as presented, accurately represented the principle(s) or working rule(s) that should govern the determination of the effective sentence(s) for the case(s) in the problem before them and, if not, in what way it was in error. These questions did not prompt the judges to address any aspects of sentencing policy not incorporated in the model. To attempt to correct this, judges were also asked to say whether there were additional principles or working rules relevant to sentence determination in the problem before them. The reflective retrospective reporting was kept separate from the immediate retrospective reporting and, indeed, the fact that the judges were to be asked to make these latter reports was not intimated to them until they had completed the first session in which they determined sentences for the cases comprising the sentencing problems and gave the verbal protocols. There was a cogent reason for this, namely, if in the first session the judges had been required to reflect on their approach at the end of each problem, this experience might have inclined them in the immediate retrospective reports for subsequent problems to reflect on their thought processes rather than to report accurately the content of these processes.

Techniques: administration

Procedure – sentences for the sentencing problems and the verbal protocols – first sentencing exercise

In Victoria, Australia, the types of case used in the sentencing problems are normally determined in the County Court (cf. the Supreme Court or the Magistrates' Courts). Accordingly, the author formally sought the permission of the Chief Judge, who agreed to the study and offered to approach individual judges to seek their co-operation. The author asked him to select eight judges who generally would be regarded as experienced in criminal work and who might be prepared to participate in a study examining the feasibility of providing judges with more detailed guidance in sentencing. (At this time there were about forty-five judges who, on roster, exercised the criminal jurisdiction of the County Court. There were no women on this Court at the time of the study.) The Chief Judge sent a list of eight names to the author, who in turn contacted these judges to explain the study to them and to confirm their offer of co-operation. The judges were told that the aim of the study was to investigate, with a view to developing a system of guidance, the method/ approach followed by judges in determining what is appropriate by way of sentence. It was explained that the exercises undertaken by a group of County Court judges for the author in 1987 were concerned with how judges determine sentence for cases comprising single counts and multiple counts belonging to the same statutory offence category, whereas the focus of this study was cases consisting of multiple counts from different offence categories. The judges were told that their participation in this study would require a substantial commitment: it was made clear that this study would require their participation in two sessions in their chambers, taking up to a total of about four hours, in which they would be asked to solve problems relating to this aspect of sentencing, and as well they would be asked to determine sentences for about forty fictitious cases which would be left with them to work through in their own time. It was stressed to the judges that this was a feasibility study only and that should detailed guidance be introduced the information gathered from them as part of this study would not be incorporated in that system.

Clearly, this sample of judges was not representative of the County Court judges who at this time determined criminal matters. This was not seen as a problem because the project was a feasibility study only. Rather, the bias was intentional and regarded as a strength; it was thought that this group would be more likely to have a greater understanding of the judicial approach to sentencing the multiple offender – the intent of the study, after all, was to tap judicial wisdom not to expose judicial ignorance – and would be less likely to be troubled by the abstract nature of the task. The eight judges were told how the sample had been selected. Four of the judges who participated in this study had also completed the sentencing exercises in Lovegrove's (1989) first study.

The author arranged individual appointments for the first exercise; at this time the judges were asked whether they would permit their answers in this and the second exercise to be tape-recorded, a request to which all agreed. Each judge was assigned an identification number and retained this number throughout this series of studies.

The forty-one sentencing problems were presented using the notation explained previously (see Tables 4.1 and 4.2) on index cards (75 × 125 mm), one problem per card, and comprising Problems 1–17, Problems 21(1–6), 22(1–4) and 23(1–4), and finally, Problems 30(1–10). Problems 1–17 were presented first, in random sequence, there being a different order for each of the judges, with two constraints: first, the problems comprising at least one case with multiple counts of a particular offence category or with three offence categories (viz., Problems 8, 9, 10, 12, 13 and 17) followed the problems not meeting these criteria (these nominated problems would appear to be conceptually more difficult than the others; now it was felt that the early presentation of these more complex cases might militate against the judges' adapting readily to the presentation of the problems in skeletal form); secondly, Problem 14 was always presented first (it appeared that this problem was conceptually the easiest and its early presentation might facilitate the judges' adapting to the form in which the sentencing problems were presented). Problems 22(1–4) followed Problems 21(1–6) and the former were in turn followed by Problems 23(1–4), but within this sequence each group of related problems [22(1–4), etc.] were presented in a different random order to each of the judges. Finally, Problems 30(1–10) were presented, again in a different random sequence across the judges.

The instructions for the judges' verbal protocols were closely based on the specimen directions of Ericsson and Simon (1984). Verbal protocols were not required for all of the problems associated with Problems 21, 22 and 23. Across and within each of these three groups of related problems, most of the comprising problems had the same structural form and, accordingly, addressed the same set of principles. It was felt that the judges' views regarding the matters raised could be tapped by several representative problems, and so it was only for Problems 21(2), 21(6), and 23(4) that verbal protocols were sought from the judges.

The judges were encouraged to take a break of several minutes after work periods of half, one, and one-and-a-half hours, and where a judge had not completed this exercise in two hours he was encouraged to conclude the session forthwith and to complete it in a second session in the near future.

The author administered this exercise. He introduced the session with the following instructions and directions; these were not read formally and verbatim but presented in point form in a natural conversational manner.

This exercise is the first in a series of three designed to investigate how judges determine what is appropriate by way of an effective (maximum) sentence for an offender who has been found guilty on more than one count and at least two of the counts belong to different statutory offence categories (e.g., a case in which an offender is to be sentenced on two counts of armed robbery and one count of burglary), and the offences are properly regarded as separate transactions which, while not part of a spree, do not incorporate one or more counts from the offender's distant past. As you are aware consideration is being given to providing the courts with more detailed guidance so that judges will have more assistance in the task of determining the types and levels of sentence appropriate to the various types of case for which they are required to impose penalties. In order to develop a system of guidance, it is necessary to understand how judges construe information about cases – the method/approach judges adopt – in order to determine sentences. The information gathered in this series of studies will be analyzed for that purpose. Your responses will not become part of a system of guidance.

The exercise takes the form of forty-one sentencing problems. The majority of these problems ($n = 25$) comprise one case, and the rest, two cases. Information about each of the cases is confined to a skeleton description: you are given the legal categories of offence to which the constituent offences belong, the number of counts of each of the offences, (generally) the maximum sentence appropriate to each of the offences standing alone (where for an offence category there are multiple counts of a particular offence, the maximum sentence appropriate to the main offence within the offence category and the effective maximum sentence appropriate to the offence category) – you must assume that the given sentences are the quanta which you would have set for these offences – together with a very brief statement about the extent of the offender's criminal history and mitigation. While in most of the sentencing problems you are given the appropriate maximum sentences (and appropriate effective maximum sentences), in some instances you will be asked to fix these sentences on the basis of a very brief description of the seriousness of the circumstances surrounding the offence. Unless instructed to the contrary, you are to assume that the offender has a very serious record of relevant prior convictions together with little by way of personal mitigation (e.g., the offender is not young, did not play a minor role in the offences, etc.); also, you are to assume that in each case the offender pleaded guilty – he initially denied the charges to the police but changed his position when confronted with the evidence during the interview. It may be helpful for you to envisage the nature and level of seriousness of a set of offence characteristics (e.g., degree of organization, nature of violence, amount of money stolen, etc.) which, in view of the assumed offender characteristics, you would regard as warranting the quantum of sentence fixed for each particular offence category; for offences of moderate seriousness you should assume that the case facts in respect of each offence characteristic make an approximately equal contribution to the total seriousness of the offence (i.e., the offence is moderately serious in terms of the value of the theft, degree of organization, etc.).

There is a sound reason for presenting the cases in the form of a skeletal rather than a comprehensive summary description. The purpose of this study is to investigate how judges aggregate two or more sentences of known quanta; now, if the cases were presented as factual descriptions the quanta of sentence deemed to be appropriate to the offences in each case would be expected to vary significantly across the sample of judges.

I shall present the cases to you, in turn, singly or in pairs, on cards. Please treat each case as independent of the others and assume that each of the cases relates to a different offender.

In most of the sentencing problems you are asked to determine an effective (maximum) sentence for each case, and where concurrency is appropriate make the necessary orders. Please exercise your discretion in accordance with sentencing law and sentencing policy (and practice) as it is to be found currently in relevant statutes and appellate judgments: fix each sentence as though you were making the determination for an actual case being heard by you in your Court. Please show how you constructed the total sentence, i.e., set out the separate quantum contributions of each of the offence categories in each case; you may, as part of this process, modify the type and quantum of sentence considered appropriate for those offences which when standing alone warrant non-custodial sentences. Write your sentences with the corresponding problem numbers on the separate sheets of paper provided for this purpose. You are not required to give reasons for your decisions. In those instances in which two cases are presented together you are encouraged to fix different sentences if one case is in your view more serious than the other, even though the margin be small. You are not required to fix a minimum sentence for any of the cases. In the final group of sentencing problems your task is to select the principal offence in each of the problems.

In this study I am also interested in having a record of your thoughts as you determine what is appropriate by way of sentence for each case (or pair of cases) or as you select the principal offence. So that I can obtain this information I should be grateful if, immediately upon your having determined a sentence for a case (or sentences for a pair of cases), or having selected a principal offence, you would tell me all you can remember about what you were thinking from the time you read the description of the case (or cases) until you made your decision. I am interested in what you can remember, not what you think you must have thought. If you are able to tell me about your thoughts in the sequence in which they occurred while you were working towards your decision, please do so. Tell me if you are uncertain about the accuracy of any aspect of your recall. When you make your report I do not want you to attempt to redo the task or to explain how you reached your decision; just report all that you can remember thinking about as you worked towards your decision; it does not matter if your thoughts do not appear to follow a coherent sequence.

At this point, the judge was given the opportunity of asking questions about any aspects of the task which were perhaps unclear to him; matters arising during the presentation of the instructions or in the course of the session and leading to confusion in the mind of the judge were promptly clarified.

The judge was then taken through the exercise, card by card. For Problem 14, the judge was told he may assume for the offence of armed robbery that there were personal extenuating factors associated with this offence (e.g., the offender played a minor role), if he thought that the non-custodial sentence was not appropriate for an offender with a serious criminal record and little personal mitigation; a similar assumption was considered appropriate for the offence of burglary in Problems 14 and 15.

For cases in Problems 11, 21, 22 and 23 the judge was not given the value of the sentence (where applicable, the effective sentence) appropriate to the armed robbery. Rather, in Problems 21(1–2) the judge was asked to set a sentence for a single count of armed robbery in which the circumstances surrounding the offence (e.g., the violence and organization) would place it at the most trivial level of seriousness for this offence and which was committed by an offender with a very serious record of relevant prior convictions together with little by way of personal mitigation. This was the sentence set for the counts of armed robbery in Problems 21(1–2). And in Problems 11, 21(5–6), 22 and 23 the judge was asked to set a sentence for a single count of armed robbery in which the circumstances surrounding the offence would place it at the highest level of seriousness for this offence and which was committed by an offender with a very serious record of relevant prior convictions together with little by way of personal mitigation. This was the sentence set for the counts of armed robbery in Problems 11, 21(5–6) and 22, and as the sentence for the principal counts of armed robbery in Problem 23. Finally, in Problems 23(3–4) the judge was asked to set a sentence for an offender who had committed multiple counts of armed robbery in which the circumstances surrounding the individual counts and the number of counts would place it at the highest level of seriousness for this category of offence (i.e., additional counts would have little if any effect on the effective sentence) and who had a very serious record of relevant prior convictions together with little by way of personal mitigation; the judge was also asked to specify the number of multiple counts he had assumed to be associated with the principal offence when he set this sentence. These were the values set as the effective sentences and assumed number of counts, respectively, for the offence of armed robbery in Problems 23(3–4). For Problems 21(3–4) the assumed sentences for the single counts of armed robbery were midway between the sentences fixed for the upper and lower limits for the single counts of this offence. These former sentences were fixed by the author in the light of the judge's responses regarding these latter sentences. Similarly, for Problems 23(1–2) the assumed quanta of sentence for the component covering cumulation for the multiple counts of armed robbery were governed by the sentences already fixed by the judge for the upper limits for single and multiple counts; and for these problems the judge was also asked to specify the number of counts appropriate to these quanta.

In Problem 11, also, the judge was not given the value of the sentence appropriate to the burglary. Rather, he was asked to set a sentence for a single count of burglary in which the circumstances surrounding the offence (e.g., the organization and the value of the theft) would place it at the highest level of seriousness for this offence and which was committed by an offender with a very serious record of relevant prior convictions together with little if anything by way of personal mitigation. This was the sentence set for the count of burglary in Problem 11.

To test the prediction in Problem 11 it was necessary to determine empirically the quanta of sentence available to the components of seriousness associated with multiple counts of armed robbery and burglary. The data necessary to calculate this value for armed robbery were available from the judges' responses to several of the other problems; however, for burglary, it was necessary to ask each judge to set a sentence for an offender who had committed multiple counts of burglary in which the circumstances surrounding the individual counts and the number of counts would place it at the highest level of seriousness for this category of offence and who had a very serious record of relevant prior convictions together with little by way of personal mitigation. This figure and the sentence appropriate to a single count of burglary in which the circumstances of the offence would place it at the highest level of seriousness for this offence are the data necessary to determine the quanta of sentence for the component available to the seriousness associated with multiple counts of burglary on the dimension representing the seriousness of this legal offence category.

In Problem 14 the judge was asked to consider the first two offences comprising the case. If he determined that a term of imprisonment was appropriate, then the problem was not taken further. However, if he did not fix a term of imprisonment, then he was asked to reconsider the case and have regard to the first three offences; this sequence was repeated until he imposed a term of imprisonment or it became clear that even with additional counts the judge would not consider imprisonment to be appropriate.

The judge's task in Problem 30 was to select the principal offence; he was to consider the count(s) of armed robbery and the count(s) of burglary as together comprising a case. The judges were also asked whether the term principal offence was synonymous with the term foundation sentence.

On the presentation of each card the notation describing the case or cases was explained to the judge. For the first problem the judge was asked to indicate whether he regarded any of the quanta of sentence set for the offences in the problem as being outside the range he would consider appropriate. (This was given as a general instruction to apply to all of the problems in the exercise.) If this difficulty arose in a problem, then the sentences considered inappropriate were to be adjusted so that they fell within the judge's working range while maintaining the same relativity between the other sentences to the extent necessary to test the hypothesis.

Similarly, for cases comprising multiple counts of one of the offences, the judge was asked to raise objection if in his view the assumed number of counts was not appropriate to the quantum of sentence fixed for the component covering cumulation for the multiple counts; again, this number was to be modified so as to accord with the judge's views.

In Problems 8 and 9 the quanta of sentence set for the offences in the cases were based on the assumption that the limiting values for a single count and for multiple counts of the legal offence category of armed robbery were of the order of twelve and eighteen years, respectively. For judges whose sentencing practices were substantially inconsistent with these assumptions, the consequential inappropriate quanta of sentence were to be adjusted so that they fell within the judge's working range while maintaining the same relativity between the other sentences to the extent necessary to test the hypotheses.

Where it appeared that a count assumed to be primary, or at least not secondary, to another count in a case was not accorded the same priority in the mind of the judge, then he was questioned on this point. If a judge did not accept the assumed priority of the constituent offences, the problem was to be modified so that it accorded with the judge's approach, as long as the change did not vitiate the testing of the hypothesis. For Problem 3 the judge was in the first place specifically asked to comment on the relative seriousness of the legal offence categories of burglary and rape.

The author had a number of blank cards ready so that the problems requiring modification could be presented in the normal fashion.

During the administration, the judge was permitted, but not instructed, to refer back to completed problems.

Upon finishing this exercise the judge was asked whether he had found the case descriptions to be disconcertingly artificial and the factual circumstances of any of the cases to be unrealistic and improbable, and whether he had experienced any other difficulties in completing these problems. If the judge replied in the affirmative on any of these points, he was asked to explain the nature of the difficulty experienced and to consider how it might have affected his answers. Finally, the judge was asked to refrain from discussing the exercise with his brother judges until all the judges who were participating in the study had completed the three exercises.

Procedure – reflective retrospective reports – second sentencing exercise

Once a judge had completed the first exercise the author arranged an appointment for a second session, and again supervised the administration of the exercise.

The cards from the first exercise were again used to present the sentencing problems. For all the judges the order of presentation was the same: the sentencing problems were presented in the following sequence – Problems 1–17, presented one at a time, then Problems 21(1–6), presented together, followed by Problems 21(5–6) and 23(1–4), again presented together, after which came Problems 22(1–4), also presented together, and finally, Problems 30(1–10), presented in serial order. Problems 21(1–6) were set out in a column-and-row format to help the judges to apprehend the comparisons under investigation: so, the first column comprised Problems 21(1) and 21(2), in descending order, and the first row comprised Problems 21(2), 21(3) and 21(5) from left to right. A similar format was adopted for the two other groups; Problems 22(1) and 22(2) and Problems 21(5) and 21(6) comprised the first columns, and Problems 22(1) and 22(3) and Problems 21(5), 23(1) and 23(3), respectively, the first rows.

The author introduced the session with the following instructions and directions; these were not read formally and verbatim but presented in point form in a natural conversational manner.

> This exercise is the second in a series of three designed to investigate how judges determine what is appropriate by way of an effective (maximum) sentence for an offender who has been found guilty on more than one count and at least two of the counts belong to different statutory offence categories (e.g., a case in which an offender is to be sentenced on two counts of armed robbery and one count of burglary), and the offences are properly regarded as separate transactions which, while not part of a spree, do not relate to the distant past.
>
> In this exercise you will be presented with the sentencing problems from the first exercise, again represented on the same set of cards. The notation describing each case has the same meaning as it did in that first exercise.
>
> The problems in the first exercise were formulated to explore possible sentencing principles and working rules which may govern how judges determine the effective (maximum) sentence in this type of case. Each problem tests different principles or rules, or previously presented principles or rules in a different context. I shall present each problem to you in turn and explain the relevant principle(s) or rule(s) being investigated in the problem and how it/they applies/y to the determination of the effective sentence. Once I have completed this exposition for a card I should be

grateful if you would tell me whether it is a correct interpretation of what is correct by way of approach to sentence determination in the given circumstances and, if it is not, please explain how it is in error. Also, if additional principles or rules apply to the problem, please state and explain them.

I should stress that the statement of the various principles and rules in a positive manner is not even intended to convey so much as a hint that they carry the imprimatur of authority; they are presented in this form to give them precision and clarity in order to facilitate their clear acceptance or rejection. That these principles and rules can in no way be regarded as authoritative follows from their provenance. You will be aware that the appellate court has formulated only a few general principles for this type of sentencing problem. Nevertheless, several academic lawyers have studied appellate decisions in this type of case and on this basis have attempted to set out a framework governing the determination of effective sentences. The principles and working rules I am putting to you cover the general policy enunciated by the appellate court, the framework developed by those academic writers, and my attempt to draw inferences from this work to provide the precision that a quantitative analysis demands.

The card with the first problem was presented to the judge, together with a verbal description of the meaning of the notation and the assumed offender characteristics. The judges were not reminded of the effective sentences they had imposed or, for Problem 30, the principal offences selected, in the first exercise. At this point, the judge was given the opportunity of asking questions about any aspects of the task which were perhaps unclear to him; matters leading to confusion in the mind of the judge were promptly clarified. In subsequent problems where the notation may not have been understood it was explained fully.

Where a judge's answer appeared to be incomplete or unclear in respect of the element of policy under test, or was one of simple disagreement, he was asked to clarify the point being made by him or to explain his disagreement. The questions were framed so as to be as content-free as possible and thereby not provide prompts to the judge about aspects of sentencing policy. No pressure was placed on a judge to elaborate his answer, so as to avoid possible embarrassment to him over his not having insight into his decision.

Finally, the judge was reminded to refrain from discussing the exercise with his brother judges until all the judges who were participating in the study had completed the three exercises.

CHAPTER SIX

Judges' thoughts on sentencing the multiple offender

This chapter presents and analyzes the judges' responses to the sentencing problems testing the decision model describing how effective sentences are determined for multiple offenders whose counts are separate transactions and offence categories. The data comprising the judges' answers take three forms: (1) quanta of sentence imposed for the cases comprising the sentencing problems; (2) verbal protocols in the form of immediate retrospective reports of their thoughts as they determined sentences for the cases; (3) reflective retrospective reports comprising direct comments on the validity of the decision model's principles and working rules as they apply to each of the sentencing problems. It is clear from the discussion of the role and nature of each of these three sets of data in the previous chapter that they are complementary for the purposes of interpretation. For example, the quanta of sentence imposed by a judge may be consistent with the model's predictions and yet the thought processes governing his decision quite at variance with the principles and rules hypothesized by the model to underlie the solution to that problem. It was appropriate, therefore, that the three sets of data be analyzed together. The data comprising the sentences for the cases and the associated verbal protocols are from the first sentencing exercise and the data base of reflective reports is from the second exercise. In Chapter 4 fourteen propositions or general predictions were derived from the decision model and related to the sentencing problems as a means of testing the model's validity (see Tables 4.1, 4.2 and 4.3). Since the purpose of the analysis at this point is to test a general or common model of judicial decision making for the sentencing of multiple offenders, in respect of which model each problem tests but an element, rather than to develop one or more models so as separately to account for the decision making of each of the judges for each of the individual problems, each of the fourteen propositions is examined in turn on the basis of the responses, taken together, of the eight judges to the problem(s) relevant to it.

In respect of each of the eight propositions with quantitative implications, a specific prediction was derived from the proposition for the problem or each of the problems used as a direct test of it. The specific predictions are presented first so as to facilitate the reader's comprehension of each analysis.

The propositions associated with quantitative predictions are considered first (nos. 2, 3, 4, 6, 8, 10, 12 and 13), then the qualitative propositions (nos. 1, 5, 7, 9 and 11) and, finally, the responses relating to the definition of the principal offence are analyzed (Proposition 14).

The quantitative tests of the decision model

Proposition 2

PROBLEM 1 Prediction: a greater proportion of the sentence for the burglary will be made concurrent in the first case.

PROBLEMS 21(1–6) Prediction: the quantum of sentence made cumulative upon the principal offence, for a given level of seriousness of the secondary offence, will decrease as the seriousness of the instant principal offence increases. (It should be borne in mind that the quanta of sentence representing the three levels of seriousness of the principal offence in these problems varied across the eight judges, because each judge was asked to fix sentences he considered appropriate to these levels – trivial, mid-level and upper limit for a single count – and the cases were presented to a judge using his sentences; also note, the results, in terms of the degree of cumulation as a proportion, are based on the mean for the two levels of seriousness of the secondary offence, at each level of the principal offence.)

PROBLEMS 7 AND 8 These are indirect tests of the second proposition and for this reason only the qualitative data are relevant.

When the responses of the eight judges to this subset of problems are considered together there appears to be strong support for the proposition that there is a monotonically decreasing relationship between the quantum of sentence for the main count of the principal offence and the degree of cumulation of the sentence for a secondary offence. Nevertheless, there is almost certainly significant disparity between the judges in respect of the magnitude and shape of the relationship.

First consider the quantitative answers to Problems 21(1–6). For seven (nos.

1–7) of the eight judges there was a monotonically decreasing relationship between the sentence for the principal offence and the degree of cumulation (proportion of the sentence for the secondary offence made cumulative), when sentence varied across the range of seriousness available to the offence characteristics of a single count of the legal offence category of the principal offence; for three (nos. 3, 4 and 7) of these judges the decrease in cumulation was confined to the change from the low to the medium level of seriousness on the principal offence. There were dramatic individual differences between the responses of these seven judges. The percentage decrease in the cumulation ranged from the order of 40–50 percent (Judges 2 and 3) to 2–3 percent (Judges 4 and 7); moreover, there were obvious differences between the judges in the percentage of the secondary offence made cumulative at the low and high levels of seriousness of the principal offence; for example, at the high level the percentage ranged from approximately 50 percent (Judges 3 and 7) to 10 percent (Judges 2 and 4). There were no obvious relationships between these disparities and the quanta of sentence fixed by these judges for the low and high levels of seriousness for the offence characteristics of a single count of the principal offence. Clearly, these data relating to disparity and the degree of cumulation should be regarded as indicative rather than definitive in view of the skeletal form in which the cases were presented. Judge 8's response took the form of a curvilinear relationship – not open to a ready and simple interpretation in this context – and is clearly inconsistent with the proposition.

In relation to these problems four (nos. 1, 2, 4 and 8) of the judges gave pertinent verbal protocols for Problem 21(6), apparently carrying the implication that a greater proportion of the sentence for the secondary offence could have been made cumulative had the sentence for the principal offence not been so high, the reason being, according to Judge 2, that at that level of sentence there would be concern about a crushing effective sentence. One judge (no. 2) gave a relevant protocol to Problem 21(2), and it was consistent with his response to Problem 21(6): here he contemplated total cumulation because the sentences for the comprising counts were low. The absence of a pertinent protocol for one or both of these problems should not be taken as casting doubt on the validity of the proposition; the reason for this is that it is the subset of problems [nos. 21(1–6)] taken together which provides a direct test; individual problems do not offer variation in terms of the seriousness of the principal offence and, accordingly, a protocol making reference to Problems 21(2) and 21(6) cannot be required as a condition of the validity of this factor.

In respect of the reflective reports for these six problems seven (nos. 1, 2, 4, 5, 6, 7 and 8) of the eight judges agreed with the author's statement of the proposition describing the judges' hypothesized approach to this set of problems. Two (nos. 1 and 7) of these judges expressed the effect on cumulation of this proposition in their own words. It was only Judge 3 who denied the validity of the proposition, well, at least rejected its practical significance – this judge thought that the proportion made concurrent would be approximately the same across the three levels of the principal offence.

Next, consider the data relating to Problem 1. Three (nos. 1, 2 and 7) of the judges' answers showed no inconsistency across the three indices – sentence, verbal protocol and reflective report – and were consistent with the second proposition; in his protocol and report Judge 2 reasoned that there would be less concern over the crushing effect of cumulation in the second case. Indeed, the quantitative and qualitative responses of these three judges to Problems 21(1–6) also favored the proposition. The failure of Judge 7 to provide a pertinent protocol for Problem 1 suggests that his response may have been intuitive rather than based on the conscious application of a reasoned principle, although his express statement of the relationship between the degree of concurrence and the seriousness of the principal offence in his reflective report covering Problems 21(1–6) clearly demonstrates that his answer was reliable.

Judges 5 and 6 appear to have determined concurrency in accordance with the second proposition. Although for both judges the quantitative answer was at variance with the prediction (they both ordered equal concurrence for the two cases), these may have been arithmetical aberrations on the judges' parts; for one (no. 5) of these judges gave a pertinent verbal protocol expressly stating that greater concurrence was appropriate in the first case, and the other judge (no. 6) expressed the import of the second proposition in his own words, relying on the concept of a crushing sentence, in his reflective report. Moreover, these two judges' sentences for Problems 21(1–6) were consistent with the prediction and they both concurred with the author's statement of the application of the proposition to these six problems. Nevertheless, the fact that Judge 6 did not provide a verbal protocol for Problem 1 does raise doubts about the soundness of his understanding of this aspect of policy.

On balance, it would appear that Judge 4 did not accept that the second principle correctly describes how concurrency should be determined: the evidence favors the view that to this judge the proportion of the sentence for the secondary offence made concurrent should not vary with changes in the sentence for the principal offence across the range of seriousness available to the offence characteristics of a single count of the legal category of that offence. This view was stated expressly in his verbal protocol and reflective report for Problem 1 and is not inconsistent with the quanta of sentence he imposed in Problems 21(1–6), where the proportion made cumulative dropped only 2 percent (13 to 11) across the range of seriousness of the principal offence. Against this are this judge's verbal protocol for Problem 21(6) and agreement with the author's statement of the application of the proposition to these six problems; however, the points should be made that (1) although his protocol could be taken to imply that a greater degree of cumulation would not be inappropriate where the sentence for the principal offence was lower, this was not expressly stated, and (2) his reflective report was no more than an agreement with the author's statement of the proposition, and this must be considered as weaker evidence than a restatement of the proposition in his own words. Judge 4's quantitative answer to Problem 1 – ordering less concurrence in the first case – appears to be an aberration on his part in view of his other answers. It seems reasonable to conclude that this judge did not have a robust understanding of his approach to this aspect of policy.

Judges 3 and 8 gave answers to the problems relating to the second proposition which are characterized by inconsistency and are hard to interpret, although some of their answers are consistent with the proposition. In regard to the former judge's answers: for example, the set of sentences he imposed for Problems 21(1–6) are consistent with the prediction, but in the reflective reports for these six problems and for Problem 1 he expressed the view of no relationship between the proportion of the sentence for the secondary offence made concurrent and the sentence for the principal offence. For Judge 8, his responses did not offer hard evidence either in support or in rejection of the second proposition: his qualitative answers when given – his verbal protocol for Problem 21(6) and his simple statements of agreement in both reflective reports – supported its validity, but his practice was not consistent with the predictions in both instances.

In relation to Problems 7 and 8, the majority of the judges did not give pertinent verbal protocols or reflective reports. Since these problems are only indirect tests, this is of no consequence. Nevertheless, the responses given here by three (nos. 1, 2 and 5) of the judges – all to Problem 7 – are consistent with the conclusions drawn on the basis of their earlier answers in support of the proposition; Judge 5 in his report gave an explicit account of the idea of scope for cumulation – a degree of cumulation for each count which represents less of a reduction on the appropriate sentence, where the sentence for the principal offence is lower.

In summary: it could be reasonably concluded that five (nos. 1, 2, 5, 6 and 7) of the eight judges determined concurrency in accordance with the second proposition and concurred with its validity. Moreover, it may well describe Judge 3's practice, although he clearly did not endorse it. Contrarily, Judge 8 was prepared to concur with the second proposition but it is not consistent with his actual concurrency orders. It is only Judge 4 who expressly endorsed an alternative approach and whose sentences clearly were not in accordance with the proposition – for this judge concurrency orders for the sentence for the secondary offence were not related to the sentence for the principal offence. Nevertheless, only two (nos. 1 and 2) of the judges' understanding of the principle and application of this element of policy could be described as deliberative, stable and coherent.

Proposition 3

PROBLEM 2 Prediction: a lesser proportion of the sentence for the arson will be made concurrent in the first case.

PROBLEM 5 Prediction: a lesser proportion of the sentence for the secondary offence (burglary in the first case and armed robbery in the second) will be made concurrent in the first than in the second case.

PROBLEM 11 This is an indirect test of the third proposition and for this reason only the qualitative data are relevant. An inspection of the judges' verbal protocols and retrospective reports revealed that they made no pertinent comments regarding the third proposition; since this problem is an indirect test, this is of no consequence.

When the responses of the eight judges to this subset of problems are considered together there is no substantial support for the proposition that there is a monotonically increasing relationship between the seriousness of the legal category of the principal offence and the degree of cumulation of the sentence for a secondary offence.

First consider the quantitative and qualitative answers to Problem 2. Seven (nos. 1, 2, 3, 4, 5, 6 and 8) of the judges imposed quanta of sentence inconsistent with the prediction: they ordered equal concurrence. Their responses showed that for them the seriousness of the legal category of the principal offence is not related to the degree of cumulation of the sentence for a secondary offence. Only one (no. 7) of the judges ordered greater cumulation for the case in which the legal category of the principal offence was more serious, an answer predicted on the basis of the decision model.

Five (nos. 1, 2, 5, 6 and 8) of the seven judges whose answers negated the hypothesis provided pertinent verbal protocols; all were consistent with their sentences and expressly or impliedly conveyed the point that the legal category of the principal offence does not in itself affect the proportion of the sentence for the secondary offence made concurrent, it being the quantum of sentence appropriate to the principal offence that is critical in determining the effective sentence. Two (nos. 3 and 4) of these seven judges did not provide a pertinent protocol; this leaves the basis of their decision an open matter and raises doubts about the extent to which it was deliberative. Although Judge 7's sentence is consistent with the prediction, his verbal protocol reveals that his thinking is at variance with the rationale for the third proposition. According to the decision model, a greater proportion of the sentence for the secondary offence can be made cumulative when the principal offence belongs to a more serious legal offence category, because the dimension representing the latter offence's seriousness covers a wider range of sentence and, accordingly, there is greater scope for cumulation; this reasoning is clearly incongruous with the judge's thinking that greater cumulation should be made because armed robbery is a more serious offence than burglary and an armed robbery in association with an arson is a more serious combination.

Regarding the reflective reports, six (nos. 1, 2, 3, 4, 5 and 6) of the seven judges whose quantitative answers negated the hypothesis disagreed with the author's statement of the proposition describing the judges' hypothesized approach to this problem and in fact gave reasons consistent with their quantitative answers and, for the four with pertinent verbal protocols, answers consistent with these also. The two (nos. 3 and 4) of these six judges, who did not give a verbal protocol, made up for that omission in their reflective reports by offering a basis for the determination of sentence in the problem, this suggesting that their setting of the quanta of sentence also may have had a deliberative component; moreover, these two judges in their reflective reports revealed an approach to the problem consistent with the four others, and Judge 8 in his protocol. Judges 7 and 8 agreed with the author's statement of the third proposition as it applied to this problem; for the latter judge this represented an inconsistency with his quantitative answer and his verbal protocol and, for the former judge, an inconsistency with his verbal protocol.

Next, consider the data relating to Problem 5. The answers of four (nos. 1, 2, 3 and 5) of the judges showed no inconsistency across the three indices – sentence, verbal protocol and reflective report – and their answers negate the third proposition that the legal category of the principal offence determines the degree of concurrence: they fixed equal effective sentences. Indeed, the responses of these four judges to Problem 2 led to the same conclusion. Again, Judge 3 did not provide a pertinent verbal protocol, but on this occasion did not make up for it with an account of his thinking in the reflective report. While this provides support that this judge's sentencing practice was stable in regard to this element of the model, it favors the view that it was intuitive rather than based on the conscious application of a reasoned principle. Judges

1, 2 and 5 all made the point, explicitly or implicitly, that the effective sentence for a case depends on the sentences appropriate to the comprising counts, not the legal offence category of the principal offence.

Judge 4's sentences and accompanying verbal protocol were consistent with one another and against the third proposition; they are consistent with the view of the above four judges. However, this judge's reflective report is inconsistent with his quantitative answer and verbal protocol; but the import of his report – the seriousness of the legal category of the secondary offence determines the degree of concurrence – is contrary to the hypothesized decision model also. In Problem 2 this judge's sentences and reflective report supported the conclusion that the legal category of the principal offence is unrelated to the degree of concurrence. On balance it would seem that Judge 4's sentencing practice was stable and at one with the above four judges on this element of the decision model – at variance with the model – although his failure to provide a pertinent verbal protocol in Problem 2 and his inconsistent reflective report in Problem 5 suggest that he did not have a robust and coherent understanding of his approach.

Judge 8's pattern of responding across the three indices is the same in this problem as in the previous problem – he provided a pertinent verbal protocol, consistent with his quantitative answer (equal effective sentences), and contrary to the hypothesized decision model, and yet agreed with the author's statement of the third proposition as it applies to the problem. Three considerations suggest that the quantitative answers and verbal protocols provide the true picture of this judge's thinking here: first, the reflective reports were simply acknowledgments of agreement against express statements of his reasoning in the verbal protocols; secondly, this judge may be a yea-sayer, since his responses to the second proposition also exhibited inconsistent reflective reports of simple agreement; thirdly, all his quantitative answers and protocols are consistent with one another. Again, it would seem reasonable to conclude that this judge's sentencing practice was stable and at one with the above five judges but his understanding of his approach was not unshakable.

Judge 6's quantitative answer confirmed the prediction of the decision model but his reflective report negated it and indicated a process of reasoning consistent with the above judges; he did not provide a pertinent protocol. Since this reflective report is consistent with his quantitative answer and both qualitative answers in Problem 2, this does suggest that his determination of the effective sentences for Problem 5 may have been an aberration, although the fact that they were not accompanied by a pertinent protocol raises doubts about the solidity of his view in regard to this element of the model.

Judge 7's quantitative answer confirmed the prediction of the decision

model, although his verbal protocol demonstrated that the basis of his reasoning
– a similar percentage of the burglary made concurrent in both cases – differs
from the model's account, namely, armed robbery as a principal offence
provides greater scope than burglary for cumulation. This judge in his reflective
report negated the author's statement of the third proposition, indicating that
the effective sentences would be the same, a response inconsistent with his
sentences for the cases and the accompanying verbal protocol. In regard to his
responses to Problem 2, the sentencing practice shows stability but the four
qualitative responses reveal conflicting approaches and reasoning. Clearly,
Judge 7 did not demonstrate a coherent understanding of this aspect of policy.

In summary: there was negligible support for the third proposition – not one
of the verbal protocols or elaborated reflective reports contained favorable
evidence. Among seven of the eight judges there was overwhelming support
for an alternative view on this element of the model, namely, the seriousness of
the legal category of the principal offence does not in itself affect the
proportion of the sentence for the secondary offence made concurrent with it.
For four (nos. 1, 2, 3 and 5) of the judges the support for this position was
unequivocal, and Judges 1, 2 and 5's understanding of the principle and
application of this element of policy could be described as deliberative,
coherent and stable; for three judges (nos. 4, 6 and 8) it was that the evidence
on balance favored this alternative view. Judge 7's practice was consistent with
the model, but his reasoning was not; indeed, it was not possible to discern a
common basis of approach for this judge to this element of policy.

Proposition 4

PROBLEM 3 Prediction: the same proportion of the sentence for the
secondary offence (burglary in the first case and rape in the second) will be
made concurrent in both cases.

The first point to note is that all the judges gave a pertinent verbal protocol
and an expanded reflective report; moreover, seven showed considerable
consistency in their responses across the three indices – sentence, verbal
protocol and reflective report. Judge 8 again made a reflective report which
was inconsistent with his sentencing practice and accompanying protocol,
further confirming his tendency to yea-say; accordingly, his verbal protocol is
perhaps the true record of his approach.

Only Judge 1 answered in accordance with the prediction based on the
fourth proposition that the seriousness of a secondary offence is defined by its
quantum of sentence and is independent of the seriousness of its legal offence
category. Even though this judge independently agreed that rape is a more

serious offence category than burglary, he ordered the same degree of cumulation in each case, and justified his approach on grounds consistent with this proposition. Problem 4 was presented as a control for Problem 3, its critical characteristic for this purpose being that the secondary offence of indecent assault shares with rape a similar relationship to armed robbery *vis-à-vis* the nature of the criminality but is more similar than rape to burglary in regard to the seriousness of its legal offence category. On the basis, then, of Judge 1's approach to Problem 3, it would be expected that he would view Problem 4 as turning on the same point and again order a similar degree of cumulation in both cases: he in fact ordered the same cumulation.

In the responses of three of the other judges there was no express or implied rejection of the proposition, although their determination of the effective sentences was contrary to the prediction derived from the fourth proposition. Judges 2, 5 and 8 independently agreed that rape is a more serious offence category than burglary and set a higher effective sentence in the case in which the rape is the secondary offence; yet these judges justified their sentencing on the ground that, in the case comprising the armed robbery and the rape, there is greater variation in the nature of the criminality, but they made no mention of the idea that a higher sentence might be warranted because rape is a more serious offence. There was no evidence then that these judges disagreed with the view that the sentence for the secondary offence defines its seriousness and that the seriousness of that offence is independent of its legal offence category, or disagreed with the consequence of this, namely, the seriousness of the legal category of the secondary offence does not in itself affect the degree of cumulation. Rather, for these judges Problem 3 raised a matter of policy not contemplated by the model. It is that the degree of cumulation is related to the similarity/variation in the nature of the criminality of the legal offence categories comprising the case: greater variation in the offending requiring more cumulation. In regard to Problem 4, the fact that indecent assault is more similar than rape to burglary in the seriousness of its legal offence category should not have caused these three judges to adopt a different approach and reach different effective sentences there, for indecent assault shares with rape a similar relationship to armed robbery regarding the nature of the criminality, and it was this matter on which Problem 3 turned for this group. An inspection of the data revealed similar reasoning and an identical set of concurrency orders.

Judge 4, like Judges 2, 5 and 8, ordered greater cumulation of the sentence for the rape than the burglary, and in both his verbal protocol and reflective report it was clear that a reason for this was similarly the greater variation in the nature of the offending. However, his reflective report suggested that there may have been a second factor exercising his mind: his reference to rape as a more serious offence category than burglary as a ground for greater cumulation in the second case. It would appear that this problem raised for him, as it did for Judges 2, 5 and 8, the same matter of policy not contemplated by the model; nevertheless, this judge, unlike these three others, rejected the fourth proposition that for the purposes of cumulation the seriousness of a secondary offence is independent of its legal offence category. Regarding Problem 4, it would be expected that the difference in the effective sentences imposed by Judge 4 for the two cases in Problem 3 would be maintained by him there, since it represents the same pattern of variation in the nature of the criminality. And a difference was maintained. Actually, the degree of cumulation of the sentence for the rape in Problem 3 was somewhat greater than for the indecent assault in Problem 4; this is consistent with his thinking, since both material factors – seriousness and variation – are present in Problem 3 but only one – variation – characterizes Problem 4. In his verbal protocol and reflective report for Problem 4, this judge gave the basis of his decision as being that the greater variation in the nature of the criminality of armed robbery and indecent assault warranted greater cumulation.

There was one judge (no. 7) whose sentencing practice and reasoning clearly contradicted the fourth proposition: for this judge the degree of cumulation depended on the seriousness of the legal category of the secondary offence, and on this basis he ordered greater cumulation of the sentence for the rape than the burglary. In regard to Problem 4, the critical point is that indecent assault is more similar than rape to burglary in regard to offence seriousness and, accordingly, it would be predicted that this judge would fix similar effective sentences in the two cases. Judge 7 was consistent with this prediction. In the verbal protocol he stated that the fact that armed robbery and indecent assault are different types of offence is not material to the determination of the effective sentence and, in his reflective report, he expressly agreed with the application of the fourth proposition and its consequence that the effective sentences should be the same in both cases.

Judge 6, like Judge 7, ordered greater cumulation of the sentence for the rape than the burglary and in both his verbal protocol and reflective report it is clear that a reason for this was similarly the greater seriousness of rape as a legal offence category. It follows that this judge's approach is contrary to the fourth proposition. However, his reflective report suggests that there may have been a second factor exercising his mind: his reference to armed robbery and rape as different types of offending as a ground for greater cumulation in the second case. Perhaps, like Judges 2, 4, 5 and 8, his concurrency orders were influenced by the similarity/variation in the nature of the criminality of the legal offence categories of the cases' constituent offences. Regarding Problem 4, it would be expected for the reasons given above that the difference in the effective sentences imposed by Judge 6 for the two cases in Problem 3 would be maintained by him there. And a difference was maintained; actually, the degree of cumulation of the sentence for the indecent assault in Problem 4 was somewhat greater than for the rape in Problem 3, although the converse effect might have been anticipated since in Problem 4 only one of the two material factors in Problem 3 was present. In his verbal protocol for Problem 4 this judge observed that armed robbery and indecent assault are entirely different types of offence; however, in the reflective report he agreed with the author's statement of the application of the fourth proposition to this problem but the reason he advanced and its relevance were not clear. There is, perhaps, an air of uncertainty in this judge's understanding of this element of policy.

Judge 3's responses are manifestly at variance with the fourth proposition. He imposed a higher effective sentence for the case comprising the count of rape and justified it on the ground that the second case is more serious because there is more violence; now, since the quanta of sentence considered appropriate to the burglary and the rape are the same, this reveals that to this judge the seriousness of a secondary offence is not defined by its quantum of sentence and is not independent of its legal offence category. The basis of his reasoning in his reflective report was consistent with this approach. In his verbal protocol accompanying his determination of sentence in Problem 4, he explained his order of greater cumulation of the sentence for the indecent assault on the grounds that this instance of the offence must have been particularly vile to have warranted four years (note, four years is 80 percent of the statutory maximum for this offence). For this judge, then, this problem raised an element of policy not contemplated by the model, namely, that the seriousness of a secondary offence as it relates to the degree of cumulation depends on the quantum of sentence as a proportion of the statutory maximum, perhaps the upper limit of actual sentencing practice, for its legal offence category. Such reasoning is contrary to the fourth proposition, and is a variation of the view that the seriousness of a secondary offence is dependent on the seriousness of its legal offence category. In his reflective report he indicated that the degree of cumulation of the sentences for the indecent assault and the burglary would be approximately the same and less than for the rape, his reason being that indecent assault has a statutory maximum of five years. (Note, for rape the statutory maximum is ten years.) This clearly reflects a view that the degree of cumulation of the sentence for an offence is dependent on the seriousness of its legal offence category. It should be noted that this is inconsistent with his practice where the degree of cumulation of the sentence for indecent assault and rape were similar and greater than for burglary; and incongruous with burglary's maximum of fourteen years. Nevertheless, despite the apparent contradictions in his reasoning, all the answers of this judge are consistent with the view that the degree of cumulation of the sentence for the secondary offence cannot be determined without reference being made to the legal category of offence to which it belongs.

PROBLEM 6 This is an indirect test of the fourth proposition and for this reason only the qualitative data are relevant.

In relation to Problem 6, the eight judges provided at least one pertinent protocol or report and answered in a way which was generally consistent with and indeed reinforced the conclusions based on their responses to Problems 3 and 4. Nevertheless, Judge 7 justified greater cumulation for the case in which the rape was present in terms of the greater variety in the nature of the criminality, whereas in Problem 3 he relied on the greater seriousness of the offence category of rape to argue for greater cumulation; of course, the variation across the counts is greater and the relative significance of each comprising count is less in Problem 6. (Since this is an indirect test, the absence of a qualitative answer is of no significance.)

In summary: the answers of four (nos. 1, 2, 5 and 8) of the eight judges were in accordance with the fourth proposition that the seriousness of a secondary offence is defined by the quantum of sentence appropriate to it and is independent of the seriousness of its legal offence category. Against this, for Judge 7 and, perhaps, Judges 3, 4 and 6, greater cumulation of the sentence for a secondary offence is warranted where that offence is an instance of a more serious offence category. Of equal significance, in the responses relating to the fourth proposition, is the finding that for a clear majority of the judges these problems raised a point of policy not contemplated by the model, namely, the effect of variation in the nature of the criminality of the constituent offences on the degree of cumulation. For three of the judges (nos. 2, 5 and 8) the solutions to Problems 3 and 4 turned exclusively on this point and it was material to Problem 6; two of the judges (nos. 4 and 6) differed from these three only in that there was some evidence that they saw the seriousness of the legal category of the secondary offence as also of relevance, and another of the judges (no. 7) referred to variation in the nature of the criminality as material in Problem 6 but did not mention it as a justification for his approach in Problem 3 and denied its relevance in Problem 4. It was only Judge 1 who expressly disavowed its relevance as a factor in cumulation, and this was in his report in Problem 6. The nature of the relationship between the variation in the nature of the criminality of the principal and secondary offences, as one factor, and the degree of cumulation of the sentence for the secondary offence(s), as the other factor, requires further exploration: presumably it would be a monotonically increasing relationship of some sort, but how it would operate when there were more than two offences is unclear; and there is the problem of defining and measuring the factor of variation in the nature of the offending across the counts comprising a case.

It was only Judges 1, 2, 5 and, perhaps, 7 who appeared to have a clear and firm understanding of this element of policy – again not a majority.

Proposition 6

PROBLEM 19 Prediction: the effective sentence will be the same in both cases.

There was little support for the sixth proposition that where a secondary offence comprises multiple counts its effective sentence defines the seriousness of these counts considered together for the purposes of cumulation. Only two (nos. 3 and 5) of the judges imposed sentences in accordance with the prediction; these two gave no accompanying pertinent protocol but their agreement in their reflective reports with the author's application of the sixth proposition to this problem is consistent with their quantitative answer. The failure of these two judges to produce pertinent verbal protocols suggests that their responses were perhaps intuitive rather than based on the conscious application of a reasoned principle. The sentencing practice of the six other judges is inconsistent with the prediction, and their reasoning, as expressed in their verbal protocols, is clearly at variance with the sixth proposition. For five (nos. 1, 2, 4, 7 and 8) of these judges the import of their protocols is that where there are multiple secondary counts belonging to the same legal offence category, and what would be the appropriate effective sentence for these counts considered together is the same as that appropriate to a single secondary count, the cumulative effect of the former would be greater than the latter when added to a principal offence. Nevertheless, two (nos. 1 and 8) of these five judges in their reflective reports showed an apparent change in their approach to this problem in their endorsing of the sixth proposition. It is suggested that perhaps not much weight should be attached to these two responses and that, accordingly, the sentences and protocols are the true indication of the approach of these two judges. It was concluded earlier that Judge 8 may be a yea-sayer; perhaps this is another instance of that behavior. And regarding Judge 1, his agreement with the author's statement of the proposition may be an artifact of the form in which the critical matter in the problem was presented, namely, the grouping of the multiple secondary counts belonging to the same legal offence category and then the fixing of an effective sentence appropriate to their cumulative effect as an offence category standing alone; indeed, his report can be read as an agreement with the principle on the ground that the given construction of the sentence for the multiple secondary offences in the presentation of the case left him no option. Indeed, Judge 5's agreement "by definition" may similarly be artifactual. Finally, Judge 6 was clearly equivocal in his approach to this problem. His sentencing practice and protocol indicated that a single serious count may outweigh multiple less-serious counts in seriousness, yet in his reflective report he expressly asserted the converse. Apparently, this judge did not have a coherent and robust understanding of this element of policy.

In summary: the evidence is overwhelmingly against the validity of the sixth proposition; only two (nos. 3 and 5) of the judges sentenced in accordance with it and neither one of them articulated his approach. Without doubt, Judges 2, 4, 7 and, perhaps, 1 had a clear view on the policy matter raised by this problem.

Proposition 8

PROBLEM 10 Prediction: a greater proportion of the sentence for the burglary will be made concurrent in the first case.

PROBLEMS 21(5-6), 23(1-4) Prediction: the quantum of sentence made cumulative upon the principal offence, for a given level of seriousness of the secondary offence, will decrease as the seriousness of the extra counts of the principal offence increases. (It should be borne in mind that the quanta of sentence representing the three levels of seriousness of the component covering the extra counts of the principal offence in these problems varied across the eight judges, because each judge was asked to fix sentences he considered appropriate to these levels – nil, mid-level and upper limit for the extra counts of the principal offence – and the cases were presented to a judge using his sentences; also note, the results, in terms of the degree of cumulation as a proportion, are based on the mean for the two levels of seriousness of the secondary offence, at each level of the extra counts of the principal offence. Note, the "nil" level of seriousness for the extra counts of the principal offence is equivalent to the upper limit of seriousness for a single count of the principal offence.)

PROBLEMS 8 AND 9 These are indirect tests of the eighth proposition and for this reason only the qualitative data are relevant.

When the responses of the eight judges to this subset of problems are considered together there appears to be reasonably strong support for the proposition that there is a monotonically decreasing relationship between the quantum of sentence cumulative upon the sentence for the main count of the principal offence and arising from extra counts of the principal offence and the degree of cumulation of the sentence for the secondary offence. Nevertheless, there is almost certainly significant disparity between the judges in respect of the magnitude and shape of the relationship.

First consider the quantitative answers to Problems 21(5–6), 23(1–4). For six (nos. 1, 2, 3, 4, 6 and 7) of the eight judges there was a monotonically decreasing relationship between the sentence cumulative upon the main count of the principal offence and associated with the extra counts of this offence and the degree of cumulation (proportion of the sentence for the secondary offence made cumulative), when the sentence cumulative on the main count varied across the range of seriousness available to multiple counts of the legal offence category of the principal offence; for one (no. 2) of these judges the decrease in cumulation was confined to the change from the low to the medium level of seriousness of the extra counts of the principal offence. There were dramatic individual differences between the responses of these six judges. The percentage decrease in the cumulation ranged from the order of 40–50 percent (Judges 3 and 7) to 10 percent (Judges 2 and 4); moreover, although there were obvious differences between the judges in the percentage of the secondary offence made cumulative at the low level of seriousness of the extra counts of the principal offence – at this level the percentage ranged from approximately 50 percent (Judges 3 and 7) to 10 percent (Judges 2 and 4) – at the high level the cumulation was uniformly very low, in fact for all but one of these six judges it was zero and for this judge it was only about 10 percent. There were no clear relationships between the previously mentioned disparities and the quanta of sentence fixed by these judges for the low and high levels of the extra counts of the principal offence. Clearly, these data relating to disparity and the degree of cumulation should be regarded as indicative rather than definitive in view of the skeletal form in which the cases were presented. The responses of Judges 5 and 8 took the form of a curvilinear relationship – not open to a ready and simple interpretation in this context – and patently inconsistent with the proposition.

In relation to these problems there were pertinent verbal protocols for Problem 23(4) for five (nos. 1, 4, 5, 7 and 8) of the judges, and the apparent implication of their statements is that a greater proportion of the sentence for the secondary offence could have been made cumulative had the quantum of sentence for the principal offence and its associated multiple counts not been so high. The absence of a verbal protocol for this problem should not be taken to cast doubt on the validity of the proposition; the reason for this is that it is the subset of problems [nos. 21(5–6), 23(1–4)] taken together which provides a direct test; individual problems do not offer variation in terms of the seriousness of the extra counts of the principal offence and, accordingly, a protocol making reference to the variation cannot be required as a condition of the validity of this factor.

In respect of the reflective reports for these problems, the eight judges agreed with the author's statement of the proposition describing the judges' hypothesized approach to this set of problems, and five (nos. 1, 2, 3, 5 and 7) of these judges expressed the import of this proposition in their own words. Judges 2 and 5, respectively, referred to the notions of crushing sentence and scope for cumulation in opting for little by way of cumulation. Nevertheless, Judge 3 thought that almost complete concurrence would be appropriate across the three levels of seriousness in view of the fact that the associated quanta of sentence were so high.

Next, there are the data relating to Problem 10. Two (nos. 1 and 7) of the judges' answers showed no inconsistency across the three indices – sentence, verbal protocol and reflective report – and are consistent with the eighth proposition. Indeed, the quantitative and qualitative responses of these two judges to Problems 21(5–6), 23(1–4) also favored the proposition.

Almost certainly Judge 6 determined concurrency in accordance with the eighth proposition. In Problem 10 his sentences concur with the prediction and in his reflective report he offered in his own words an express statement of the effect of this proposition in regard to concurrency for this problem. Moreover, his sentencing practice in Problems 21(5–6), 23(1–4) is in agreement with the prediction and, also, he endorsed the author's statement of the eighth proposition in regard to this set of problems. In fact, the only index not providing evidence in favor of the proposition was his verbal protocol for Problem 10. And the basis of his approach to this problem, as expressed, cannot be taken as evidence for or against this proposition. The reason for this is that his explanation of his approach did not address and, accordingly, could not be related to the point on which the problem turns. Now, prima facie, a judge's failure to refer to the aspect of the model in a direct test is regarded as casting doubt on its significance. It would be wise, perhaps, to resist that conclusion here. For the judge's line of reasoning, in which he determined the appropriate quantum of cumulation for the sentence for the secondary offence in relation to what he estimated to be the mean quantum of cumulation for the each of the extra counts of the principal offence, may well have been induced by the form in which the quantum of sentence relating to the multiple counts of the principal offence was presented in relation to the sentence for the main count of the principal offence; the form of presentation was one which he would not have experienced before and in his attempting to deal with the problem promptly he may have allowed its form of presentation to determine his pattern of thought. If this was so, then the judge's expressed approach to the problem would be an artifact of the mode in which it was presented and, accordingly, could not be taken as negating the proposition.

Judge 4's responses were similar to those of Judge 6 and the preceding comments are similarly applicable here. By way of exception, in his reflective report Judge 4 did not provide in his own words an express statement of the application of this proposition to Problem 10, but the report did, nevertheless, carry the implication that a greater proportion of the sentence for the secondary offence could have been made cumulative had the quantum of sentence for the principal offence and its associated multiple counts not been so high. In addition he made this comment in his protocol for Problem 23(4). And so it would appear reasonable to conclude that for Judge 4, too, the eighth proposition described the appropriate approach to this aspect of policy.

For one (no. 8) of the judges there is no convincing evidence that his determining of concurrency for a sentence for a secondary offence was related to the quantum of sentence cumulative upon the sentence for the main count of the principal offence and arising from extra counts of that offence. Regarding Problem 10, not one of his responses on the three indices favored the proposition; in sentencing, he ordered equal concurrence. In Problems 21(5–6), 23(1–4) his sentencing practice was characterized by a curvilinear relationship across the range of seriousness on multiple counts of the principal offence. His verbal protocol there, while not inconsistent with the proposition, was not an express endorsement of it; moreover, his simple agreement with the author's statement of the application of the eighth proposition to this subset of problems may no more than confirm this judge's previously noted tendency to yea-say.

In Problem 10 Judge 5 ordered equal concurrence of the sentences for the secondary offence in the two cases, in contrast with the prediction of greater concurrence in the first case. While he did not provide a pertinent verbal protocol here, his reflective report for this problem was an express statement of the relationship predicted on the basis of the eighth proposition. And a similar pattern of responding was found in his answers to Problems 21(5–6), 23(1–4): his sentencing practice was curvilinear rather than monotonically decreasing, yet in his protocol for Problem 23(4) there was implicit recognition of, and in making his reflective report he expressly applied, the eighth proposition in accordance with the decision model. It would appear that the approach regarded by Judge 5 as applying to the ordering of concurrency in this problem is accurately captured by the eighth proposition but that this judge did not give effect to it in practice, a finding suggesting that he had difficulty in applying policy to actual sentencing problems; and his failure to provide a pertinent protocol for Problem 10 further emphasizes the lack of clarity in his understanding of this matter.

The responses of Judges 2 and 3 were equivocal in regard to their support for the eighth proposition. In Problems 21(5–6), 23(1–4) both judges' sentencing practice conformed to the predicted relationship and both, in their reflective reports, expressed the import of the eighth proposition in their own words, although Judge 3 doubted that the magnitude of the effect would be of practical significance. Against this, the responses of both these judges in Problem 10 offered little or no evidence favoring the eighth proposition's validity. Indeed, Judge 3's answers clearly negated it – he ordered equal concurrence of the sentences for the secondary offence in the two cases, provided no verbal protocols, and in his reflective report expressly disavowed the appropriateness of the author's application of the eighth proposition to this problem. Judge 2's sentencing practice here was clearly contrary to the prediction – he ordered less, not greater, concurrence. However, his qualitative answers were not explicitly at variance with the proposition; his verbal protocol could be read as implying that a greater proportion of the sentence for the secondary offence could have been made cumulative had the quantum of sentence for the principal offence and its associated multiple counts not been so high – a crushing sentence being the subject of his concern – and his reflective report suggested an approach determined by the form in which the problem was presented, a response, as it was explained for Judges 6 and 4, not necessarily inconsistent with the proposition. Clearly, these two judges did not have a stable approach to this element of policy.

In relation to Problems 8 and 9, the majority of the judges did not give pertinent verbal protocols or reflective reports. Since these problems are only indirect tests, this is of no consequence. Nevertheless, Judges 1 and 6 gave pertinent responses and these were consistent with the conclusions drawn on the basis of their earlier answers. In his reflective report for Problem 9, Judge 6 referred to cumulation being by way of decreasing gains.

In summary: on balance the evidence favors the validity of the eighth proposition. It can be asserted confidently that Judges 1 and 7 approached this aspect of sentencing policy in accordance with the decision model, and a similar conclusion of support is warranted for Judges 4 and 6, although with somewhat less confidence, the doubts being associated with possible methodological problems. For Judge 5, his qualitative answers offered express agreement, yet his quantitative answers were at variance with the predictions. Judges 2 and 3, too, showed disparity in their answers, but it took a different form: their answers demonstrated support for the proposition's validity in Problems 21(5–6), 23(1–4); however, similar confirmation was not to be found in their responses to Problem 10. Against this, there is only one judge (no. 8) whose sentencing and statements across problems either negate or offer negligible support for the validity of this aspect of the decision model. Nevertheless, the evidence indicates that only two of the judges – Judges 1 and 7 – had a deliberative, stable and coherent approach on this element of policy.

Proposition 10

PROBLEM 6 Prediction: there will be a limiting effective sentence and it will be the same in both cases.

PROBLEM 7 Prediction: the effective sentence will be greater in the first case than in the second case by any amount equal to the difference between the quanta of sentence for the two principal offences (i.e., $4\frac{1}{2}$ years).

PROBLEM 11 Prediction: the effective sentence will be greater in the first case than in the second case by an amount equal to the difference between the quanta of sentence for the two principal offences, each being at the upper level of seriousness for the offence characteristics of a single count in their respective offence categories, plus the difference between the quanta of sentence available to the components of multiple counts for the principal offences of armed robbery and burglary on the dimensions representing the seriousness of these two legal offence categories. (Remember, the predicted difference varied across the judges, since each judge was first asked to impose the quanta of sentence he considered appropriate to two levels relating to the above components – the sentences appropriate to a case at the upper limit of seriousness for the offence characteristics of a single count (the lower limit for multiple counts) and a case at the upper limit of seriousness when it comprised multiple counts of the principal offence – for these two offence categories, and the cases were presented to a judge and his responses were analyzed using these sentences.)

The tenth proposition comprises three elements relating to the general proposition that where a case comprises multiple secondary offences cumulation of the sentences for these secondary counts is made in regard to a notional limiting quantum of sentence above which extra counts would have a negligible additional effect on what would be the running effective sentence for the counts considered up to that point. The three elements are: (1) the limiting quantum of cumulation is the same whether the multiple secondary counts belong to the legal category of the principal offence or are equally or less serious offences belonging to a different legal category; (2) the limiting quantum of cumulation for the multiple secondary counts is independent of the quantum of sentence appropriate to the principal offence; and (3) the limiting quantum of cumulation is defined as the component available to multiple counts of the principal offence on the dimension representing the seriousness of the legal category of the principal offence, and its value varies across legal categories of the principal offence. These three elements are directly addressed by Problems 6, 7 and 11, respectively. When the responses of the eight judges to this subset of problems are considered together, the conclusion that the general proposition cannot withstand the weight of evidence is inescapable.

In relation to the first element, the responses of only one judge (no. 5) were consistent across the three indices – sentence, verbal protocol and reflective report – and in support of the position that there is a limiting quantum of cumulation for multiple secondary counts of a principal offence and the limit is the same for a case comprising equally serious multiple secondary counts but belonging to a variety of offence categories. Even though this judge believed that there is greater criminality arising from the variation in the nature of the offending associated with the second case, he expressly affirmed that in the limiting case this counts for nought; according to him, the purpose of the limit is to avoid the imposition of a crushing sentence on an offender. On the contrary, Judges 2 and 4 in their responses explicitly disavowed this element of the proposition on the ground that greater criminality should be partially reflected in the effective sentence, and in the second case the presence of the rape, an offence of a different nature, marks greater criminality. Judge 2 noted in his verbal protocol that there is not a limiting sentence which must not be exceeded; the effective sentence must reflect the offender's criminality, to the extent that it is not crushing. Actually, Judge 4 fixed equal effective sentences in the two cases but stated that the presence of a serious rape in the second case would require a higher effective sentence there; in effect, then, he rejected the notion of a limiting sentence as it was used in this problem. The five other judges showed equivocation regarding this element of sentencing policy in the sense that their responses manifested an inconsistency of approach across the two sessions. Three (nos. 3, 7 and 8) of these five judges imposed the same effective sentence in both cases as predicted, and the two who provided pertinent protocols (Judges 7 and 8) based their thinking on reasons in accordance with the tenth proposition. And two (nos. 1 and 6) of these five judges imposed different sentences in the two cases, contrary to the prediction; Judge 6 fixed a higher effective sentence in the second case, explaining the outcome in terms of the greater variety in the nature of the offending and, accordingly, greater criminality of the case, whereas Judge 1 arrived at a higher sentence in the first case on the ground that repetition of a particular offence is more serious. However, these five judges expressed a view contrary to their original position, in their reflective reports: Judges 1 and 6 favored the proposition, and Judges 3, 7 and 8 were against it, the latter two on the ground that the greater variation in the nature of the offending required a higher effective sentence in the second case, Judge 3 apparently concerned about the seriousness of the rape and also invoking the idea that cumulation is constrained nevertheless by the requirement to avoid a crushing sentence. Since all the judges except Judge 6 offered a reasoned account of their agreement or disagreement with the author's statement of the application of the tenth proposition to this case, weight must be given to this evidence. (It should be noted that in the first session, Judge 3, and in the second session, Judges 1 and 6, did not even impliedly convey whether they considered one of the two cases to be more serious.)

In view of the finding that the majority of the judges revealed an inconsistency of approach across the two sessions and the eight judges are more or less evenly divided in approach when their responses are considered within each of the sessions, it appears that the first element of this proposition (Proposition 10) may have raised a matter of policy about which these judges as a group did not have a stable and preferred view. Of course, it is possible that this inconsistency of approach is apparent and not real, an artifact of the nature of the problem: judges are accustomed to dealing with concrete problems in sentencing, and it is possible, therefore, that the instruction to them to include an unspecified number of imaginary additional counts was too abstract and induced instability in their decision making. Again, there was only a minority of the judges (nos. 2, 4 and 5) who demonstrated a deliberative and coherent understanding of their approach.

Now consider the second element of the tenth proposition, namely, the limiting quantum of cumulation for the multiple secondary counts is independent of the quantum of sentence appropriate to the principal offence. It follows from this that the limiting quantum of cumulation is the same in the two cases in Problem 7, so that the two effective sentences would be expected to differ only according to the difference between the sentences appropriate to the principal offences, i.e., $4\frac{1}{2}$ years.

Not one of the eight judges imposed sentences in the two cases or offered pertinent verbal protocols consistent with this element of the tenth proposition.

And in respect of the reflective reports there was no more than tenuous support to be found for the hypothesized decision model. Only two of the judges were prepared to endorse the author's application of the decision model to the problem. Judge 7 agreed that the effective sentence would be lower in the second case than the first, though it be comprised of more counts, and that its limiting value would probably be equal to the quantum of sentence for the principal offence plus the quantum of cumulation he had fixed for the component available to multiple counts; however, he did not refer to the limiting sentence appropriate to the first case. This judge's agreement amounted to little more than his mouthing of part of the author's statement of the application of the decision model to this problem; moreover, his sentences and accompanying verbal protocol represent an approach at variance with this present position. As well, Judge 8 simply voiced his agreement with the author's statement, again inconsistent with the approach he adopted in the first session but true to his previously noted tendency to yea-say.

Nevertheless, in the responses of six of the eight judges (the exceptions being Judges 7 and 8), and expressed with greater or less coherence, completeness and explicitness, it was possible to detect a common alternative approach to this element of sentencing policy. What follows is a clarified version of this alternative approach, described by the principles and having the consequences set out as follows: (1) there is not a limiting effective quantum of sentence with an absolute value above which cumulation of the sentences for multiple secondary offences cannot be made on the sentence for the principal offence; (2) rather, what is appropriate by way of an effective sentence in a case is the resultant effect of two contrary considerations, namely, more serious and extra multiple counts require additional discrete quanta of sentence, and the potentially crushing effects on the offender of the additional quanta of sentence appropriate to the greater seriousness and number of the multiple counts must be minimized; (3) accordingly, the higher the possible effective sentence – the sum of the sentences appropriate to the principal and multiple secondary counts – the greater the degree of concurrence for each of the appropriate sentences associated with the multiple secondary counts, the increase being tailored to satisfy the preceding two considerations; (4) since the sentence for the principal offence is not subject to concurrency orders, it determines what scope there is for the sentences appropriate to the secondary counts to be reflected in the effective sentence. Now, assuming the validity of this approach, the following two predictions would be made for Problem 7: first, where there was an equal number of equally serious multiple secondary counts in the two cases, the quantum of cumulation for these counts would be greater in the second case, since a greater proportion of the appropriate sentence for each of the multiple secondary counts could be made cumulative, although the effective sentence would be greater in the first case; secondly, where there was a greater number of multiple secondary counts in the second case and with a sufficient number of these counts, a point would be reached when the effective sentence would approach, perhaps equal, the effective sentence appropriate to the first case, since greater criminality requires a higher sentence until the point at which this consideration and the consideration of the crushing effects of the sentence are for practical purposes balanced.

Judge 1's sentencing practice and qualitative responses are consistent with these predictions and, indeed, the contents of his verbal protocol and reflective report covered in express terms much of the alternative approach just formulated. It is not clear whether he was assuming the same or a different number of multiple secondary counts in the two cases and, in any case, whether this distinction would be in his mind material to effective sentence.

Similar comments are apposite to the verbal protocol and reflective report of Judge 2, whose qualitative answers were consistent with, but added to and almost completed, the approach to decision making outlined by Judge 1; he also gave a numerical illustration of the application of the policy in his reflective report. It is surprising, then, that his sentencing practice in the first session was at variance with the approach clearly expressed both in his verbal protocol (and reflective report) – he ordered less cumulation in the second case – and this prompts the conclusion that his sentence for the second case may have been the result of an aberration in his numerical thinking.

Regarding Judge 5, his sentences accord with the predictions based on the alternative approach; although his verbal protocol conveyed nothing of significance, his reflective report represented an account and explanation of the application of the alternative policy pursued by the former two judges, including the notion of the scope for cumulation, and, as well, incorporated the consequences for this approach of a different number of multiple counts in the two cases.

To the extent the positions adopted by Judges 3, 4 and 6 were articulated in their reflective reports, it is apparent that they are consistent with the approach discerned in the responses of the previous three judges. Both Judges 3 and 4 dealt with the matter of the effect on effective sentence of a different number of multiple counts in the two cases in accordance with the alternative approach. And Judge 3's report offered something by way of explanation for this element of policy – the need to balance higher cumulation for greater criminality with its potentially crushing effects; also, his sentence and protocol were not inconsistent with the alternative approach – he thought the effective sentences would be approximately the same were there a sufficient number of multiple secondary counts in the second case. More significant was the observation of Judge 6, who recognized in his report that there was greater scope for cumulation in the second case. Nevertheless, in view of the fact that Judge 3's verbal protocol said little, that Judge 4 experienced difficulty in determining sentence in this problem, and that Judge 6 did not determine sentence in accordance with this approach – he ordered greater cumulation in the first case – nor referred to this approach in his protocol, it would appear that these judges had a largely intuitive and limited understanding of this element of policy.

Judge 7's sentencing – equal effective sentences – and verbal protocol were clearly inconsistent with the approach he expressed in his reflective report (see the earlier discussion), but because of the vague terms in which his protocol was expressed it was not possible to discern the basis of his decision.

Judge 8 in his verbal protocol offered a reasoned decision for his determination of the effective sentences in the two cases: it was that where there is a series of multiple and equally serious secondary offences the limiting sentence should not exceed the quantum equal to the sentence for the principal offence plus the sentence appropriate to one of the multiple counts. Clearly, the basis of this judge's approach and the proposed alternative to this element of the decision model are conceptually quite different. His approach here is also inconsistent with his endorsement of the application of the decision model in his reflective report.

To the extent that each judge offered a reasoned approach to the determination of the effective sentences in this problem, Judges 7 and 8 were the only ones whose thinking in at least one of the two sessions did not fit in with the alternative pattern discerned in the approaches of the other judges. In its present form Judge 8's approach could not be regarded as a significant contribution to the development of a detailed decision model, offering as it does no more than a crude indication of what order of magnitude might be appropriate by way of a limiting sentence; moreover, it cannot handle cases in which the multiple secondary counts are not of the same level of seriousness.

In summary, then, there was no evidence of consequence in support of the second element of the tenth proposition. Rather, from the collective responses of those judges who gave a more or less detailed approach to the matters of policy raised by the problem, an alternative decision strategy was readily discernible. In respect of this aspect of the decision model, there is not a limiting quantum of cumulation to be independent of the quantum of sentence appropriate to the principal offence; rather, the degree of cumulation for the sentences associated with the multiple secondary counts is monotonically and decreasingly related to the quantum of sentence appropriate to the principal offence. Judges 1 and 2, certainly, and, perhaps 5, displayed considerable clarity of thought in their understanding of this alternative approach.

Finally, there is the third element of the tenth proposition: the limiting quantum of cumulation for the multiple secondary counts is defined as the component available to multiple counts of the principal offence on the dimension representing the seriousness of the legal category of the principal offence, and its value varies across legal categories of the principal offence. It will be recalled that each of the judges was required to fix a value for this component as a quantum of sentence for both armed robbery and burglary. Also, the quanta of sentence assumed to be appropriate to armed robbery and burglary as principal counts in the first and second case, respectively, in Problem 11 were fixed by each of the judges. Accordingly, it would be predicted that, for a particular judge, the effective sentence would be greater in the first case than in the second case by an amount equal to the difference between the quanta of sentence considered, by that judge, to be appropriate to the upper limits of seriousness for the two principal offences plus the difference between the quanta of sentence considered, by the same judge, to be available to the components of multiple counts for the principal offences of armed robbery and burglary on the dimensions representing the seriousness of these two legal offence categories. (It should be noted at the outset that the sentencing practices of Judges 2 and 3 could not be considered in relation to the analysis of Problem 11 because each adopted one basis for fixing the quanta of sentence he considered appropriate to cases falling at the upper and lower limits of the component available to multiple counts for burglary and a different basis for armed robbery.)

Not one of the judges imposed sentences in the two cases or offered pertinent verbal protocols consistent with this element of the tenth proposition. And in respect of the reflective reports, there was no substantial support to be found for the hypothesized decision model. In fact five (nos. 1, 2, 4, 5 and 6) of the judges, to the extent that they commented on the model, implicitly or expressly disavowed it: the quantum of cumulation for the multiple secondary counts was said not to be governed by the hypothesized component available to multiple counts of the principal offence, the appropriate increase being regarded as less in the first case (Judge 1), less in the first case and greater in the second (Judge 2), the same in both cases (Judge 4), greater in the second case (Judge 5), and potentially greater in both cases (Judge 6). Judge 3's report was not intelligible. Only Judges 7 and 8 supported it, but then only as a simple acknowledgment of the author's statement of the application of the model to this problem, a position further weakened by the fact that their view here is inconsistent with their sentencing practices in the first session.

In regard to sentencing practice, the source of this failure of the judges to confirm the prediction can be seen by examining the sentencing data, especially in regard to the quantum of sentence fixed for the hypothesized component available to multiple counts of the principal offence, which is the basis of the prediction. The quantum of cumulation ordered for the multiple counts associated with the armed robbery as the principal offence in the first case was less than that fixed for the hypothesized limiting quantum for armed robbery for four (nos. 4, 5, 6 and 8) of the six judges, and the quantum of cumulation ordered for the multiple counts associated with the burglary as the principal offence in the second case was greater than that fixed for the hypothesized limiting quantum for burglary for three (nos. 1, 6 and 7) of the six judges. Of course, the prediction for this part of Problem 11 was that the quantum of cumulation ordered for armed robbery and for burglary would be equal to that considered appropriate to the hypothesized limiting quantum for each offence category. Not one of the judges sentenced in accordance with this aspect of the proposition; this was for both armed robbery and burglary. Clearly, the hypothesized component available to multiple counts of the principal offence on the dimension representing the seriousness of the legal category of the principal offence does not define a limiting (or determining) value for the quantum of cumulation open to multiple secondary counts; this quantum of cumulation is clearly independent of the legal category of the principal offence.

The striking feature of the judges' sentencing practices in the first session is that for five (nos. 1, 4, 5, 6 and 8) of the six judges the observed disparity between the effective sentences in the two cases was less than expected. This prompted a comparison of the quantum of cumulation for the multiple secondary counts in the first case (armed robbery as the principal offence) with the same parameter in the second case (burglary as the principal offence). For five of the six judges the cumulation was greater in the latter instance and for Judge 5 these quanta were the same in both cases. This finding is, of course, contrary to what would be expected on the basis of the hypothesized decision model, since the quantum of cumulation for the component available to multiple counts on the dimension representing the seriousness of the legal category of the principal offence was determined by five of the six judges (the exception being Judge 4) to be equal (Judge 7) or greater (the four others) for armed robbery than burglary. Nevertheless, it is in accordance with the alternative decision strategy discerned in the responses of a majority of the judges to Problem 7. A basic element of the alternative approach is that the degree of cumulation for the multiple secondary counts is monotonically and decreasingly related to the quantum of sentence appropriate to the principal offence. Now, in the present problem, since each of the six judges fixed a much lower quantum of sentence for the burglary than for the armed robbery, as the principal offence, it would be expected on the basis of the alternative decision strategy that a greater quantum of cumulation would be ordered when the multiple secondary counts were associated with the burglary than with the armed robbery.

In respect of the verbal protocols, of the five judges who ordered greater cumulation for the multiple secondary counts where burglary was the principal offence, there was only one judge (no. 8) whose verbal protocol conveyed a significant part of the alternative decision strategy. Judge 6 captured a minor element of the alternative approach; as well, a fundamental element of the alternative strategy was implicit in Judge 2's protocol. There were no other pertinent protocols.

Regarding the reflective reports, there was a similar picture: only one judge (no. 2) provided a substantial account of what he considered to be the policy governing this problem, and it too was in accordance with the alternative decision strategy; Judge 1 captured an element of the alternative approach.

The general lack of depth and scope in the pertinent verbal protocols and reflective reports suggests that the judges' thinking in regard to this problem was largely intuitive rather than insightful. Nevertheless, that evidence for the alternative approach was to be found in one form or another in the responses of a majority of the judges augurs well for the reliability of the relevant observations. The intuitive nature of their thinking here can be contrasted with Problem 7 – in terms of the alternative decision strategy Problems 7 and 11 are conceptually almost identical problems, tapping the same elements of policy – where the judges' qualitative answers demonstrated a greater tendency to deliberation. In Problem 11 there is an additional distinction between the two cases, namely, the legal category of the principal offence, and perhaps this additional factor rendered the problem confounding and thereby obstructed deliberation and induced intuition.

In summary, then, there is no evidence of consequence in support of the third element of the tenth proposition. Rather, the responses of the judges here appeared to be consistent with the alternative decision strategy discerned in the data for Problem 7. In this alternative approach, contrary to the decision model, there is not a limiting quantum of cumulation to be dependent on the legal category of the principal offence; rather the degree of cumulation for the sentences associated with the multiple secondary counts is related to the quantum of sentence appropriate to the principal offence according to a monotonically decreasing function. The judges' responses were not generally characterized by deliberation and coherence in relation to this element of policy.

Across Problems 6, 7 and 11 the evidence is against the tenth proposition that where a case comprises multiple secondary offences cumulation of the sentences for these secondary counts is made in regard to a notional limiting quantum of sentence, whose value depends on the legal category of the principal offence but not on the sentence for that offence, and above which extra counts would have a negligible additional effect on what would be the running effective sentence for the counts considered up to that point. In Problems 7 and 11 an alternative decision strategy appeared to fit the data; in essence it is that what is appropriate by way of an effective sentence in a case is the resultant effect of two contrary considerations, namely, increases in criminality require additional discrete quanta of sentence, and the potentially crushing effects on the offender of this extra punishment must be minimized, this within the constraint that the sentence for the principal offence determines the scope for cumulation. Five (nos. 1, 2, 5, 6 and 8) of the eight judges, in explaining in their own words what they thought to be correct by way of approach to determining the effective sentence in this type of problem, on at least one occasion clearly set out a strategy taking the form of this alternative decision model. Their sentencing across the two problems was not always in accordance with this approach and they did not always discern its applicability to the two problems across the four sessions, yet no other logical or substantial alternative was proposed nor could it be detected. Their thinking was halting, clearly, but its direction unmistakable. And the responses of two (nos. 3 and 4) of the other judges were not characterized by a strategy but to the extent that they expressed an approach at least were consistent with the alternative decision model on one or more occasions. Regarding Problem 6, it will be recalled that it was not possible to establish a preferred view, indeed even a stable view, among the judges when their responses were considered in relation to the first element of the tenth proposition. This prompts the question whether there is order in the judges' responses to Problem 6 in relation to the proposed alternative decision strategy. The answer must be in the affirmative. In the first session four of the seven judges who saw one of the cases as potentially more serious were prepared to order a higher sentence for that case; and in the second session, these respective figures are five and six. More importantly, five of the judges when they did take the view that one case was potentially more serious were prepared to order a greater effective sentence for the greater criminality; Judges 7 and 8 were inconsistent with respect to the appropriateness of a higher sentence for greater criminality in the limiting condition; it was only Judge 5 who consistently disavowed this approach. These findings, of course, accord with the alternative decision strategy; and Judge 2 described how this approach applies to Problem 6 where greater criminality is assumed to be associated with one of the cases.

Proposition 12

PROBLEM 13 Prediction: a greater proportion of the sentence for the arson will be made concurrent in the first case.

PROBLEMS 22(1–4) Prediction: the quantum of sentence made cumulative upon the principal offence, for a given level of seriousness of the tertiary offence, will decrease as the seriousness of the secondary offence increases. (It should be borne in mind that the quantum of sentence representing the level of seriousness of the principal offence in these problems varied across the eight judges, because each judge was asked to fix a sentence he considered appropriate to this level – upper limit for a single count – and the cases were presented to a judge using his sentence; also note, the results, in terms of the degree of cumulation as a proportion, are based on the mean for the two levels of seriousness of the tertiary offence, at each level of the secondary offence.)

PROBLEM 12 This is an indirect test of the twelfth proposition and for this reason only the qualitative data are relevant. The results can be reported simply: there were no pertinent verbal protocols or reflective reports regarding the twelfth proposition; since this problem is an indirect test, this is of no consequence.

It should be noted, Judge 3 said that he could not determine sentences for the cases in this set of problems unless further facts about the offence of arson were provided, his reason being that the circumstances surrounding the offence of arson are so varied.

When the responses of the seven judges to this subset of problems are considered together there is only limited support for the proposition that there is a monotonically decreasing relationship between the quantum of sentence cumulative upon the sentence for the main count of the principal offence and arising from a secondary offence and the degree of cumulation of the sentence for a tertiary offence.

First, consider the quantitative answers to Problems 22(1–4). For only one judge (no. 1) was the degree of cumulation of the sentence for the tertiary offence, as predicted, less when the sentence for the secondary offence was greater; in regard to the six others, for Judges 6, 7 and 8 there was no difference on the dependent variable and for Judges 2, 4 and 5 the observed difference was in the opposite direction to the prediction. The last of these three outcomes has no apparent theoretical significance. Indeed, there are no good reasons to regard the two outcomes of difference as anything but noise in the data and, accordingly, to interpret the data as indicating that in these cases the seriousness of the secondary offence did not affect the degree of cumulation ordered for the tertiary offence. For the seven judges, mean degree of cumulation for the tertiary offence of arson, across the two levels of seriousness of the secondary offence, was of the order of 30 percent of the sentence considered appropriate to it; only two of the judges departed significantly from this – the mean cumulation for Judge 1 was lower (approximately 10 percent) and for Judge 7 it was higher (50 percent). This disparity is not related to the sentence considered by these judges to be appropriate to the principal offence of armed robbery or the degree of cumulation ordered for the secondary offence of burglary.

In respect of the retrospective reports for these cases, all of the judges agreed with the author's statement of the proposition describing the hypothe- sized approach of the judges to this set of cases, but only two (nos. 4 and 6) of these judges expressed the effect of this proposition in their own words.

Next, there are the data relating to Problem 13. The seven judges all ordered the same degree of cumulation of the sentence for the tertiary offence in the two cases despite the variation in the seriousness of the secondary offence, contrary to the prediction derived from the twelfth proposition. And of the six judges (nos. 1, 2, 5, 6, 7 and 8) who provided a pertinent verbal protocol none indicated an approach consistent with the hypothesized decision model. There was some apparent support for the twelfth proposition in the reflective reports but this evidence in itself could not be regarded as weighty: four (nos. 1, 5, 7 and 8) of the judges agreed, but their responses were no more than simple statements of acceptance of the author's application of the proposition to this problem and contrary to their practice in the first session; moreover, Judge 5 asserted that the principle would not have much practical effect, at least for the quanta of sentence assumed for the cases in Problem 13, and it has already been noted that Judge 8 has a tendency to yea-say. In opposition to this weak support, there were three elaborated reflective reports (Judges 2, 4 and 6) disavowing the validity of the author's application of the hypothesized decision model to this problem; it is only Judge 2 who offered insight into the approach to sentencing in these reflective reports.

Clearly, the sentencing data for Problem 13 and Problems 22(1–4) offered no evidence that the twelfth proposition has any practical significance in the determination of effective sentences. In Problems 22(1–4) only one judge (Judge 1) sentenced in accordance with it, but in Problem 13 this judge, and again the six other judges, did not determine concurrency orders as predicted on the basis of the hypothesized decision model. And the verbal protocols for Problem 13, with the exception of Judge 1's, did not refer to a decision strategy; indeed, the general absence of pertinent references to the relative proportion of the sentence for the count of arson made concurrent in each case suggests that it was not based on a deliberative application of policy. At first blush, at least, there is no pattern to be found in the judges' responses for the reflective reports: for Problem 13 there is simple agreement by a majority and considered disagreement by a minority with the proposition, whereas for Problems 22(1–4) there is unanimous agreement and with two (nos. 4 and 6) of the judges expressing the effect of the proposition in their own words – two of the three judges who elaborated – brief though it was – on their disagreement in Problem 13. However, some consideration suggests that a resolution may be possible. In Problem 13 the author's statement of the application of the proposition covered both the hypothesized approach to decision making and its effect, but in Problems 22(1–4) the author's emphasis was on effect, namely, a greater degree of concurrence of the sentence for the tertiary offence is required where the sentence for the secondary offence is higher. It may be, then, that the judges were prepared to accept in principle that there should be less cumulation of the sentence for the tertiary offence where the secondary offence is more serious but were confused by or rejected the policy basis for this outcome as it is explained in the hypothesized decision model. Nevertheless, the facts that the view, regarding the relative proportion of the sentence for the count of arson made concurrent in each case, expressed by the three judges (nos. 2, 4 and 6) in the reflective reports for Problems 22(1–4) represented a change in the position taken by them in their reflective reports for Problem 13, and that there was only one pertinent reflective report in Problems 22(1–4) offering a reason for this outcome (Judge 4), reinforce the view that the judges did not have a deliberative and coherent understanding of the element of policy represented in this set of problems. But why was the view that there should be less cumulation of the sentence for the tertiary offence in the first case not reflected in the sentencing data? Perhaps, because in cases comprising three counts and these levels of sentence it would require awkward arithmetical calculations and ungainly concurrency orders.

While there was no evidence of weight in the data in support of the hypothesized element of policy for which these problems are a direct test, there was a hint in the data of the operation of an alternative approach. It is to be found in one verbal protocol (Judge 1), one reflective report (Judge 2), both for Problem 13, and one reflective report (Judge 4) for Problems 22(1–4). In these responses the notion is introduced that, notwithstanding the fact that the greater seriousness associated with the multiple counts requires a higher effective sentence, there must be a greater degree of concurrence of the sentences for these multiple counts than there would otherwise have been to minimize the potentially crushing effects of cumulation. This is, of course, consistent with the alternative decision model, proposed as a result of the analyses of Problems 7 and 11 for the tenth proposition. However, here, evidence of its applicability is limited for Judge 1 to the effect on orders of concurrency of greater seriousness arising from extra multiple secondary counts and for Judge 2 to the effect on the orders of concurrency of greater seriousness arising from more serious multiple secondary counts. Judge 1 did not acknowledge, as the alternative decision model would require, that there be somewhat greater concurrence of the sentences for the multiple secondary counts in the first case than the second partially to allow for the more serious burglary; and Judge 2 did not acknowledge, as the alternative decision model would require, that in the first case there be greater concurrence not only of the sentence for the burglary but also for the arson to allow for the more serious burglary. Perhaps these judges did not fully outline or implement the alternative decision model here because it would have required awkward arithmetical calculations and ungainly concurrency orders. In relation to Problems 22(1–4) it should be noted that this alternative decision model would require that there be greater concurrence of the sentence for the tertiary offence when the secondary offence was more serious, a proposition agreed to by all of the judges as a valid principle, but not expressed in their sentencing practice, perhaps for the reason given previously. In this respect, Judge 4 noted that the greater cumulation required in cases 22(3) and 22(4) to reflect the more serious count of burglary necessitated that there be greater concurrence of the sentence for the arson.

In summary: there was some limited support in principle for the effect of the twelfth proposition, but not the decision model hypothesized to account for it, and there was negligible evidence that it was of consequence for sentencing practice. Three judges (nos.1, 2 and, perhaps, 4) in their responses provided some recognition of the applicability of the alternative decision strategy identified in the analysis of the tenth proposition.

Proposition 13

PROBLEM 14 Prediction: a term of imprisonment will be imposed in this case.

PROBLEM 15 Prediction: the effective sentence of imprisonment will be greater in the first case.

PROBLEM 16 Prediction: the effective sentence will be the same in both cases; custodial sentences will be imposed for the secondary offences and a proportion of these sentences will be made cumulative.

The thirteenth proposition, comprising two elements, deals with an offence at a level of seriousness just short of that warranting a custodial sentence if it stood alone, and relates to how its seriousness would be treated for the purposes of cumulation were it a secondary offence. The first element is that it would be regarded as having a minimum level of seriousness defined as a very short term of imprisonment, and the second element is that this term is independent of the seriousness of the instant offence. When the responses of the eight judges to this subset of problems are considered together, there are clear and express views for and against the first element, although few of the judges show stability across problems regarding this matter; however, there was negligible support for the second element.

Problems 14, 15 and the first case in Problem 16 provide evidence relating to the first element.

In Problem 14, three (nos. 2, 6 and 7) of the judges were prepared to impose an effective sentence of imprisonment (and, accordingly, sentences of imprisonment for each of the constituent counts) in a case comprising a series of counts each of which if standing alone would be at a level of seriousness just below that warranting a custodial sentence. The verbal protocols of these three judges clearly state (Judge 7) or carry the implication (Judges 2 and 6) that the seriousness associated with such counts cumulates when they are presented together for the purposes of determining an effective sentence for the case. It is as if these judges, having decided that a term of imprisonment was appropriate as an effective sentence, in accordance with the thirteenth proposition fixed a sentence of imprisonment for each of the constituent counts, and then determined an effective sentence for these counts. The device of fixing a minimum level of imprisonment as the level of seriousness of otherwise non-custodial individual counts, simply because they comprise a case of multiple offending, is a means of handling the problem of how to cumulate the seriousness associated with these individual counts; it is artificial in the sense that it is unrelated to the hypothesized framework for the scaling of the seriousness of individual offences in terms of their offence and offender characteristics (see Chapter 2). In respect of the reflective reports, there is a twist in Judge 2's account of how an effective sentence of imprisonment may be appropriate for a case comprising individual counts at a level of seriousness which, if standing alone, would just fall short of that warranting custody. In this account of his, seriousness of the individual counts does not cumulate.

Rather, it is that the second count, as part of a case comprising multiple counts, is considered more serious than it would be were it standing alone, because the first count is then a prior conviction and this then renders the second count more serious; consequently, as part of a case it is no longer at a level of seriousness for which a non-custodial sentence is appropriate. This approach, clearly, is within the hypothesized framework for the scaling of seriousness of individual counts. Judges 6 and 7 in their reflective reports simply assented to the author's statement of the application of the thirteenth proposition to this problem, a position consistent with their responses in the first session.

For Judges 1 and 5, contrarily, an effective sentence of imprisonment was considered to be never appropriate for a series of counts each of which would not individually warrant imprisonment. The thinking evident in their verbal protocols is, according to Judge 5, that the seriousness of an individual count is not greater merely because it is presented with other counts and the appropriate sentence must be imposed for each count and, in Judge 1's view, that the seriousness associated with individual counts each not warranting custody should not be cumulated when they are presented together for the purpose of determining an effective sentence for the case. These two judges' responses are consistent across the three indices – sentencing practice, verbal protocol and reflective report – and are unambiguously at variance with the thirteenth proposition.

The non-custodial effective sentences of Judges 4 and 8, too, are inconsistent with the prediction based on this proposition. However, their reasoning raises a problem: their view was that there must be a strong and special mitigating factor personal to the offender – Judge 8 cited rehabilitation prospects – for a non-custodial sentence to be appropriate to an armed robbery and, in these circumstances, the significance of this factor for what is appropriate by way of an effective sentence for the offender would not be diminished by the consideration of additional counts. Now this, of course, is a reasonable approach to this problem, but Problem 14 could not serve as a valid test of the prediction unless the contrary assumption is accepted, namely, that there is not a strong and special factor personal to the offender in this case. Consequently, no weight could be placed on their responses in the first session as either support for or disconfirmation of the proposition. The possibility that these two judges may actually approach the determination of the effective sentence in this type of case as predicted is raised when their responses in the second session are considered. When the author stated how the proposition applied to this problem, the two judges were told to exclude the count of armed robbery from the series of counts comprising the case. Under these circumstances both judges in their reflective reports assented to the statement. In fact one of Judge 8's comments underscores the difference in approach between those who considered a custodial sentence to be an appropriate effective sentence in this type of case and those who did not. Judge 8 expressly stated that it is correct by way of approach to view the case as a whole – globally – when assessing its seriousness as a basis for sentence; now this, in effect, requires that seriousness of individual counts be cumulated. By way of contrast, Judges 1 and 5 determined sentence on the basis of seriousness in relation to individual counts, which prevents the cumulation of seriousness across the counts comprising a case.

In the first session Judge 3 declined to do Problem 14 on the grounds that he could not envisage an armed robbery for which a non-custodial sentence would be appropriate. And his reflective report is so redolent of uncertainty that a conclusion about his approach is not warranted.

The discussion now turns to Problem 15, in relation to the first element of this proposition. On the basis of the answers given for Problem 14, it would be expected that Judges 2, 6 and 7 would fix a custodial sentence for the secondary offence of burglary and order a degree of cumulation on the sentence for the principal offence of armed robbery. Judges 2 and 7 did; Judge 6 did the former but not the latter. The approach of Judge 2, as expressed in his verbal protocol, is consistent with the thirteenth proposition that when a count at a level of seriousness just short of a custodial sentence is presented with a second count, the seriousness of the two counts should be cumulated for the purpose of determining an effective sentence for the case. It is not possible to discern the basis of Judge 7's approach in his verbal protocol and his thinking is perhaps better regarded as intuitive rather than deliberative. Nevertheless, in the reflective report these two judges effectively did not endorse the author's statement of the application of the thirteenth proposition to this problem: they were inclined to the view that a sentence of imprisonment would be fixed for the secondary offence but would be made fully concurrent with the sentence for the principal offence, Judge 2 giving as his reason that the sentence for the burglary would pale beside that for the armed robbery. Clearly, in regard to this element of the hypothesized decision model, the position of Judge 7 cannot be regarded as clear and robust, nor that of Judge 2 stable.

Judge 6, contrary to expectation, did not sentence in accordance with the prediction based on this proposition; rather, his sentencing was in line with the five other judges. These judges fixed a custodial sentence for the secondary offence of burglary but ordered that it be made fully concurrent with the sentence for the armed robbery. Three (nos. 1, 5 and 6) of these six judges in their verbal protocols offered a clear reason for their chosen course of action: it appears grounded in practical considerations, namely, in view of the fact that the offender is to serve a nine-year sentence on the count of armed robbery not one of the possible non-custodial options for the burglary could be considered appropriate in conjunction with such a sentence. It may have been for these three judges that in principle a non-custodial sanction was the preferred sentencing option for the burglary. If this interpretation is correct, then the approach of these judges is clearly at variance with the thirteenth proposition. These six judges maintained this position in their reflective reports. Of these six, Judges 3, 4 and 8 did not give either a clear explanatory verbal protocol or a reflective report and, accordingly, there are no grounds for concluding that they had more than an intuitive understanding of their approach to this problem.

Judges 4, 6 and 8's reflective reports here were inconsistent with those they gave in the previous problem; this inconsistency also held for Judges 2 and 7.

The judges' responses for the first case in Problem 16 in relation to the first element of this proposition can be commented upon similarly. On the basis of the answers given for Problem 14, it would be expected that Judges 2, 6 and 7 would fix a custodial sentence for the secondary offence of intentional damage to property and order a degree of cumulation on the sentence for the principal offence of armed robbery. Judge 2 did, Judges 6 and 7 did the former but not the latter. The approach of Judge 2, as it was expressed in his verbal protocol, is consistent with the thirteenth proposition that when a count, at a level of seriousness just short of a custodial sentence, is presented with a second count, the seriousness of the two counts should be cumulated for the purpose of determining an effective sentence for the case. Nevertheless, in the reflective report, this judge did not endorse the author's statement of the application of the thirteenth proposition to the problem: he was inclined to the view that a sentence of imprisonment would be fixed for the secondary offence but would be made fully concurrent with the sentence for the principal offence. Clearly, in regard to this element of the hypothesized decision model the position of Judge 2 cannot be regarded as stable.

Judges 6 and 7, contrary to expectation, did not sentence in accordance with the prediction based on this proposition; rather, their sentencing was in line with the five other judges. For these judges the presence of the count of property damage did not result in an effective sentence of imprisonment for the case greater than that considered appropriate to the armed robbery alone. With one exception these judges fixed a custodial sentence for the secondary offence of intentional damage to property but ordered that it be made fully concurrent with the sentence for the armed robbery; Judge 8 achieved this result by imposing a fine for the count of property damage. Three (nos. 1, 5 and 6) of these judges in their verbal protocols offered reasons for their chosen course of action, grounded in a common practical consideration, namely, in view of the fact that the offender is to serve a nine-year sentence on the count of armed robbery, not one of the possible non-custodial options for the property damage could be considered appropriate in conjunction with such a sentence. It may have been for these three judges that in principle a non-custodial sanction was the preferred sentencing option for the property damage, but that it was considered inappropriate purely on practical grounds. If this interpretation is correct, then the approach of these judges is clearly at variance with the thirteenth proposition. Judge 3 also offered a pertinent verbal protocol and it too was grounded in practical considerations, namely, it would be pointless to order that a small amount of the custodial sentence fixed for the property damage be served cumulatively on the sentence for the armed robbery, since the latter sentence is so long. Nevertheless, this thinking may be consistent with the thirteenth proposition, since a custodial sentence was fixed for the property damage and there is an implicit hint in the reasoning of this judge that in principle a short amount of cumulation of the sentence for the secondary offence was preferred but its appropriateness rejected purely on practical grounds. Of these seven judges, it was only Judges 3 and 8 who did not maintain their positions in the reflective reports. In fact, in the second session Judges 4 and 7 gave an indication of the basis of their thinking; it, too, was that on practical grounds there was no appropriate non-custodial alternative. Their approach, then, like the approach of Judges 1, 5 and 6, and for the same reasons, is apparently contrary to the thirteenth proposition. Regarding Judges 3 and 8: in the second session, Judge 3 indicated that a fine, not a concurrent sentence of imprisonment, was appropriate for the secondary offence, whereas Judge 8 now preferred concurrent imprisonment to a fine. Judge 3 and Judge 8's express change of heart demonstrates that they did not have a clear and stable understanding regarding what is correct by way of approach to this problem. It was only Judge 8 who did not provide a verbal protocol or reflective report in which the reason for his approach was apparent.

In summary, the evidence regarding the validity of the first element of the thirteenth proposition is mixed. Judge 2's sentencing practice and associated reasoning favored the hypothesized decision model, but in the second session for the latter two problems his position showed some instability. Then there were two judges (nos. 1 and 5) whose understanding and application of principle were resolutely to the contrary. These were the only two whose thinking could be described as stable, coherent and deliberative. Another judge (no. 6) responded as though Problem 14 was conceptually different, i.e., required a different approach, from Problems 15 and 16(1), favoring the decision model in the former problem but rejecting it in the latter two. This conclusion may also apply to Judges 4 and 8, but must be regarded as uncertain, since they did not provide valid responses for the first session of Problem 14 and Judge 8 did not offer any explanatory pertinent protocols or reports for Problems 15 and 16(1). Finally, there is contradictory evidence of inconsistent quality to be found in the responses of the two other judges. Judge 3 did not provide usable data for Problem 14, but on balance his approach was contrary to the hypothesized decision model in the two other problems. Judge 7 favored the decision model in the first problem (no. 14), rejected its application in the third (no. 16), and responded inconsistently across the two sessions for the second (no. 15).

The evidence relating to the second element of the thirteenth proposition is to be found in Problem 16. The evidence is overwhelmingly against the second element of the thirteenth proposition. The common view, expressly stated, is that the difference in the seriousness of the secondary offences of property damage in these two cases should be reflected in the sentences considered appropriate to them. Five (nos. 1, 2, 4, 5 and 6) of the judges showed consistency across the two sessions in relation to this matter, and the three others proposed this approach in one of the two sessions. Four (nos. 1, 2, 4 and 6) of the judges took the view, in at least one of the sessions, that where the secondary offence was not serious it would not be appropriate to impose a custodial sentence even though it be made fully concurrent, but they showed some uncertainty as to what course should be followed.

The data having been analyzed in respect of the eight propositions with direct quantitative implications, the analysis now turns to the five qualitative propositions. The former primarily cover those aspects of the hypothesized decision model's structure relating to the algebraic rules for computing effective quanta of sentence. In contrast, the latter deal with those aspects of the model's structure relating to the strategy to be adopted to determine what is appropriate by way of an effective sentence. The former propositions operate within the decision framework defined by the latter. Nevertheless, a strategy cannot always be deduced from the computational rules nor from a verbal protocol or reflective report pertinent to only the quantitative aspects of a problem. The qualitative aspects must, therefore, be considered separately. Moreover, where a judge's responses to a problem cover both strategy and computation, their implication for the decision model can be communicated more readily and clearly by means of separate analyses.

The qualitative tests of the decision model

Proposition 1

All the problems, but especially Problems 1–17, relate to this proposition, most as direct tests and the others as indirect tests (see Table 4.3). This proposition states that in each case a principal offence is selected to provide the foundation sentence upon which the effective sentence is built – the appropriate sentences for the secondary and subsequent offences are added with a degree of cumulation to the sentence for the principal offence.

The judges without exception, in their sentencing practices, verbal protocols and reflective reports across these problems, were in accord with the hypothesized decision model to the extent that their approach in each case was that one offence provided the base sentence and the offender would serve the whole of the sentence appropriate to that offence; in general, a proportion of each of the sentences for the other offences comprising the case was made concurrent with the base sentence so that the offender would serve only part of the sentences appropriate to these other offences; these part-sentences for the extra counts were added to the whole of the base sentence, the sum being the effective sentence for the case. Two judges (nos. 6 and 7) expressly stated that this approach was grounded on practical considerations (see the discussion for Proposition 14).

However, the first part of this proposition, in which it is stated that in each case a principal offence is selected to provide the foundation sentence, requires qualification in the light of some of the judges' verbal protocols and reflective reports (again, see the discussion for Proposition 14). Judge 3 stated that he does not select a principal offence as a base for building an effective sentence; for him, where a case comprises multiple counts concurrency orders are made in relation to the first count on the presentment. And Judges 1, 5 and 8 made the point that in some cases one offence is not more serious than the others or there are several offences more serious than the others, and in these circumstances the first offence on the presentment or any one of the offences, or one of the more serious offences, respectively, is selected to provide the foundation sentence.

Proposition 5

Problem 17 alone relates to this proposition; it acts as a direct test.

Only two (nos. 2 and 4) of the eight judges were able to verbalize the strategy they would adopt in this type of problem to determine appropriate effective sentences. Judge 2 set out his approach clearly in both sessions: it is that when there are multiple secondary counts, even though they belong to the same legal offence category, an appropriate sentence must first be fixed for each of these counts and then a degree of cumulation ordered for each sentence on the sentence for the principal offence. Judge 4 in his verbal protocol expressly disavowed the appropriateness of first fixing an effective sentence for the multiple counts of the secondary offence. This approach is clearly contrary to the fifth proposition that, where the multiple secondary counts to be added to the principal offence belong to the same legal offence category, they are considered together as a secondary offence and are not added separately to the principal offence.

Proposition 7

Three problems – Problems 8, 9 and 10 – relate to this proposition; Problem 10 is a direct test, and 8 and 9 are indirect tests.

According to the seventh proposition, where there are multiple counts of the principal offence the degree of cumulation of the sentence for a secondary offence is determined first by reference to the sentence for the main count of the principal offence and then the quantum of sentence cumulative upon this sentence and arising from the extra counts of the principal offence. Considering the eight judges' responses across the three problems there was not even one instance of a hint that the degree of cumulation for the secondary offence was determined in this way. Moreover, one judge (no. 2) expressly stated in his reflective report for Problem 8 that it is not proper to determine the degree of cumulation of the sentence for the secondary offence after and on the basis of what quantum might be added in respect of the multiple counts of the principal offence considered alone. (It must be remembered that two of these three problems provide only an indirect test of this proposition, for which the omission of a verbal report is of less significance.) Nevertheless, two alternative decision strategies were found in the data.

Judge 1 described one of these strategies on all but one of the occasions he was given an opportunity of providing a verbal protocol or reflective report for one of the three problems (it was the report for Problem 8). The strategy can be described simply: it is that the degree of cumulation of the sentence for the secondary offence is determined in regard to the effective sentence for the principal offence, i.e., the sum of the quantum of sentence appropriate to the main count of the principal offence plus the quantum of cumulation for the additional counts of the principal offence; it is a one-stage process, and differs from the two-stage process postulated by the decision model. Problem 8 brings the distinction between the sentence for the principal count and the quantum of cumulation of the sentences for the additional counts of the principal offence into focus. In his verbal protocol for this problem Judge 1 expressly rejected the two-stage approach, saying that it is not relevant to cumulation of the sentence for the secondary offence that the nine-year sentence for armed robbery covered three counts in one case but only one in the other. Clearly, Judge 1 had a deliberative, coherent and quite stable understanding of this aspect of policy as it applied in these problems.

Three (nos. 3, 7 and 8) of the other judges, on the occasions on which they did provide a pertinent protocol or report, described a strategy apparently identical with Judge 1's approach. That two (nos. 3 and 8) of them gave only one pertinent qualitative response – a reflective report in Problem 8 and a protocol in Problem 10 – and the other (no. 7) offered but two – verbal protocols in Problems 8 and 10 – does suggest that these judges did not have a clear understanding of what is correct by way of approach to this type of problem.

The view that the degree of cumulation of the sentence for the secondary offence is determined in relation to the effective sentence for the principal offence was the strategy most frequently endorsed as appropriate to this aspect of sentencing policy. The conclusion that this was the judges' preferred approach is strengthened by two other findings: first, as explained, it was for four of the eight judges the only strategy to which they referred; and secondly, five (nos. 1, 3, 4, 6 and 7) of the seven judges who provided at least one pertinent qualitative response for Problem 8 – the problem, it will be recalled, that brings the contrary effects of the two components of the effective sentence for the principal offence into focus – described this one-stage strategy as the basis of their decision in at least one of the two sessions.

This discussion now turns to the second of the two decision strategies to be found in the data; Judge 2 described this strategy or pursued an approach consistent with it in both sessions for each of these three problems. The detail in his description of this strategy and the consistency with which he asserted its applicability across superficially different types of problem attests to the fact of this element of his sentencing policy being deliberative and robust. The rules governing his approach are set out in detail in his reflective report for Problem 9 and verbal protocol for Problem 10, with the application of these rules illustrated on these two and the four other occasions: (1) in the determination of what is appropriate by way of cumulation on the sentence for the principal offence (the main count of the principal offence) it is first necessary to determine appropriate sentences for each of the multiple counts comprising the case (i.e., the secondary offences and, where applicable, the individual additional counts of the principal offence); (2) cumulation is made separately for each of these sentences but not sequentially, rather it is made in regard to what is the appropriate effective sentence for the case; (3) the degree of concurrence for each count is tailored to achieve a balance between the requirements of there being some cumulation of the appropriate sentences for each of the multiple counts and yet there not being a crushing sentence; (4) in the tailoring of the concurrency orders to achieve this end, a similar proportion of the sentence for each of the multiple counts is made cumulative. This strategy, which may be described as a global approach, is clearly at variance with the sequential view which is implicit in the seventh proposition; indeed, Judge 2 expressly disavowed this approach on several occasions, including his reflective report for Problem 8.

Judge 4 also – in his reflective reports for Problems 9 and 10 – indicated his preference for an approach in which cumulation of sentences for individual counts is made in regard to what is an appropriate effective sentence for the case. As far as it goes, this is consistent with the views of Judge 2, although no detail was given and, accordingly, Judge 4's understanding of this matter must be regarded as largely intuitive. This, together with the fact that on one occasion – his verbal protocol for Problem 8 – he accounted for his concurrency orders in terms of Judge 1's reasoning, and on several occasions did not offer a pertinent protocol or report, clearly demonstrated that Judge 4's understanding of this approach was not robust.

Judge 5 perhaps demonstrated an embryonic form of Judge 2's thinking in regard to this aspect of policy; he recognized for the three problems – each time in a verbal protocol – that cumulation of the sentences for all multiple counts is made in relation to the main count of the principal offence, as did Judge 2, but unlike this judge was unable to explain how the sentences for the individual multiple counts are cumulated to reach an effective sentence appropriate to the case. Since he made no reference to the quantum of cumulation fixed for the additional counts of armed robbery, there is no evidence to favor the view that Judge 5's strategy was the first of the two stages represented in the seventh proposition. The fact that this judge was able to give no more than a partial account of his approach to this problem, and on three occasions did not offer a pertinent reflective report, reveals that his understanding of this approach was extremely limited.

The view that the concurrency orders are determined separately for each multiple count but yet jointly in regard to what is the effective sentence appropriate to the case is the second of the two decision strategies espoused by the judges as alternatives to the seventh proposition. This policy cannot be said to have received strong endorsement from the judges taken as a group; it was referred to by only two of the judges (nos. 2 and 4) and elaborated and used consistently by only the former. It will be recalled that the appropriateness of the approach of first fixing a sentence for each of the comprising multiple counts was avowed by the two judges (nos. 2 and 4) who gave an account of their thinking in the problem testing Proposition 5, where in the presentation of that problem an effective sentence was set for the multiple counts of the secondary offence. And it is, of course, consistent with and elaborates the alternative decision model discerned in the analyses for Proposition 10.

Judge 6, in his reflective report for Problem 8 and verbal protocol for Problem 9, adopted Judge 1's strategy. Nevertheless, on two other occasions he did outline an approach which clearly did not rely on the effective sentence for the armed robbery as the reference point, but the principle underlying his responses was not apparent. Clearly, his understanding of the policy matters raised by these problems is weak.

In summary: there is no support in the data for the seventh proposition. Two alternative approaches to decision making were discerned in the judges' responses: one is that the degree of cumulation of the sentence for the secondary offence is determined in relation to the effective sentence for the principal offence; the other is that the degree of cumulation of the sentences for the additional counts of the principal offence and the secondary offences is determined separately for each count but yet jointly in regard to what is appropriate by way of the effective sentence for the case. It should be noted, however, that the first of these two strategies, unlike the second, does not provide a general principled approach to the determining of an effective sentence for a case comprising multiple counts, since no method is offered for determining concurrency orders for the extra counts of the principal offence, rather it is problem specific. This former approach was endorsed more frequently and by a greater number of the judges. Nevertheless, the support for both approaches was not strong. For each approach there was only one judge (nos. 1 and 2, respectively) who could be said to have a robust and deliberative understanding of their view. The majority of the judges provided no evidence that they could articulate and apply a coherent approach for dealing with the element of sentencing policy raised by this type of problem. Of course, it is possible that one reason for this is that the form in which the problem was presented disorientated them – the grouping of the multiple counts of the principal offence is something which the judges would not have experienced before. And it even may be that the first strategy is an artifact of this representation of the problem.

Proposition 9

Six problems – Problems 13, a direct test, and 6, 7, 9, 11 and 12, indirect tests – relate to this proposition. (Judge 3 did not do Problems 13, and 9 and 12 because, for the reason given previously, he found the count of arson made the determination of sentence problematic.)

According to the ninth proposition, where a case comprises multiple secondary counts, the offences belonging to separate legal offence categories are added to the principal offence in turn, first the sentence for the secondary offence, then the tertiary offence, and so on, cumulation being by way of decreasing gains. (It should be noted that the notion of cumulation by way of decreasing gains relates to the calculation of the effective sentence; this proposition does not require that the actual concurrency orders reflect this process.) Considering the eight judges' responses across the six problems the conclusion must be that the evidence favoring this ninth proposition is weak.

In regard to the ninth proposition, only two (nos. 4 and 6) of the judges described a decision strategy consistent with the hypothesized decision model. Judge 4 in his verbal protocols for Problems 9 and 11 and in his reflective report for Problem 12 almost certainly determined concurrency for the sentences appropriate to the multiple secondary counts sequentially, in one case in each of these problems expressly considering first the sentence for the burglary and then, apparently independently, the sentence for the arson. However, in his reflective report for Problem 13 this judge put a view contrary to this strategy, stating that, notwithstanding that more serious counts require a higher effective sentence, the degree of cumulation of the sentences for the multiple counts in a case cannot be determined independently of what is appropriate by way of the effective sentence appropriate to the case. It should be noted that for this judge sentences may be provisionally fixed for the multiple counts comprising a case and then to some extent modified, along with the initial concurrency orders, as part of the process of tailoring to achieve an appropriate effective sentence for the case. Similarly, Judge 6 seemed to follow a sequential strategy in which cumulation was by decreasing gains. In his verbal protocol for Problem 7 his approach was clearly to add quanta of sentence for the comprising counts, in turn, with increasing concurrency, and in his reflective report for Problem 9 he spoke of cumulation by decreasing gains when the running effective sentence is high. However, in his reflective report for Problem 13, Judge 6 adopted another tack for this type of problem; he determined concurrency for the second multiple secondary count (the arson) before the first multiple secondary count (the burglary), this approach obviously being contrary to the "sequential" strategy. Both these judges on more than one occasion sentenced in accordance with a sequential determination of concurrency orders; however, on at least one occasion they adopted a contrary strategy and on the majority of occasions did not offer a pertinent protocol or report. (It should be noted, however, that most of these omissions relate to problems providing only an indirect test of the proposition, for which the omission of a verbal report is of less significance.) Without doubt, these two judges did not demonstrate that they had a clear and firmly established view on this element of sentencing policy. And the fact that they are the only judges to offer any evidence favoring the ninth proposition says little for its validity.

Again, an alternative strategy for handling this aspect of the determination of an effective sentence was found in the responses to these problems. For five (nos. 1, 2, 3, 5 and 8) of the judges, when they provided a pertinent protocol or report, this was their expressed approach; for one other (Judge 4) it was one of several approaches adopted for these problems, as discussed above. Across the judges this alternative was expressed with varying clarity, completeness and consistency. In terms of these criteria, Judge 2 was the leading exponent of this alternative strategy; he made reference to at least a significant element of it in a protocol or report for four of the six problems on five of the twelve occasions. Before outlining this strategy it is as well to note that Judge 2 expressly eschewed the sequential view: in his verbal protocols for Problem 6 and 7 he stated that it is not correct to determine sequentially what appears to be a reasonable degree of concurrence for each of the counts comprising the case in the hope that the resulting effective sentence will be appropriate. Judge 8 expressed a similar note of caution in his protocol for Problem 11. This approach as described by Judge 2 has the following elements: (1) concurrency orders in respect of the appropriate sentences for the multiple secondary counts in a case are fixed so that the resulting effective sentence is appropriate to the seriousness of the counts considered together; (2) higher effective sentences are required for more serious cases, seriousness arising from the number of multiple counts and the seriousness of these counts and the principal count; (3) notwithstanding the preceding point, the potentially crushing effects of cumulative sentences must be minimized; (4) as the seriousness of a case increases so there must be greater concurrence, as a proportion of the sentences for the multiple counts, in order to avoid a crushing sentence; (5) for each of the multiple counts in a case, the proportion of the sentence made concurrent is approximately the same. This approach is, of course, the same global strategy discerned in the analysis for Proposition 7.

The responses of Judge 1, taken together, show that he too had a comprehensive and detailed understanding of this element of policy; while the grasp of this approach shown by Judges 3, 4, 5 and 8 was superficial and limited in scope, suggesting that, for this group of four, their understanding of this element of policy was not well developed. And, as explained before, Judge 4 wavered in his commitment to this alternative. This approach was the only alternative offered to the ninth proposition and was referred to in part or in whole more frequently and consistently than the approach to this element of policy described in the hypothesized decision model. Nevertheless, the large number of occasions on which all of the judges, some more than others, failed to offer a pertinent protocol or report does suggest that its applicability was not always appreciated.

Judge 7 was unable to verbalize a decision process for the determination of sentence in this type of problem.

In summary: there was no substantial support in the data for the ninth proposition. However, in the evidence an alternative approach was readily discernible: it indicated a global approach, rather than a sequential approach, in which concurrency orders in respect of the sentences for multiple secondary counts are fixed so that the resulting effective sentence is appropriate to the seriousness of the counts considered together and is not crushing. Although all except two of the judges on at least one occasion pointed to the appropriateness of the alternative approach, only two (nos. 1 and 2) of the judges demonstrated a detailed and comprehensive understanding of it, but not even these two demonstrated that they appreciated its application across the range of problems.

Proposition 11

Three problems – Problems 13, a direct test, and 9 and 12, indirect tests – relate to this proposition.

This proposition states that, where there is a secondary offence, the degree of cumulation of the sentence for a tertiary offence is determined by reference first to the sentence for the main count of the principal offence and then to the quantum of sentence cumulative upon this sentence and arising from the secondary offence. Acceptance of this proposition requires the validity of the ninth proposition, it being a necessary but not sufficient condition here that the determination of concurrency orders for a series of multiple counts is determined sequentially. The three problems (nos. 9, 12 and 13) used to test the present proposition also relate to the ninth proposition and, accordingly, it is appropriate to recall the conclusions reached in relation to the hypothesis of sequential cumulation. None of the judges' responses in Problem 13 and only two (nos. 4 and 6) of the judges in their responses to Problems 9 and 12 provided evidence in favor of the ninth proposition. Of these data, it is only Judge 6's reference in his reflective report for Problem 9 to cumulation by way of decreasing returns, which is at least consistent with the eleventh proposition, decreasing gains being a necessary outcome of the strategy proposed in this proposition; however, he did not give any clue as to the approach producing this outcome. Slim evidence, indeed, for the validity of the eleventh proposition. And it is apparent from Judge 4's two favorable references to the hypothesis of sequential ordering of cumulation – his protocol for Problem 9 and report for Problem 12 – that in determining cumulation for the tertiary count no reference was made to the cumulation fixed for the earlier counts on the presentment, evidence against the validity of the eleventh proposition. And, it should be borne in mind, the global approach to the determination of concurrency in a case comprising a series of multiple counts, for which there was substantial evidence in the data relating to the ninth proposition, describes a pattern of reasoning at variance with the eleventh proposition.

In summary: there was no substantial evidence in favor of the eleventh proposition.

The principal offence

Proposition 14
Proposition 14's validity is tested by Problems 30 (1–10).

Two judges (nos. 2 and 4) in Session 1 selected the principal offence in accordance with the hypothesized decision model: the principal offence being the offence with the higher appropriate sentence (effective sentence for principal offences comprising multiple counts) and, where these two quanta were equal, the more serious legal offence category. (Of course, in this approach, where the principal offence comprised multiple counts, the foundation sentence – the sentence upon which the effective sentence is built – would be the sentence for the most serious of the counts comprising that principal offence.) These judges, in selecting the offence category with the greatest instant criminality and, then, statutory seriousness, thereby had the opportunity of determining an effective sentence for a class of offender (an armed robber, or a burglar, in these examples), defined according to the nature of the offence characterizing the criminality of the case. In Session 2, these two judges followed a different formula from the one governing their decision in the first session: here, the foundation offence was the count with the higher appropriate sentence and, where these two quanta were equal, the statutorily more serious legal offence category. By way of contrast with the first session, their selection of the principal offence turned on the seriousness of counts considered individually, not in regard to the instant seriousness of an offence category. This formulation does not as readily permit the interpretation that these judges could then determine an effective sentence for a class of offender; rather, it appears that an effective sentence in effect would be determined for an offender.

Judge 7 showed the same variation as the previous two judges, except that he adopted the criteria "higher effective sentence," then, "more serious category of offence" in the second session and the criteria "higher sentence," then, "more serious category of offence" in the first session. In his verbal protocol in the first session, the reason he gave for using the count with the higher sentence as the foundation offence was that it affords an arithmetically easier means of expressing the concurrency orders. He was the only judge in the second session to sentence in accordance with the hypothesized decision model.

Two other judges (nos. 1 and 8) used the criterion of "higher effective sentence" as the first of two or more criteria for selecting the principal offence in one of the two sessions. In the second session Judge 8 added the criteria "greater number of counts," then, "more serious category of offence," while in the first session Judge 1 added the criterion "greater number of counts." Again, the use of these additional criteria in association with that of "higher effective sentence" suggests that in these instances the judges were determining an effective sentence for a class of offender, defined according to the nature of the offence characterizing the criminality. In this respect it is interesting to note that Judge 1 in his verbal protocol for Problem 30(8) said, in selecting the burglary as the principal offence, that he would regard the offender as a "substantial burglar." In the other session these two judges followed a different formula: in the second session for Judge 1 and the first session for Judge 8, the foundation count was the count with the higher appropriate sentence, and if two or more counts satisfied this criterion, then one of these counts was arbitrarily chosen to provide the base sentence (Judge 8) or the first of these counts on the presentment was assigned this role (Judge 1).

The five judges who founded their decision regarding the principal offence on the effective sentence did this in only one of the two sessions, and on the other occasion made the offence with the higher sentence the basis of their selection. This latter strategy was followed by the remainder of the judges (nos. 3, 5 and 6). Judges 3 and 6 in the second session added the criterion "more serious category of offence" and Judge 6 in the first session added the criterion "less serious category of offence" as a tie-breaker (Judge 6's reasoning being that where the sentences for the main counts of armed robbery and burglary were equal, the burglary qua burglary was more serious than the armed robbery qua armed robbery). In his verbal protocol in the first session, Judge 6, like Judge 7, justified his using the count with the higher sentence as the foundation sentence on the ground of practicality. In his reflective report in the second session Judge 5 noted that for him the notion of the principal offence as the foundation sentence was of practical significance only when there was a substantial difference between the quantum of sentence appropriate to one of the counts and the sentences for the other counts comprising the case; he added that when such a disparity did exist, an effective sentence is being determined for a class of offender (armed robber, burglar, etc.), his reason no doubt being that in these circumstances this offence characterizes the criminality of the case. Where one count does not stand out as principal, then the first count on the presentment is normally taken as the foundation sentence, according to this judge. In his determining whether one of the offences was substantially more serious, Judge 5 did appear to show inconsistency across the cases. And Judge 3 in his reflective report in the second session stated that he does not select a principal offence as a base for building an effective sentence; for him, where a case comprises multiple counts, concurrency orders are made in relation to the first count on the presentment.

It should be noted that within a session the judges exhibited a high degree of consistency across the problems in applying their criteria for the selection of the principal offence. In the first session Judge 5 (the matter of whether the difference between the two sentences was substantial aside) and Judge 3 each showed one aberration, and in the second session Judges 3, 6 and 7 each showed what appeared to be a slip in one instance. Two points should be made in relation to this matter. It is possible that some of these supposed errors were not real: perhaps the judges discriminated between the two offences in terms of factors, or the interaction of factors, not contemplated by the hypothesized decision model, and these additional considerations would have emerged had the appropriate pairs of offences been included in the list. Secondly, the decision rule ascribed to each judge was the one which when applied to his responses showed the fewest inconsistencies. It is possible, therefore, that some of the judges actually were attempting to apply a rule different from the one imputed to them, but applied it less reliably; this was not thought to be a significant problem, because the decision strategy inferred from a judge's choice of principal offence was compared with his verbal protocols and reflective reports, and each strategy was based on responses to ten pairs of offences, not an insubstantial number for a simple decision.

In view of the consistency shown by each judge within a session it would be expected that reasoned explanations would have been readily apparent in their verbal protocols and reflective reports. And so they were: there were no judges in the first session who did not in this way provide evidence of a deliberative approach, although it should be noted in parenthesis that it was not often stated in the crisp, formulaic manner reported in this analysis.

Nevertheless, that apart, it could not be concluded that as a group these judges had a stable and robust understanding of this aspect of sentencing policy. Not one of the judges applied the same criteria across the two sessions, and only Judges 3, 5 and 6 used the same criterion as the basis of their selection (for these three, in each session, it was the count with the higher appropriate sentence).

The substantial disparity within and between the judges' sentencing practices in respect of Problems 30(1–10) demonstrates that sentencing policy relating to the choice of a foundation sentence on which to cumulate sentences in cases comprising multiple counts is an open question, and a matter requiring resolution. Nevertheless, considered in general terms, there was a majority position: there were five judges in the first session and six in the second for whom the basis of the selection was the count with the higher sentence; and it was the only criterion to be used by a judge – there were three, in fact – in both sessions.

In summary: the data provided little or no support for the fourteenth proposition; nor was it possible to discern a clearly favored and precisely defined alternative.

CHAPTER SEVEN

An alternative sentencing decision model for the multiple offender

The sentencing problems were developed and then administered to a sample of judges as a means of testing the hypothesized decision model describing how judges determine effective sentences for multiple offenders whose counts are separate transactions and offence categories and once appropriate sentences have been fixed for the multiple counts. A detailed analysis of the results is presented in the previous chapter: there the data are interpreted in terms of fourteen propositions, which cover those aspects of the decision model represented in the sentencing problems. One of the purposes of this chapter is to set out in general terms the fate of the model at the hands of the analysis; the second is to present information and discuss matters relating to the administration of the problems; the third is to state in a rounded-out and systematic form the principles of the alternative decision model discerned in the judges' responses and, then, to comment on its validity and limitations; and the fourth and final purpose of this chapter is to assess the extent to which this aspect of judicial sentencing is deliberative and to interpret the nature of judicial intuition, this being done in the light of the qualitative data from the sentencing problems, the latter with the aid of relevant theory.

Hypothesized decision model

Regarding the hypothesized decision model: first, the propositions for which there was substantial support are listed; secondly, the propositions which were rejected or for which the judges' position was equivocal are listed. The criterion for support or rejection is that there were at least five of the eight judges whose responses across the set of problems on balance favored or were against, respectively, the proposition; where, in regard to support or rejection, the eight judges were equally divided between themselves or there was not a majority position and the responses of at least one of the judges were inconsistent across the problems relating to a proposition, the judges' view was defined as equivocal.

Propositions – supported

PROPOSITION 1 In each case a principal offence is selected to provide the foundation sentence upon which the effective sentence is built – the appropriate sentences for the secondary and subsequent offences are added with a degree of cumulation to the sentence for the principal offence.

PROPOSITION 2 There is a monotonically decreasing relationship between the quantum of sentence for the main count of the principal offence and the degree of cumulation of the sentence for a secondary offence.

PROPOSITION 8 There is a monotonically decreasing relationship between the quantum of sentence cumulative upon the sentence for the main count of the principal offence and arising from extra counts of the principal offence and the degree of cumulation of the sentence for a secondary offence.

It should be remembered that in respect of each of the latter two propositions there were only two judges – Judge 1 was one of the two judges in each instance – who could explain the principle underlying their approach, who showed consistency in applying this principle across the problems relating to the proposition, and whose sentencing practice gave effect to that principle. The responses of the other judges making up the majority support for these two propositions were characterized by intuition, inconsistency and incoherence; for each of these judges it was the case that in their responses across the set of problems there was significant support for the proposition. By way of contrast, the support for the first proposition was overwhelming and decisive.

Propositions – unsupported

PROPOSITION 3 There is a monotonically increasing relationship between the seriousness of the legal category of the principal offence and the degree of cumulation of the sentence for a secondary offence. (The majority view was against this proposition.)

PROPOSITION 4 The seriousness of a secondary offence is defined by its quantum of sentence and is independent of the seriousness of its legal offence category. (The judges' view was equivocal in respect of this proposition.)

PROPOSITION 5 Where the multiple secondary counts to be added to the principal offence belong to the same legal offence category they are considered together as a secondary offence and are not added separately to the principal offence. (The majority view was against this proposition.)

PROPOSITION 6 Where a secondary offence comprises multiple counts its effective sentence defines the seriousness of these counts considered together for the purposes of cumulation. (The majority view was against this proposition.)

PROPOSITION 7 Where there are multiple counts of the principal offence the degree of cumulation of the sentence for a secondary offence is determined first by reference to the sentence for the main count of the principal offence and then the quantum of sentence cumulative upon this sentence and arising from extra counts of the principal offence. (The majority view was against this proposition.)

PROPOSITION 9 Multiple secondary offences belonging to separate legal offence categories are added to the principal offence in turn, first the sentence for the secondary offence, then the tertiary offence, cumulation being by way of decreasing gains. (The majority view was against this proposition.)

PROPOSITION 10 Where a case comprises multiple secondary offences cumulation of the sentences for these counts is made in regard to a notional limiting quantum of sentence above which extra counts would have a negligible additional effect on what would be the running effective sentence for the counts considered up to that point; the limiting quantum of cumulation is the same whether the multiple secondary counts belong to the legal category of the principal offence or are equally or less serious offences belonging to a different legal category; the limiting quantum of cumulation for the multiple secondary counts is independent of the quantum of sentence appropriate to the principal offence; and, the limiting quantum of cumulation is defined as the component available to multiple counts of the principal offence on the dimension representing the seriousness of the legal category of the principal offence, and its value varies across legal categories of the principal offence. (The judges' view was equivocal in regard to the first element, and was in the majority against the second and third elements of this proposition.)

PROPOSITION 11 Where there is a secondary offence the degree of cumulation of the sentence for a tertiary offence is determined first by reference to the sentence for the main count of the principal offence and then the quantum of sentence cumulative upon this sentence and arising from the secondary offence. (The majority view was against this proposition.)

PROPOSITION 12 There is a monotonically decreasing relationship between the quantum of sentence cumulative upon the sentence for the main count of the principal offence and arising from a secondary offence and the degree of cumulation of the sentence for a tertiary offence. (The majority view was against this proposition.)

PROPOSITION 13 An offence at a level of seriousness warranting a non-custodial sentence if it stood alone would as a secondary offence and for the purposes of cumulation be regarded as having a minimum level of seriousness defined as a very short term of imprisonment, a term independent of the seriousness of the instant offence. (The judges' view was equivocal in regard to the first element, and was in the majority against the second element of the proposition.)

PROPOSITION 14 The principal offence is the offence with the highest effective sentence and, if two or more offences satisfy this criterion, then (1) the offence belonging to the most serious legal offence category, and (2) the offence belonging to the legal offence category with the highest number of counts, are introduced in order as the criteria. (The majority view was against this proposition.)

Of those propositions for which there was majority rejection, it was in fact the case that there was not one instance where the responses of any of the judges across the problems relating to a proposition showed overwhelming support for it.

In view of this summary of the empirical evidence from the sentencing problems, the inescapable conclusion is that the hypothesized decision model describing how judges sentence multiple offenders has been roundly rejected. Even though three of the fourteen propositions – one with qualitative implications and two with quantitative implications – were supported, the model cannot be regarded as but a wreck. Indeed, the support for the two quantitative propositions is of little consequence. The reason for this is readily apparent from the already mentioned distinction between the nature of the quantitative and the qualitative propositions (see the previous chapter). The former cover those aspects of the hypothesized decision model's structure relating to the algebraic rules for computing effective quanta of sentence. By way of contrast, the latter deal with those aspects of the model's structure relating to the strategy to be adopted to determine what is appropriate by way of effective sentence. The quantitative propositions operate within and must be consistent with the decision framework defined by the qualitative propositions. Now, since the four qualitative propositions providing the framework for the computation rules were knocked out by the data, the two remaining quantitative propositions cannot be placed on the canvas that is to become the picture of judicial decision making for the sentencing of multiple offenders. Fortunately, in the judges' verbal protocols and reflective reports for problems relating to both quantitative and qualitative propositions it was possible to discern an alternative decision model. The discussion returns to make a somewhat formal presentation of this model after dealing with matters relating to the administration of the sentencing problems and the analysis of the data.

Methodological considerations

Four matters relating to the methods adopted for the presentation and analysis of the sentencing problems require additional information and discussion: (1) the administration of the problems; (2) the judges' comments on these two sentencing exercises; (3) the analysis of the data; and (4) the size of the sample of judges. Many of the matters discussed here were raised in Chapter 5.

The administration of the problems

The administration of the first sentencing exercise proceeded smoothly and with a minimum of fuss.

All of the judges apparently understood the instructions – they required little clarification at the beginning and during the test – and the notation was readily intelligible and accepted as a valid way of representing the necessary details about a case. The need for practice on a few illustrative problems was uniformly and unreservedly rejected; and the fact that they all were immediately comfortable with the task justified this decision.

The eight sessions were conducted early June to mid-July, 1991; for six of the judges the length was approximately one-and-a-half hours, and for the other two, two and two-and-a-half hours. Each judge was offered a short break on several occasions during the course of the session, but all declined.

Four (nos. 2, 4, 7 and 8) of the judges did each of their verbal protocols as an immediate retrospective report (or primarily in this way with some concurrent reporting interspersed); for the others the converse was true. The instructions to the judges were for an immediate retrospective report. The author's observations of the judges as they undertook this task suggested this was a wise decision: the judges found that it was necessary to give the problems careful consideration and some found some of the problems required intense concentration. Those judges who, despite the instructions, thought aloud, were not stopped from doing this, because they were obviously comfortable and apparently found it undemanding.

All except Judge 8 gave the appearance of being well motivated; nevertheless, this judge did give thought to the exercise, his attitude perhaps denoting defensiveness. In fact, Judges 2, 4 and 7 manifested mild stress during the session, well, perhaps exaggerated concern over their performance. The time and thought given to each problem demonstrated that the problems were not considered routine and that they raised significantly different points of policy, requiring considerable mental application, but all able to be solved to the judge's own satisfaction and without the momentum of the administration being lessened.

The author intervened during the period in which a judge was working on a problem in any one of three circumstances: (1) where there was a period during which the judge did not think aloud or for which he did not volunteer an account of his thinking, he was asked to provide a record of his thoughts; (2) when a judge arrived at a conclusion, sometimes apparently after little thought, sometimes after a series of verbalizations not clearly related to the conclusion, he was asked how, in terms of his thinking, he arrived at that conclusion; and (3) where it was possible that a judge's response had import for the element of policy raised by the problem but was not clear, he was asked for clarification; for example, in Problem 3 if a judge said "the rape there is serious," he would be asked whether his comment related to the quantum of sentence, category of offence, or both. The second intervention was made more than on the odd occasion for Judges 4 and 7, and frequently for Judge 8; the first and third interventions were made occasionally for most if not all of the judges. However, on these interventions, judges were not pushed to respond or to elaborate a response, since what was wanted was a record of their thoughts at the time, not a *post hoc* justification of an intuition.

None of the judges said that they were not able to give a complete and accurate record of the information they heeded as they worked towards the solutions to the problems, although for most if not all of the judges there were occasions on which there was little deliberative thought to report, the approach being largely intuitive. Of course, it is impossible to know for immediate retrospective reports (prompted or not) the extent to which an account comprises record rather than justification.

In the presentation of the problems it was not necessary to modify the cases in any significant way. All the judges accepted the quanta of sentence set for the offences in all the problems as being within the range they would consider appropriate, with the exception of two judges for Problem 14. And for one judge the count of arson in Problems 9, 12, 13 and 22(1–4) made the determination of sentence problematic there. Both of these matters are explained in the analysis. There were a few instances for cases comprising multiple counts of an offence category where the judge thought that the assumed number of counts was not appropriate to the quanta of sentence fixed for the component covering the cumulation of the additional counts; when this problem arose the judge was told to assume a number he considered to be appropriate, and in no instances did this hinder the testing of the proposition. Two judges (nos. 5 and 6), in fixing a quantum of sentence appropriate to a case whose seriousness placed it at the lower limit on the dimension representing the seriousness of the legal offence category of armed robbery, indicated a sentence of six months as appropriate. Now, Problems 21(1) and 21(2) require for the count of armed robbery a sentence of at least two years, so that the count of burglary is not principal. Accordingly, for both judges these two cases were presented as comprising an armed robbery for which the appropriate sentence was two years; fortunately, this course did not undermine the validity of the test of the second proposition, because both judges agreed that an armed robbery for which a sentence of two years was appropriate would be a trivial instance of this offence.

Where a judge required clarification regarding the task of setting sentences considered appropriate to the limiting values for single and multiple counts of the legal offence categories of armed robbery and burglary, he was told that he should not let his imagination run wild and imagine a case at a level of seriousness which would be regarded as extremely rare or unusual.

The second sentencing exercise, like the first, proceeded expeditiously. The eight sessions were conducted late June to mid-August; each one ran for approximately one hour, with no breaks. For six of the judges the second exercise followed one to three weeks after the first, for the other two, five and eight weeks.

Where a judge, in responding to the author's statement of the application of the hypothesized decision model, gave a reason for his agreement or disagreement and the import of his thinking was not clear or was incomplete in respect of the element of policy being tested, he was asked to clarify or expand his point. Similarly, a judge was asked for his reasoning when his response was one of simple disagreement. These interventions by the author were not common.

The judges' comments on the sentencing exercises

None of the judges indicated that they had found any of the case descriptions to be disconcertingly artificial nor any of the factual circumstances associated with the cases to be unrealistic and improbable. Nevertheless, there were a number of pertinent comments. Four of the judges (nos. 2, 3, 5 and 7) observed that some of the assumed sentences were appropriate to levels of seriousness rarely encountered; Judges 2, 5 and 7 noted, however, that this factor would not render their answers invalid in these instances, Judge 2's reason being that the same principles apply at the high as at more moderate levels of seriousness. Also, four of the judges (nos. 2, 3, 4 and 5) reminded the author that in sentencing actual cases more thought is given to the determination of what is appropriate by way of quantum of sentence, not infrequently authorities and colleagues are consulted and, in some instances, the decision is an agonizing one. Again, Judges 2, 4 and 5, despite this qualification, were confident that their answers reflected what they thought was correct by way of approach to the determination of effective sentence. In fact, it was only Judge 3 who claimed that these two matters necessarily invalidated his answers; indeed, he went so far as to suggest that his answers were perhaps no better than guesses for the problems in which these factors were operative. This judge also identified a third factor, and believed that it would similarly bring into question all his answers. To this judge, sentencing has a significant emotional component, which interacts with one's reasoning in the determination of sentence; clearly, where as in this exercise the judge is not sentencing flesh and blood – offender and victim – then the emotional component is missing and, accordingly, thought processes are being studied in the absence of a potentially significant influence. The argument against the relevance of this point is that even if this factor was responsible for a relatively small general increase or decrease on what otherwise would be considered appropriate by way of sentence, its effect would not be expected to vary between cases. Now, of course, it is only this variation which has the potential to invalidate the problems as tests of the model. Finally, Judge 6 felt that for validity these exercises require the assumption that sentencing can be considered as a primarily deliberative process, whereas in his mind sentencing must be largely intuitive since the relevant considerations and their potential interactions are manifold and vary infinitely from case to case; the source of his unease, he argued, arose from the fact that the problems tested the propositions by focusing on one element of sentencing policy, this forcing the judge into a mental strait-jacket. It is not clear how this could be so, since the judges were nonetheless imposing sentences for complete not part cases and were free to approach the case(s) comprising each problem as they pleased.

The analysis of the data

The author transcribed the judges' responses from the tape-recordings and produced a more-or-less verbatim record; this record was checked for accuracy and completeness by the author himself against a second playing of the tape-recordings. The interpretations of the judges' responses by the author in relation to the hypothesized decision model were made on the basis of this record.

An ever-present danger in this type of analysis is the possibility of the author's memory playing a role in his producing consistency of interpretation of a judge's responses in regard to a proposition (where several problems related to the one proposition) or even the complete decision model. The fact that the analysis of the data was fragmented and over an extended period did not provide conditions favorable to this undesirable outcome; specifically: (1) each interpretation of a judge's relevant responses was made in regard to only an element of the model (proposition), of which there were a considerable number; (2) to assess a proposition it was necessary to examine only a small part of a protocol or report; (3) the analysis was made, protocol then report, across judges within a problem, problems being examined sequentially within each proposition, as presented, and propositions being examined sequentially, again as presented in the previous chapter; and (4) the analysis was conducted over a three-month period alongside of the author's regular academic duties.

A second danger to a valid analysis lies in the author's possible predisposition to interpret the data in a way favorable to the hypothesized decision model. The form of the present analysis would not readily admit of this type of error. Since each segment of a judge's verbal protocol or reflective report addressed a specific element of policy directly represented in the problem, the leeway for the author's subjective interpretation was minimal or not significant. And the quantitative aspects of the decision model were tested objectively by means of the comparisons between the actual quanta of sentence imposed by the judges and the sentences predicted on the basis of the model.

To test the reliability of the analysis, the author checked his interpretations of the judges' responses in relation to the model. This commenced several weeks after the analysis had been completed for the last proposition, and it ran for two to three weeks; it was conducted in the same way and under the same conditions as the initial analysis. The author read the judge's responses to each problem, determined what if anything was pertinent to the relevant proposition, and then checked whether it had been accurately interpreted in the analysis. In six instances a judge's verbal protocol or reflective report for a problem was considered to be relevant where previously it had not, and in three instances the original interpretation of a response was modified. These alterations were spread across problems, propositions and judges. Numerically, of course, nine is a very small fraction of the total number of interpretations. None of the changes required a consequent modification of the conclusions relating to the proposition being tested, and in only two instances was it necessary to modify the interpretation of the approach followed by the judge in regard to the proposition. Clearly, the interpretations of the protocols and reports were done with a high degree of reliability.

These comments regarding the reliability and validity of the analysis and applying to the testing of the hypothesized decision model do not extend to the alternative decision model, whose uncertain foundation is of an apparent approach discerned by the author primarily in the responses of a small number of the judges to several of the problems. In appreciating the status of the alternative model, the nature of its data base must be understood. In the reflective reports these data were generated when a judge disagreed with the author's statement of the application of the hypothesized decision model to a problem and in its stead outlined in more or less detail his view of what is correct by way of approach in determining an effective sentence. Under these circumstances a judge might easily overlook or be unaware of elements of policy or detailed considerations relating to these elements. In the verbal protocols these data are a judge's account of his thinking as he determined the effective sentence for a problem – the principles and working rules enunciated by him and contrary to the hypothesized decision model. Now, to the extent that this principle applies beyond the element of policy represented and directly tested by the problem, its completeness and precision are open to doubt, its scope and generality unknown. And for a response to a problem providing only an indirect test of a proposition, there is no check at all in respect of these matters on the validity of the proposed approach.

The size of the sample of judges

Some may question whether a sample of eight judges was adequate for the testing of the decision model. In view of the results obtained, the answer is unquestionably in the affirmative. Rejection of the fundamental structure of the decision model by eight experienced judges, representing a complement of the order of forty-five, is surely sufficient to regard the model as mortally wounded. Similarly, the characteristic of judicial experience favors the validity of the conclusion that judicial decision making in regard to the sentencing of the multiple offender is largely intuitive and exhibits a degree of inconsistency within and across judges and some incoherence between thought and action. Indeed, sample selection based on experience allowed the option of a small sample, an alternative compatible with the economical use of scarce judicial resources and with empirical efficiency.

Nevertheless, in the light of the finding that the thinking of most judges appears to be largely intuitive, this strategy carried the inherent risk of there being no judges with a sufficiently deliberative understanding of their approach to provide enough data upon which to build an alternative decision model. Fortunately, that outcome did not occur here, but it was close, there being only two judges providing quite detailed and comprehensive data for this purpose.

Alternative decision model

The alternative decision model for the sentencing of multiple offenders incorporates both a decision strategy and a set of computational rules for the determination of effective sentences in cases comprising offences from separate transactions and different legal offence categories. It is based primarily on the responses of Judges 1 and 2 to the problems testing Propositions 7 and 9 (qualitative) and Proposition 10 (quantitative). The following statement of the alternative decision model brings together, though in a rounded-out and systematic form, its various elements as they are to be found in the responses to these problems; it was expressed by the judges with varying detail, completeness and consistency across the problems, but nevertheless it appears as generally coherent across and within the occasions when and to the extent that it was expressly recognized as correct by way of approach to these problems.

This alternative approach is governed by the following principles:

(1) an appropriate sentence of imprisonment must first be fixed for each of the multiple counts; the principal offence is the offence with the highest sentence, but when two or more offences have equally high sentences, any one of these counts is treated as the principal offence;

(2) then, the proportion of each of the appropriate sentences for the multiple secondary counts to be made cumulative on the sentence for the principal offence is determined;

(3) what is appropriate by way of an effective sentence is the sum of two components – the first is the full sentence appropriate to the seriousness of the principal offence, and the second is made up of a part (proportion) of each of the appropriate sentences for the secondary counts;

(4) the determination of what is appropriate by way of cumulation is made separately for each of the multiple secondary counts, yet not sequentially,

but in regard to what is the effective sentence appropriate to the seriousness of the case viewed globally;

(5) in the global determination of sentence:

(i) there is not a limiting effective quantum of sentence with an absolute value above which cumulation of the sentences for the multiple secondary counts cannot be made on the sentence for the principal offence (at least within the levels contemplated in the present problems);

(ii) rather, the quantum of sentence appropriate to the second component of the effective sentence – the sum of the part-sentences to be added to the sentence for the principal offence – is the resultant effect of two contrary considerations: the first, an enhancing factor, is that more serious principal offences require higher effective sentences and more serious and extra multiple counts require additional discrete quanta of sentence on the sentence for the principal offence – *ceteris paribus*; the second, a constraining factor, is that the potentially crushing effects on the offender of the additional quanta of sentence appropriate to the greater seriousness and number of the extra multiple counts must be minimized;

(iii) the enhancing factor is manifest through cumulation of the sentences associated with the multiple secondary counts; cumulation is by way of decreasing gains in the quanta of sentence made cumulative for constant additional sums of the sentences appropriate to these counts;

(iv) the constraining factor is manifest through the degree of concurrence (proportion made concurrent) of the sentences associated with the multiple secondary counts; its effect is determined by the seriousness of (sentences appropriate to) the principal offence and the total seriousness of (sum of the sentences appropriate to) the multiple secondary counts; the effect of these two factors is considered sequentially, first the former, then the latter: the higher the sentence for the principal offence, the less scope there is for cumulation of the sentences associated with the multiple secondary counts – as this sentence approaches the limit of the range contemplated in the present problems, there can be increasingly little by way of cumulation – and, within this constraint, the higher the sum of the sentences for the multiple secondary counts, the greater the degree of concurrence;

(v) accordingly, the higher the sentence appropriate to the principal offence and the higher the sum of the sentences appropriate to the other counts, then the less the degree of cumulation for each of the appropriate sentences associated with the multiple secondary counts on the sentence for the principal offence, the increase in the degree of concurrence being tailored to satisfy the preceding two considerations, namely, enhancement to cover additional seriousness associated with greater criminality and restraint to avoid crushing the offender;

(6) in the tailoring of the concurrency orders to achieve this balance, in principle a similar proportion of the sentence for each of the multiple secondary counts is made cumulative.

The five sub-principles under the fifth principle are all concerned with how the degree of cumulation is made on the basis of the total seriousness of the case viewed globally. The operationalization of this element must wait until Chapter 9 where these principles are translated into quantitative form by means of an algebraic model; a full understanding of the idea of global sentencing is not possible in terms of a rule-based description, but requires a mathematical operation.

This alternative decision model must be regarded as a worthy substitute for the now-rejected hypothesized decision model. In regard to the problems testing the ninth proposition (qualitative) all except two of the judges on at least one occasion pointed to the appropriateness of this approach, and for five of the judges, when they did give an account of their thinking, this was the expressed approach. Also, for the second and third elements of the tenth proposition (quantitative) considered together, five of the judges in explaining what they thought to be correct by way of approach on at least one occasion clearly set out a strategy taking the form of this alternative decision model. As well, of the two judges demonstrating the clearest understanding of this alternative decision strategy, one gave a detailed account of its operation in relation to the seventh proposition and recognized its applicability to the fifth, and both partially outlined its application in the twelfth proposition. Moreover, in regard to the third proposition, the judges overwhelmingly favored an approach consistent with the alternative decision strategy, and tentative support for it was to be found in the data for the first element of the tenth proposition. There is a second consideration underpinning its claim as the substitute model. In the judges' quantitative and qualitative responses to the sentencing problems relating to these propositions it was the only approach offering a decision strategy and computational rules capable of being related to cases comprising multiple additional counts of the principal offence and multiple secondary counts belonging to different legal offence categories. In doing this, it provides an alternative coverage of, or renders irrelevant, aspects of decision making dealt with by these and the sixth, eleventh and fourteenth propositions. Finally, this alternative model is consistent with the three propositions from the hypothesized decision model for which there was substantial majority support.

These findings provide strong support for the alternative decision model. Notwithstanding these considerations, it must be recognized that the judges taken as a group did not demonstrate in accounts of their thinking a detailed and comprehensive understanding of this approach, did not often recognize its applicability to the problems relating to its constituent propositions and, where relevant, did not always fix sentences in accordance with it. Nevertheless, there were two judges (nos. 1 and 2) for whom this assessment unfairly underestimates the clarity of their thought.

The philosophy behind the present approach to model-building with uncertain data is to be found in the views of Francis Crick, as expressed in his reflections upon his successful attempt with Watson to determine the structure of DNA, views recorded by Judson (1979:113) in his account of their discovery.

> "The fact is ... that we knew that Bragg and Kendrew and Perutz had been *misled* by the experimental data. And therefore every bit of experimental evidence *we* had got at any one time we were prepared to throw *away*, because we said it may be misleading... The point is that evidence can be unreliable, and therefore you should use as little of it as you can. And when we confront problems *today*, we're in exactly the same situation. We have three or four bits of data, we don't know which one is reliable, so we say, now, if we discard that one and assume it's wrong – even though we have no evidence that it's wrong – then we can look at the *rest* of the data and see if we can make sense of *that*."

This discussion of the alternative decision model closes on five points. First, the evidence requires the rejection of the hypothesized decision model and warrants the alternative decision model being substituted in its stead. Nevertheless, this alternative model must be regarded as having an uncertain empirical foundation and for this reason requiring rigorous and direct testing by means of a set of especially formulated sentencing problems.

Secondly, it is important to assess how this alternative model of the judges' working rules governing the application of the totality principle – the severity of the effective sentence should be proportional to the seriousness of the offender's criminal conduct viewed as a whole – relates to the notions underpinning this principle, as discussed by Thomas (1979) and Ashworth (1992a) (see Chapter 1). It will be recalled from the discussion there that the import of the principle is that in the cumulation of sentence for the multiple offender the severity of the effective sentence should not exceed the level appropriate to the seriousness of the principal offence considered as a class of offence and should not be so great as to crush the offender; moreover, to satisfy these two requirements and ensure that more serious and extra counts receive greater punishment, cumulation of the additional sentences is by way of decreasing gains. In the analysis of the judges' responses to the sentencing problems there was no evidence of a decision structure governing the maintenance of proportionality between classes of crime in their determination of effective sentence for the multiple offender. The consequence of this is that in the alternative decision model there is no principle specifying the appropriate degree of constraint on the cumulation of sentence.

It is appropriate at this point to compare the decision strategy implicit in the alternative decision model with the framework and approach proposed by Thomas (1979) and Ashworth (1983, 1992a) on the basis of their legal analyses of English appellate judgments (see Chapter 1). Thomas's second version of the application of the totality principle seems to allow greater cumulation where the legal category of the principal offence is more serious, since the "normal bracket of sentences" are broader for more serious types of offence. And Ashworth proposes that in sentencing a multiple offender, the sentencer first adds a component of the sentence for the second count to the sentence for the principal offence, and to this running total is then added part of the sentence for the third count, and so on. However, in the decision strategy based on the judges' responses here, the legal category of the principal offence is not material to the degree of cumulation for the secondary counts and the cumulation of sentence for these counts is not determined sequentially across the counts. (Lovegrove, in press, provides a detailed discussion of the implications of the theory and findings in the present study for what legal scholars have proposed on the basis of their analyses of appellate judgments.)

Thirdly, there was a relevant aspect of decision making not contemplated by the hypothesized decision model but for which there was substantial support from the judges in their responses to the problems relating to the fourth proposition. Stated as a principle, it would take something like the following form:

> there is a monotonically increasing relationship between the variation in the nature of the criminality of the legal categories of the principal and secondary offences comprising a case and the degree of cumulation of the sentence(s) for the secondary offence(s).

This principle should be added to the ten already incorporated in the statement of the alternative decision model.

Fourthly, aspects of decision making covered by Propositions 4 and 13 of the original model, and which the alternative model does not address, require resolution; the issue is what is correct by way of approach regarding the matters dealt with by these two propositions. Indeed, confirmation of the implications of the thirteenth proposition – a custodial sentence may be deemed to be the appropriate effective sentence for a series of offences each of which if it stood alone would not be serious enough to warrant imprisonment – would require a recasting of the basis of cumulation as it is presented in the alternative model; cumulation would have to be by way of seriousness, not quantum of sentence.

Finally, there may be aspects associated with multiple offending not raised in these problems and yet possibly material to the degree of cumulation of sentence; for example, the proximity of the counts in time and the number of counts.

Intuition and deliberation in sentencing

In the introduction to this study (Chapter 1) it was predicted that the judges' verbal protocols and reflective reports would be characterized more by intuition than by deliberative thought. And so they were. When the judges were confronted with the cases in the sentencing problems they generally had little difficulty in arriving at what they considered to be appropriate effective sentences, or at least the order of magnitude of these sentences, but the records of their reasoning showed faltering thought. There were, however, two judges who demonstrated a reasonably well-integrated set of principles and working rules linked to a general decision strategy for this type of problem; but even these two, where a problem gave them the opportunity of outlining this approach, were often short on detail, left relevant matters uncovered, and apparently did not always recognize the strategy's applicability. The others, at best, could do no more than give part-strategies. Moreover, all of the eight judges, some more often and to a greater extent than others, had difficulty in giving even logical and coherent, problem-specific accounts of their approach to a particular problem, and appeared often to be attempting to formulate a solution on the run rather than applying an established policy. Not surprisingly there was much diversity of thought in these problem-specific accounts. The point is that only two of the eight judges demonstrated, and then somewhat weakly, the capability of a relevant deliberative approach to the sentencing of the multiple offender.

The questions remain: What is the nature of this intuition? Does it take the form of pattern recognition or is it weakly calculative? Consider a task which is conceptual, as is sentencing (or has a significant conceptual component to it). There is a view that when such a task is first undertaken performance is based on the slow and conscious application of given rules; here performance is unskilled and the knowledge base is said to be declarative. The effect of practice on performance is that the task in all its variations – but not ones totally outside the individual's experience – comes to be executed readily and with an appreciation of subtle distinctions, and the underlying processes are perceptual, quickly executed and cannot be verbalized; this is skilled performance and is the product of procedural knowledge. (See, generally, Chi, Glaser and Farr, 1988; Hoffman, 1992; and Klein, Orasanu, Calderwood and Zsambok, 1993; but see, especially, Gordon, 1992; and, also, Dreyfus and Dreyfus, 1986.) The clear and, for this study, important implication is that these intuitive and skilled performances have their beginnings in an explicit knowledge base; this base must be sufficiently detailed and comprehensive to permit the task to be undertaken, but will not, of course, cover the numerous variations and nuances which must be taken account of in a smooth and finely honed performance. And presumably the level of skill attained is related to the quality of the declarative knowledge. For example, both experienced ordinary drivers and professional racing drivers normally perform intuitively, but the greater skill of the latter can undoubtedly be traced in part to the higher standards of their instructional programs.

Now, in respect of this view, it might be expected that when individuals skilled in a particular task were called on to give an account of the thinking underlying their performance they could, with the help of appropriate elicitation techniques, describe it in terms at least approaching the level of the declarative knowledge base from which their expertise grew. Yet it is patently clear from the preceding summary of the content of the verbal records of the judges, who were all experienced in the criminal jurisdiction, that the thinking of only two of these eight judges even approached the level of detail and comprehensiveness required of a declarative knowledge base. Seemingly, then, judicial intuition in the sentencing of the multiple offender is not that of the skilled expert, capable of taking precise account of subtle distinctions between cases, but something different and less; the intuition of the skilled expert born of a deep task involvement and growing out of analysis, the intuition of the judge used for want of analysis. So, despite the fact that sentencing judges in describing their intuition draw on an epithet appropriate to the skilled intuitive expert – each case is a special case – they are referring to very different thought processes. Subjective experience of intuitive thought is clearly an illusory basis for judging the quality of that thought.

What then is the typical thought product of judicial sentencing expertise acquired through experience? In respect of the multiple offender, presumably judges learn from advice and experience the appropriate levels of (effective) sentence for particular combinations of individual sentences. In Victoria, a sentence is considered to be at an appropriate level as long as it falls within what is a comparatively broad range, whose upper and lower limits are defined by sentences just short of being regarded by an appellate court as, respectively, manifestly excessive and manifestly lenient (see Lovegrove, 1989). And since the Court of Criminal Appeal does not have a detailed set of principles to guide its deliberations, its standards are often based on what is in conformity with past, and intellectually largely unexplored, ways of deciding matters (as Hawkins, 1986, has described much of the discretion in legal decision making). Perhaps, then, with experience the first-instance sentencing judgments come to be made intuitively with respect to these appellate standards, themselves not characterized by precision; but this thought is patently not the finely honed decision making claimed by the judiciary to be the product of intuition. Moreover, intuitive expertise of the skilled professional is not within the reach of judges acquiring experience in the conventional sentencing system, since they are not given an analytic foundation necessary for the deep task involvement underlying skilled intuitive expertise. All this is not to deny that there are judges who of their own accord have built their sentencing practice on a more principled approach; indeed, the data from the present study suggest that there are judges who are exceptional in this respect.

This interpretation is consistent with the observation, stated at the beginning of this section, that generally the judges had a ready sense of the sentences appropriate to the cases in the sentencing problems, but that their thought was faltering. Viewed in this light, the determination of sentence has a pattern recognition quality to it; the process is perhaps akin to, but not as precise as, one's knowing the products of commonly experienced numbers. Of course, to the extent that in the cases in the sentencing problems the judges identified factors relevant to the quantum of cumulation (e.g., the sentence for the principal offence or the total of the sentences for the comprising counts), but no more, then their thinking was weakly calculative. In fact, there was clear evidence of this in the verbal records. This finding is consistent with the prediction derived from the analysis of appellate court judgments in Chapter 1. Jareborg (1993) introduced the term "roving sentencer" as a contrast to what he regarded as the desirable approach of respecting the restrictions of a decision structure. In view of the technical meaning given to intuition here, the thinking of the judges observed in the present study is perhaps better captured by the term "roving" and its connotations.

On the basis of the preceding discussion, the inescapable conclusion is that in order to ensure individualized justice for the multiple offender there must be policy development and a more deliberative approach to the determination of sentence. All this is not to imply that intuition grounded in analysis, but unsupported by a decision aid, would ensure optimal decision making in sentencing; and nor should this last statement be taken as a hint that there is not a place for intuition in association with guidelines. These matters are taken up in the last chapter.

Validity and development of the alternative decision model: the data collection

This study has now reached a point where there is an alternative model describing the principles and working rules relied on with varying awareness and comprehension by judges in order to determine, according to current sentencing policy, effective sentences for multiple offenders where the counts are separate transactions and offence categories and once an appropriate sentence of imprisonment has been fixed for each of the multiple counts. This model was formulated in the previous chapter on the basis of the judges' responses to the sentencing problems. In the sentencing of the multiple offender, principle dictates that more serious principal offences require a higher effective sentence and more serious and additional multiple secondary counts require a greater quantum of sentence to be added to the sentence for the principal offence. Nevertheless, this cumulation must not result in what would be a crushing sentence on the offender. The model, then, is also concerned with the principle governing the constraint on the cumulation of sentence, and this was discerned to be: the higher the sentence appropriate to the principal offence and the higher the sum of the sentences appropriate to each of the other (i.e., the multiple secondary) counts, then the greater the degree of concurrence for each of the appropriate sentences associated with the multiple secondary counts.

In view of the alternative model's provenance, a rigorous test of its validity requires the formulation of new sentencing problems specifically designed to test predictions from it, especially for those aspects inconsistent with its forerunner. That is beyond the scope of what is an exploratory analysis in respect of theory and method for the study of the sentencing of the multiple offender from a legal decision-making perspective. However, even a set of responses, for appropriately constructed problems, consistent with the alternative model, including imposed sentences, thought processes (verbal proto-cols) and assertions of the applicability of the model's principles (reflective reports), could be regarded as taking the development of the model and the testing of its validity only so far. Regarding development, the functions relating the variables – quantum of sentence appropriate to the principal offence and the sum of the sentences imposed on the other counts (independent variables) and the proportion of each of the sentences for the multiple secondary counts made cumulative (dependent variable) – require delineation and quantifica-tion. In relation to the testing of the model, the ultimate question is whether the model is consistent with behavior; in this instance, behavior is the effective sentences considered appropriate to cases. Of course, the strategy adopted to develop and validate a model depends on the nature of the model – a matter to be elaborated in the next chapter. The task of this chapter is to present and explain the use and construction of the set of fictitious cases developed for the purposes of the quantification and validation of the model.

The fictitious cases took the same form (comprehensive summary descrip-tions of the circumstances of the case) and were administered under similar conditions (e.g., apparently well-motivated judges) as the cases in Lovegrove's (1989) study. There was no option but the use of a fictitious-cases technique here. In Chapter 5 the point was made that it is not feasible to select a sample of cases from archival records when the cases are required to satisfy a theoretically determined set of exacting specifications; moreover, it was also argued that fictitious cases are to be preferred when one is studying what was described as ideal (cf. actual) decision making. That position, taken in the planning of the sentencing problems for the first and second senten-cing exercises, applies to the fictitious cases in this the third sentencing exercise.

Now, while, as stated above, it is true that the strategy adopted to test validity depends on the nature of the model, what holds across all approaches is that the rigor of the analysis is enhanced by greater diversity in the conditions under which the test is made, here the relevant aspect of the conditions being the structures of the cases for which sentences are to be fixed by the judges; of course, in this study the principle of diversity must be applied with the constraint that none of the cases represents an unrealistic pattern of offending. Where robustness is not guaranteed by diversity, there arises the danger that quirky consequences of the decision model may go undetected and subtle aspects of behavior may be missed. In view of the content of the alternative decision model, summarized above, the variation in the structure of the cases had to be made in regard to the quantum of sentence appropriate to the principal offence and the sum of the sentences appropriate to the other counts (in effect, the number and seriousness of these multiple counts). Concerning development, the delineation and quantification of the functions relating these two independent variables to the dependent variable also require a set of cases representative in respect of the seriousness of the offence combinations which may arise for the types of offence under study.

Once the construction of the fictitious cases – as single-count cases and as cases comprising multiple counts – has been dealt with, this chapter will conclude with a presentation of the procedural details relating to the administration of these fictitious cases. But first, a digression is appropriate to address, in the light of the aim of the present study, the problem of the validity of the judges' sentences for cases presented in the form of comprehensive summary descriptions.

The validity of the technique of fictitious cases

The external validity of fictitious exercises and simulation tasks has received critical appraisal in regard to studies of decision making in general (e.g., Levin, Louviere, Schepanski and Norman, 1983) and studies of the legal system in particular (e.g., Konečni and Ebbesen, 1992). The point of this section is to argue for the validity of judges' sentences for fictitious cases as presented in and for the purposes of the present study. (This material is taken largely from Lovegrove, 1989.) There are four potentially telling points against artificiality in the research environment.

(1) No significant consequences (or different consequences) attend the decisions, and the prisoner is a "paper" defendant. Under such conditions judges might give vent to personal biases in the absence of appellate review of sentences (e.g., a preference for harsher penalties) and curb other biases when under academic scrutiny (e.g., chivalrous sentencing of women), or other normally critical factors might not exercise their minds (e.g., considerations relating to mercy), or simply they might not pay due attention to the task.

(2) Information describing the cases is presented more simply – fewer case factors, less redundancy, no conflicting evidence, a more compact and readily comprehensible presentation of the evidence. In these circumstances the judges might give weight to factors that would otherwise be ignored because of information overload. There is another potential problem where information about common case characteristics is omitted. In such instances a judge might make inferences about these characteristics in the light of the given information.

(3) Some of the cases comprise atypical characteristics or patterns of factors. Certain factorial combinations might be difficult to judge because they rarely occur in real life. Further, the decision-making strategy in other combinations might be affected by these atypical cells. Moreover, the use of atypical case-factor levels together with the omission of common case characteristics might result in the significance of these factors being overestimated because of their then undue prominence. Finally, if the atypical cases appear to be unrealistic and comprise a significant proportion of the task, the judges might conclude that the task is irrelevant and as a consequence not apply themselves to it.

(4) Decisions are made in the absence of potentially critical features of court procedures, such as (1) the pressures to decide cases fairly and yet as quickly as possible to minimize backlogs, (2) the presentation of information about cases by personal testimony, and (3) the complexity of many cases. These differences might affect the case factors that are taken into account and the weights given to them.

Konečni and Ebbesen (1992) concluded that the appropriate data source for studies describing the process of sentencing is archival data incorporating transcripts of hearings and documents available to the judge. It is not my intention here to argue that this position is wrong but to put the view that this approach may be interpreted in an unnecessarily narrow way unless it is firmly set in a broader context. Ready acceptance of their conclusion might restrict and stifle the application of psycho-legal research for the understanding of and consequent improvement in sentencing. The issue is the extent to which the process of sentencing can be simulated and yet offer valid information. In Konečni and Ebbesen's (1979) discussion of research methods there is a guiding principle: when one studies an intact, functioning social network, such as the criminal justice system, there are certain logical and practical criteria that lead one on a priori grounds to trust the conclusions reached by one method over those reached by another. The contentious issues surrounding simulation are examined in turn on this basis. Before moving on to this, it is necessary to set in context the sort of information that is required from the present analysis.

There are at least three different aspects to the understanding of judicial decision making. First, one may seek to understand how judges actually fix sentences as they hear and determine cases in court. Secondly, one may seek to understand the decision rules judges attempt to follow, that is, how judges would apply current sentencing policy if they were free from the influence of confounding factors such as information overload. Finally, the attention of the researcher may be directed toward helping the judiciary to develop and reform sentencing policy – here, fictitious cases would be seen as a technique for assisting judges to decide afresh, perhaps in view of new considerations, the principles and working rules which should govern the determination of sentence. Research pursuing the latter two goals could be the basis of sentencing guidelines. These three faces of understanding judicial decision making may be conveniently labelled, respectively, actual, ideal and prescriptive. The present research comes within the scope of the latter two categories, although up to this point the study has addressed only the ideal orientation. Under what conditions might responses to fictitious cases offer a valid basis for understanding ideal decision making and for formulating new policy?

INCONSEQUENTIAL DECISIONS Clearly, simulation is of suspect validity where it is used as a means of identifying what judges actually do. The validity, however, of exercises directed toward understanding ideal and prescriptive judicial decision making is a different matter. In these instances the consequences of the study would be seen by the judges to be significant if they believed that the results were to be used to develop a structure for guidelines. Furthermore, in relation to the prescriptive orientation, judges would be freer to exercise their personal discretion as they imposed sentences in the light of legislation, simply because their decisions would not be subject to appeal; accordingly, these data would be expected to be a more valid representation of judges' personal preferences.

SIMPLIFICATION OF CASE DETAILS Simplification takes the form of the concise and compact presentation of information. Clearly, such a data base would not be suitable for the development of a decision model representing courtroom sentencing practices. For the study of ideal and prescriptive decision making, however, distortions caused by information overload are not wanted. Accordingly, to the extent that fictitious cases minimize information overload, in this respect they hold a potential advantage. Of course, it is critical that all the major material legal factors are present, because factors might otherwise be inappropriately weighted, in part because inferences might be made about the nature of the missing information and also because the factors present might be given undue prominence. A related trap with simulations, which must be avoided, is the tendency of some researchers to classify (summarize) information rather than to present the material as concrete, case-specific factors; for example, the describing of a burglary as well planned, rather than the listing of the characteristics of the case bearing on organization and then leaving the judge to assess the degree of organization. Where this is practised, the researcher is performing part of the judge's task and may be biasing the outcome. To avoid these undesirable outcomes, the cases here were described in terms of a detailed and comprehensive set of factors, and the task of classifying the information was left to the judge.

ARTIFICIALITY OF THE TASK Fictitious cases for which the descriptions comprise atypical case characteristics and/or omit common factors present a validity problem for the three orientations to the study of sentencing. Atypical combinations of case factors and levels of case factors are sometimes unavoidable and arise from the requirement of some statistical analyses for systematic variation in the combination of case characteristics. The statistical analysis used here was formulated so that it did not carry this difficulty, and all the cases included in the exercises were checked to ensure that they were not factually improbable nor unrealistic.

PROCEDURAL INFIDELITY The absence of the essential features of a court-room hearing would not appear to undermine in general the validity of the data as a basis for understanding ideal and prescriptive sentencing. (One critical exception might be for information relating to an offender's rehabilitation prospects and based on impressions conveyed by witnesses in court; this point is, of course, not relevant here since the study is confined to offence factors.) Indeed, for the reasons given previously, one might expect that the absence of procedural features that add complexity and immaterial information to the case might enhance the validity of the fictitious technique for these orientations. In respect of immaterial information, when the goal is the development of guidelines, it is not appropriate that legally immaterial yet emotionally and personally compelling matters, such as sympathy for distressed relatives, confound the case material. However, there is a positive point. It is that many judges appear to be comfortable with a practice analogous to the use of fictitious cases; both in England and in Australia there is support for sentencing conferences as a means of providing information about the quantum of sentence, and yet the training material there comprises fictitious cases. Moreover, judges use this approach in the courts. Surely, the use of the fictitious technique is analogous to procedures followed by the appellate courts? There, one of the judges' main sources of information about cases is the trial transcripts and associated documents, and they determine and weight material factors largely on this basis. Similarly, law reports of cases determined by appellate courts are abridged versions of the facts of these cases.

The preceding arguments defend the validity of the qualified use of simulation, according to the criteria advanced for understanding ideal and prescriptive aspects of the judicial approach to sentencing. They represent a different view of simulation than that of Elwork, Sales and Suggs (1981) and Lloyd-Bostock (1988), who state that the research methodology should be designed to eliminate artificiality as much as possible. Rather, this approach shows sensitivity to the warning of Elwork et al. (1981) and Monahan and Loftus (1982) that simulation is essential if we are to develop alternatives to existing procedures, and it is in sympathy with the view of Davis (1989) that the heart of the matter is whether the technique used to collect the data provides a valid basis for the type of conclusion the researchers have drawn. Nevertheless, it is stricter than Houlden's (1981) position that verisimilitude is not critical when the purpose of the research is to test theory and propose interventions on the basis of the theory. The present discussion also serves to qualify Greenberg and Ruback's (1992) multi-method argument: i.e., confirmation of a result across a number of different procedures gives grounds for confidence in the validity of that finding.

Lovegrove (1989) empirically tested the external validity of judges' sentences for fictitious sentencing cases. The question was whether sentences determined for real-life cases and heard as part of the normal business of the court would be similar to the sentences fixed for the same cases presented in the form of a sentencing exercise. The sample comprised thirty-six cases, heard in the County Court, in which the principal offence was burglary; there was a substantial range of case seriousness, the lowest level being well below that at which a custodial sentence was appropriate, and the mean court sentence for the highest level being just under four years. For each case all the information apparently put before the court was presented as a summary case description. The task of the nine County Court judges was to fix sentences for these cases. On the basis of these data, when compared to the sentences fixed in court, and subsequent comments about the cases by the judges, the conclusion drawn was that, in general, fictitious cases are a valid means of understanding how judges determine what is appropriate by way of sentence. The exception relates to those cases in which the quality of the plea may be decisive and vital information is in assessments based on the judge's personal observations of the offender and the witnesses. This limitation did not raise a problem for the present study, since the conditions under which the model was tested required that there be little if anything by way of mitigation associated with the personal circumstances of the offender. What is important for the present study was the finding that the inconsequential nature of the task – the offender's not being more than a paper defendant – and artificiality, to the extent that it characterized the sentencing exercises, did not appear to affect the levels of sentence considered to be appropriate.

The structure of the fictitious cases

This discussion now turns to present the fictitious cases and explain the basis of their structure and content. To maintain consistency with the previous empirical work in this study, the cases in this exercise were designed so that armed robbery would be regarded as the principal offence, while the multiple secondary counts would be burglaries, although in two instances they included armed robberies. It was necessary in some cases to forgo the preference for burglary as the sole secondary offence, in favor of combining burglary with a series of armed robberies as secondary offences (always armed robbery as principal), so that there were cases for which the sum of the sentences appropriate to the multiple secondary counts was very substantial.

In the first part (Part A) of this the third exercise the cases for which the judges were required to fix sentences comprised mainly single counts of either armed robbery or burglary, although two cases comprised multiple armed robberies; in the second and third parts (Parts B and C) of this exercise the cases presented to the judges for sentencing comprised various combinations of the counts from the first part, and the task of the judges was to fix for each case sentences appropriate to the constituent counts and an effective sentence. There was a cogent reason for asking the judges to impose a sentence for a count presented individually as a case in itself (Part A) and on a separate occasion for the same count presented as one of a number of the multiple counts comprising a case (Parts B and C); it was then possible to compare the sentences for particular counts across the two conditions and so determine whether the sentences determined in the latter condition could be regarded as appropriate sentences.

The first task, then, was to formulate patterns of offending forming the offence characteristics of individual counts of armed robbery and burglary; within each of these offence categories the patterns of offending were varied so that the counts were well distributed across their respective dimensions of offence seriousness. Following this, cases comprising multiple counts, at least one of armed robbery and one of burglary, were developed. Finally, a portrait of a fictitious offender's biography and circumstances was sketched and became the offender characteristics for these cases; again, consistent with the previous empirical work, these were held constant across cases as a very serious relevant criminal history and little by way of personal mitigation except for a plea of guilty but with no evidence of contrition. To ensure that the structure and content of the individual counts were realistic, they were based on the author's archival analyses of the sentencing of actual cases of armed robbery (Lovegrove, 1983; 1988) and burglary (Lovegrove, 1989) in which he attempted to describe, separately for each offence category, a set of dimensions, together with their defining levels, which described comprehensively the variations found in his samples of these two types of case.

Offence factors of armed robbery

The five offence factors identified in the archival studies of armed robbery (Lovegrove, 1983; 1988) were type of premises (premises), violence to the victims (violence), organization (organization), total value of the theft (value), and counts of armed robbery (counts). The following discussion is based on the analyses in respect of these factors in those studies.

First, consider the violence perpetrated by offenders; it appeared that it could be adequately characterized by one of four qualitatively different levels: actual and significant physical injury to a victim; rough and aggressive handling but without physical injury to a victim (includes a victim taken aside under threat of injury); direct, pointed and prolonged threat of injury with a weapon to a specific victim; an indirect and general threat of violence to a victim.

Secondly, there is the organization of the offence. Degree of organization was regarded as monotonically related to the number of components putatively indicative of planning/organization/sophistication of approach and characterizing the offence. The components of organization were the number of offenders, the type of weapons, the disguises worn by the offenders, whether other offences were committed to facilitate the armed robbery, the conduct of the escape, the *modus operandi* of the robbery itself, and the nature of the planning. To maintain consistency with the scaling of the seriousness of violence, four categories were created to describe the variation on this dimension. The lowest level of seriousness was intended to represent an impulsive, ill-considered and minor armed robbery, while great forethought, skill and effort were to mark the most serious category.

Thirdly, in regard to the total value of the theft, its upper and lower levels of seriousness must be considered separately for single and multiple counts. For small institutions, such as small businesses, amounts robbed under (say) $1,500 are common and over $3,000 are rare in single counts. For medium to large institutions, for example banks and building societies, an amount stolen in the order of $10,000 would not be uncommon. And, of course, a figure of $60,000 would not be unexpected in the robbery of a payroll. For multiple counts of armed robbery a working upper limit is difficult to establish, since the amount stolen depends on the number of counts and the type of premises, but certainly a total well in excess of $100,000 could be readily envisaged.

Fourthly, there is the number of counts of armed robbery. The most

Table 8.1 *Structures of the offence characteristics for armed robbery as principal offence in the fictitious cases[a]*

Case no.	Offence factors			
	Violence	Organization	Value	Type of premises
1	1	1	1	Small grocery store
2	2	2	2	Large liquor store
3	3	3	3	Building society
4	4	4	4	Payroll

Note: [a] The patterns of offending are defined in terms of the levels described in Tables 8.2 and 8.3 for violence and organization, and given in the associated text for value. Level 1 represents the lowest level of seriousness on an offence factor.

common number of counts associated with a case is one, multiple-count cases being very frequent but in a clear minority; three or four counts is not frequently exceeded, and a figure of the order of twelve is very rare.

It was necessary to introduce the characteristic of the type of premises robbed in order to provide for the typical variation in the patterns of offending on the four other offence characteristics. For example, armed robberies of premises from which substantial amounts of money are expected, and stolen, are commonly well organized, whereas robberies of individuals are frequently poorly planned, even impulsive, and commonly yield small gains. In view of the immediately preceding discussion, it was decided that four types of premises could accommodate the patterns of offending which were to be generated from the four offence factors of value, violence, organization and counts, and their defining levels. The premises were: small business (small grocery store); small business (large liquor store); building society; and a factory payroll (at the office). Four cases were developed from these factors to provide for the variation on the dimension of offence seriousness of armed robbery as a principal offence. Each case is defined in terms of three levels of seriousness, one for each of the offence factors, together with the type of premises robbed; these structures or patterns of offending in respect of the offence characteristics of the four cases are shown in Table 8.1.

In regard to these case structures, Case 4 is clearly a very serious single count of armed robbery and Case 1 is a relatively minor count of this offence category. A less serious count could be readily envisaged; for example, an incident involving little more than the impulsive snatching of a small amount of money under a veiled threat; nevertheless, it was decided to use a case a little further up the scale to decrease the likelihood of the armed robbery not being regarded as the principal offence when combined with one or more burglaries warranting imprisonment. It would be fair to conclude that four cases permit no more than the minimal level of acceptable variation on the dimension of offence seriousness of armed robbery; however, the exercise would have become impracticable and, indeed, unnecessarily demanding for an exploratory study, if there had been more than a small number of armed robbery cases.

The detailed descriptions of the four levels of seriousness for each of violence and organization are shown in Tables 8.2 and 8.3, respectively. Since the previously stated levels for each of these offence factors were without content, it was necessary for the author to compose illustrative case events to represent the various levels. For the completeness of the presentation, the levels of seriousness for the offence factor of total value of the theft are presented here, and follow directly from the preceding text: $1,050 (1), $3,050 (2), $10,100 (3) and $60,985 (4).

It will be noted from the descriptions of the levels of violence and organization in Tables 8.2 and 8.3 that in the more serious armed robberies (Cases 3 and 4), in which there are multiple offenders, the individual referred to as the offender and for whom a sentence is to be set, while a major player, is not the principal one, in that he does not perpetrate the worst aspects of the violence characterizing these offences nor is he the prime mover. This was deliberate, since it provided greater scope for these cases of armed robbery and burglary to be combined without the judges' credulity over the offender's capability and level of criminality being strained.

In the setting of these ranges for the offence factors regard was paid to the distributions on these factors of cases of armed robbery in Lovegrove's (1983; 1988) archival studies. To check that these conclusions accorded with the judges' views, they were asked whether the levels representing the lower and upper limits on the offence factors could be reasonably regarded as realistic.

Offence factors of burglary

Lovegrove (1989) presented a study of judicial sentencing of fictitious cases of burglary of a private home (see Chapter 2). The patterns of offending across those cases were based on the four offence dimensions, each defined by four levels, which appeared to describe comprehensively the variation found in a sample of actual cases of burglary; this archival study is also reported in Lovegrove (1989). The four offence factors were violence to the victims (violence); organization (organization); total value of the theft (value); and counts of burglary (counts).

Table 8.2 *Descriptions of the levels on "Violence to the Victims" for armed robbery in the fictitious cases*

Level	Description of level
1	The offender ran into the store, pulled out and pointed a knife directly at the man (the owner, aged 45) and woman (an assistant, aged 25) and told them in a firm voice to hand over the day's takings; the owner took the money from the cash register promptly and, as instructed, put it in one of the store's carry bags; the offender then ran off.
2	The offender ran into the store, pulled out and pointed a hand-gun directly at the man (the owner, aged 45) and woman (an assistant, aged 25) and told them in a firm voice to hand over the day's takings; the owner took the money from the cash registers promptly and, as instructed, put it in one of the store's carry bags; the offender shouted that there must be more money, hidden somewhere, adding in a raised voice and menacing manner that if the man did not get it quickly and hand it over then he would be shot; the owner relented quickly and said that there was a safe at the back of the store, with more money; the owner and the assistant were told to get the money, the offender following them out, with the gun appearing to be at the ready; the owner and the assistant took the cash out of a safe and put it in two more bags; the offender then ran off.
3	The offender and one of the co-offenders ran into the building society, pulling out their guns, which they waved around, and shouting obscenities, and then ordered everyone – approximately six staff and four customers – to lie on the floor; the co-offender grabbed one customer, a man aged 45, pulled him to one side, held his gun at his head, and shouted that if all the money on the premises was not handed over quickly or the alarm was set off, then the man would be shot; at this point he threw the bags he was carrying across the counter and ordered the staff to fill them up; meanwhile, the offender jumped over the counter and waved his gun around, pointing it first at one teller then another, and shouting at the staff to hurry; he threw his bags at one of the tellers and ordered him to go to the safe; when it appeared that all the money had been handed over, the offender and co-offender ran out the door; as they were leaving the premises they warned that anyone who attempted to follow them would be shot; the man taken aside was not physically injured.
4	The offender and the co-offender pulled out their guns as they entered the main office at the factory; they waved their guns in the air, told the receptionist it was a hold-up, and ordered her to walk ahead of them into the pay-office area; the co-offender pushed past the young woman and ran

into the office, shouting obscenities and waving his gun around, and then ordered everyone – two men and two women – to stand together; this offender grabbed one of the staff, a man aged 45, pulled him to one side, held his gun at his head, and shouted that if all the pay-packets and money in the office were not handed over quickly, then the man would be shot; at this point the offender entered the room; the two offenders threw down their bags and ordered two of the employees to open the safe and help load the pay-packets and loose cash into their bags; the offender waved his gun around, pointing it at the two employees who were loading the bags and shouting at them to hurry; when all the money had been handed over, the offender and the co-offender ran out the door; as they were leaving they pulled the telephone cords from the wall-sockets and warned that anyone who attempted to follow them would be shot; just as they were running past the receptionist's desk a security officer appeared in the main corridor; he instinctively drew his service revolver; as he was drawing his gun, the co-offender, who was carrying a hand-gun, shot at him and hit him in the left leg; the officer collapsed, and the offender and co-offender ran out the front door; the security officer, aged 55, suffered severe internal bleeding and underwent an operation to have the bullet removed; he has since recovered; the man taken aside in the pay-office was not physically injured.

The second co-offender pulled out his gun as he entered the security office at the gate; the post was staffed by one unarmed man; he pointed the gun at the man, aged 50, and told him that he would shoot him if he moved or attempted to set off the alarm; the co-offender pulled the telephone cord from the wall-socket; he held the officer at gunpoint until his partners arrived back at their car; at this point he ran to the car; as he turned and left the office, he warned the officer that if he attempted to follow him he would be shot.

Table 8.3 *Descriptions of the components and levels on "Organization" for armed robbery in the fictitious cases*

Level	Component	Description of component/level
1	No. of offenders	One man.
	Weapon	Kitchen knife, which the offender carried to and from the store, under his jacket.
	Disguise	A beanie with eye-slits; the offender pulled on the beanie as he entered the store and took it off in the car as he left.
	Connected offence	Nil.
	Escape	The offender ran out of the store to his own car, which he had left with the engine running in the rear car-park, and drove home.
	Modus operandi	Around 9.00 pm the offender took a kitchen knife and drove in his own car to the store; when he entered the store there were no customers, only a man and woman behind the counter; the offender went directly to the counter and pulled out the knife from under his jacket; the owner was told to hand over the day's takings and the offender pointed at the cash register, and told him to put the money in one of the store's bags; when the owner had done this, the offender then ran off.
	Planning	On the morning of the robbery the offender decided to do a "hold-up" to get some money easily; he thought that the small grocery store in a nearby shopping centre would be a good idea, especially just prior to closing time, late on a Friday night.
2	No. of offenders	One man.
	Weapon	Imitation hand-gun, which the offender bought on the morning of the robbery; he carried the gun to and from the store, under his jacket.
	Disguise	Gloves and a beanie with eye-slits; the offender pulled on the beanie as he entered the store and took it off in the car as he left.
	Connected offence	Theft of a motor car to use as a get-away vehicle; the offender stole the car on his way to the robbery, from a car-park, about two kilometers from the store and not too far from his flat.
	Escape	The offender ran out of the store to the car, which he had parked in the rear car-park and left with the engine running; he got out of the car several kilometers from the store and walked home.

Modus operandi		Around 9.00 pm the offender went to the car-park, stole the car, and drove to the store; the offender waited and entered the store when there were no customers, only a man and a woman behind the counter; the offender went directly to the counter and pulled out the gun from under his jacket; the owner was told to hand over the day's takings and the offender pointed at the three cash registers, and told him to put the money in one of the store's bags; when the owner had done this the offender said that there must be more money, hidden somewhere; the owner told him there was a safe at the back of the store, with more money; the owner and assistant were told to get the money, and the offender followed them out; when they had put this money in two more bags, the offender then ran off.
	Planning	The day before the robbery the offender decided to do a "hold-up" to get some money easily; that same morning he drove around looking for suitable premises and found a large liquor store in a nearby shopping centre offering good access, and he thought that there would be a lot of cash on the premises especially just before closing time, late on a Friday night.
3	No. of offenders	Three men, the offender and two co-offenders; one co-offender entered the building society for the robbery and, beforehand, looked for suitable premises, and prepared the weapons and disguises; the offender entered the building society with this co-offender; the other co-offender stole and drove the get-away vehicle.
	Weapons	Two unloaded shotguns; the guns were in the possession of one of the co-offenders and the barrels of the shotguns were shortened by him two days before the robbery; the guns were carried by the offender and the co-offender who went into the building society with him, and were hidden in bags as they entered and left the premises.
	Disguises	The offender and co-offender who went into the building society wore gloves and beanies with eye-slits; they pulled the beanies on as they entered the building society and pulled them off as they left, putting them in their bags; the driver of the get-away car wore gloves; the beanies and gloves were purchased two days before the robbery by one of the co-offenders.
	Connected offence	Theft of a motor car to use as a get-away vehicle; one of the co-offenders (the driver of the get-away vehicle) on the

Table 8.3   *(contd)*

Level	Component	Description of component/level
(3)	(Connected offence)	morning of the robbery walked to a car-park near his flat and stole a car for use as a get-away vehicle.
	Escape	The offender and co-offender ran out through the door of the building society to the get-away car, which was parked just at the back of the premises, with the engine running and one of the co-offenders at the wheel; they got out of the car about ten kilometers away in a quiet location, and split up, each finding his own way home.
	Modus operandi	On the morning of the robbery one of the co-offenders, the driver, walked to the car-park, stole a car, and drove directly to the flat of a girlfriend of the offender several kilometers away, where the offender and the other co-offender were waiting, hiding the car at the back of the flats; they drank for about an hour and then at about 11.00 am drove to the building society – a half-hour drive; on entering the premises they pulled out their guns and ordered the (approximately) six staff and four customers to lie on the floor; they then ordered the staff to fill up the bags, which they had brought with them, and one teller was ordered to go to the safe; when the (three) tellers had filled their bags with all the money which appeared to be in the building, they ran out the door.
	Planning	About one week before the robbery, the offender and two of his friends were drinking one evening at the flat of one of the co-offenders, when one of the two friends suggested that they do a robbery to get a lot of money easily; they decided that a bank or building society would be a good idea; one of the co-offenders, the next day, drove around looking for a bank or building society with low security and easy access such as a car-park next to the premises; this offender drove around for two hours and found a building society which seemed to be what they wanted; they decided to do the robbery at a time when they thought there might be a lot of cash on the premises – mid-morning on a Friday.
4	No. of offenders	Four men, the offender and three co-offenders; one co-offender entered the pay-office for the robbery and, before-hand, obtained employment at the factory, and prepared the weapons and disguises, and helped the driver search for a suitable car-park; the offender entered the pay-office with

this co-offender and recruited the observer; another co-offender stole and drove the get-away vehicle and held the gate attendant hostage; the fourth offender acted as the observer and met the get-away car.

Weapons

Two loaded shotguns and a loaded hand-gun; the guns were in the possession of one of the co-offenders and the barrels of the shotguns were shortened by him two days before the robbery; a shotgun was carried by the offender and the hand-gun and a shotgun by the co-offenders who went to the factory; the guns were hidden in bags as they entered and left the premises.

Disguises

The offender and co-offenders who went to the factory wore overalls, gloves and beanies with eye-slits; the two who took the money put on the beanies upon entering the main office, the driver, as he entered the security office at the gate; the driver of the get-away car wore gloves during the robbery and while driving the car; the offender and two co-offenders took off their beanies as they left the offices, and their overalls in the get-away car, putting them in their bags; the three later burnt their bags, disguises and the clothes which they wore during the robbery; the gloves and beanies were purchased two days before the robbery by one of the co-offenders.

Connected offence

Theft of a motor car to use as a get-away vehicle; two days before the robbery two of the co-offenders (one was the driver of the get-away vehicle) searched for a car-park from which they could steal a car on the morning of the robbery; they decided on a car-park at a railway station – this car-park was quiet at off-peak times and most of the vehicles there were left by their owners for at least several hours.

Escape

Just prior to leaving the pay-office, the offender and the co-offender pulled the telephone cords from the wall-sockets in the office; the telephone in the security office at the gate was also disconnected similarly immediately this co-offender had the attendant hostage; the offenders left in the stolen get-away car, which had been left with the engine running, and drove to a quiet parkland, about two kilometers away, got out of this car and walked through the reserve and met the fourth offender who was waiting for them in his own car; they all then drove to the flat of one of the co-offenders.

Modus operandi

About one hour before the robbery one of the co-offenders, the driver, went to the car-park and stole a car; he immediately drove to the flat of a girlfriend of the offender

Table 8.3   *(contd)*

Level Component	Description of component/level
(4) *(Modus operandi)*	several kilometers away, where the offender and a co-offender were waiting, hiding the car at the back of the flats; meanwhile the third co-offender drove in his own car to the factory, and parked about 400 metres away so that he could see when the security van had delivered the money; as soon as the van left he drove to the flat, told the other three, who were drinking, had a few drinks himself, and then drove to the park where he was to meet the others after the robbery; upon being alerted, at about 2.00 pm, the three others immediately drove to the factory – about a half-hour drive – stopping at the security office at the gate; the driver went straight to the office, took out his gun, and held the security officer hostage; at the same time, the offender and the other co-offender walked quickly to the main office, about 50 metres away; on entering the building they pulled out their guns, ordered the receptionist to go ahead of them, and went to the pay-office; the four employees (two men and two women) were ordered to stand together; two of the employees were ordered to open the safe and help load the pay-packets and any cash on hand into the offenders' bags, which they had brought with them, and the offenders also grabbed the pay-packets which were on the table being sorted for distribution; when all the money had been handed over, the two offenders ran out the door; when these two arrived back at the car, the third offender ran out of the security office at the gate and got into the get-away car.
Planning	Some months before the robbery, the offender and two of his friends were drinking one evening at the flat of one of the co-offenders, when one of the two friends suggested that they do a robbery to get a lot of money easily; they decided that a payroll of a large factory would be a great idea; one of the co-offenders said that he knew of one large factory – it had well over 100 employees – at which it was easy to get casual work, especially at certain times of the year when production was high; he knew that there the employees' wages were paid in cash and the payroll, he thought, would be delivered at a regular and known time to the main office from where the wages would be distributed to the various

sections of the factory for collection by the employees; he would get a job there to find out how the office was set out and payment of wages was organized; he was able to get employment within a month and worked there for about six weeks, leaving just four weeks before the robbery; two days before the robbery the offender persuaded a friend of his to take part in the robbery, his job being to act as the observer for the security van and to help them escape.

The detailed descriptions of the levels of seriousness for the offence factors of violence and organization, used in this present study for the cases of burglary as a single count, are shown, respectively, in Tables 8.4 and 8.5. These descriptions rely heavily on those developed for Lovegrove's (1989) original study.

Regarding the total value of the cash and merchandise stolen, Lovegrove's (1989) archival study of the sentencing of cases of burglary showed that for the burglaries of private homes the total amounts were well distributed up to $10,000–$15,000 (being particularly dense up to $500–$1,000), more thinly distributed between $15,000 and $50,000, and sparsely distributed to an amount somewhat in excess of $100,000. The levels of seriousness set for this offence factor were: $325 (1), $10,050 (2) and $30,650 (3). The values for levels 2 and 3 are midway (approximately) between the values defining levels 1 and 2, and 2 and 3, respectively, in Lovegrove's (1989) study; in that study this offence factor included single and multiple counts of burglary.

Four cases of single-count burglaries of a dwelling were developed from these offence factors of violence, organization and value to provide for the variation on the dimension of offence seriousness of burglary. Each case is defined in terms of three levels of seriousness, one for each of the offence factors; these structures or patterns of offending in respect of the offence characteristics of the four cases are shown in Table 8.6. When deciding upon the structures of these cases, individually and as a group, thought had to be given to ensure that in combination with armed robbery, as single or multiple burglaries, there would be a set of cases characterized by diversity yet without loss of realism. This thinking is elaborated in the next section.

Case 7 marks the lower end of the range of seriousness for burglary – an offender who did not have high expectations, gave little thought or preparation to the crime, and for whom the gains were commensurately low. It was expected that the sentence appropriate to an offence comprising these characteristics and committed by an offender with a serious record and negligible mitigation would be a short term of imprisonment (see Chapter 4).

Table 8.4 *Descriptions of the levels on "Violence to the Victims" for burglary in the fictitious cases*

Level	Description of level[a]
1	No one was home during the burglary.
2[b]	The burglar entered the home when the occupants were out; during the burglary he heard a car turn into the drive; he looked out from an upstairs window and saw a man entering by the front door; he continued to search the room, even after the owner came upstairs, until the owner entered the room, whereupon the offender moved one step toward him, waved his fist and threatened to hit him if he did "anything silly"; the burglar then immediately ran across to the window and climbed out onto the roof below and made his escape.

Note: [a] For both levels the only damage done was a broken lock on the rear door and minor disturbance, associated with the search, to the contents.

[b] This is the third level from the operational definition of violence in Lovegrove's (1989) original study.

Table 8.5 *Descriptions of the levels and components on "Organization" for burglary in the fictitious cases*

Level[a]	Component	Description of the components
1	1	The offender carried in a bag a jemmy, which he had owned for some time.
	2	The offender committed the burglary at night (committed the burglary during the day); the offender wore gloves; the offender knocked at the front door, then the back door; the offender searched the house thoroughly for cash and goods he could sell (the offender did not search the house thoroughly and was looking for cash).
	3	The offender knew a fence to whom he took the stolen goods on his way home (the offender sold the stolen goods in a local pub, some days later).
	4	The offender on his way stole a panel van from a hotel car-park near his home and, after taking the stolen goods to his fence, he left it several kilometers from his home and walked there; he left the bag and jemmy with the fence (the offender drove his own panel van).
2	5	The offender, a few days before the offence, drove around one morning in a well-to-do area, and looked for houses that seemed what he wanted, such as ones partly hidden by bushes (on the morning of the offence the offender drove to a suburb close by

		because it was handy and just picked out a house without thinking about it too much).
3	6	The offender, a few days before the offence, got in touch with a friend and asked him to help with a burglary for some "easy" money; his friend said he would be in it (the offender did not have anyone with him).
4	7[b]	The offender, a few days before the offence, got in touch with a friend and asked him to help with a burglary for some "easy" money; his friend said he would be in it; he said he had asked that friend because he knew a lot about alarm systems and the house he had especially picked had a burglar alarm – he had picked that house because he knew the people who lived there were very wealthy, the house was partially hidden by a bushy garden, and the couple of times he had gone past the house during the day and at night everything seemed quiet as though they were away; the friend brought an extension ladder with him, climbed onto the roof, removed tiles, and disconnected the alarm in the ceiling.

Note: [a] Levels 1, 2, 3 and 4 comprise components 1, 1–5, 1–6 and 1–7, respectively. For some of the components of organization, when not part of an offence, it was considered desirable in order to maximize realism and precision to set this out clearly, and so in such instances reference was made in the fictitious descriptions to events indicative of their absence; these are described in the table in parentheses. The seriousness of levels 1 and 3 represent levels of seriousness similar to their equivalent levels in Lovegrove's (1989) original study, while levels 2 and 4 are probably a little more serious than their respective levels in that study.

[b] When this component is part of the organization, no reference is made to component 6 and component 5 is modified.

Table 8.6 *Structures of the offence characteristics for single counts of burglary in the fictitious cases[a]*

Case no.	Offence factors		
	Violence	Organization	Value
7	1	1	1
8	1	2	2
9	1	4	3
10	2	3	3

Note: [a] The patterns of offending are defined in terms of the levels described in Tables 8.4 and 8.5 for violence and organization, and given in the associated text for value. Level 1 represents the lowest level of seriousness on an offence factor.

Combined cases of armed robbery and burglary

The next task in this analysis in regard to the offence characteristics for the fictitious cases was to make up a set of cases comprising one count of armed robbery as the principal offence combined with multiple secondary counts, principally of burglary. The point has already been made that these cases must be characterized by diversity. Operationally, this means that: (1) the seriousness of the principal offence of armed robbery should be well distributed across the dimension representing the possible range of seriousness of this legal offence category; (2) the total seriousness of the multiple secondary counts should show a substantial range in terms of the number and seriousness of the counts, the discriminations across this range should not be coarse, and as far as is possible at each level of seriousness there should be several cases, each comprising a different structure; and (3) to maintain realism, combined cases should not bring together an unlikely offence combination, such as a skilfully committed burglary and an impulsive, trivial armed robbery. The structures of the cases used to quantify and to test the validity of the alternative decision model were intended to give effect to these considerations.

Table 8.7 shows the structures of the cases in which the multiple secondary counts are comprised solely of burglaries. The following points cover the major considerations governing the choice of the actual combinations of armed robbery and burglary. First, for consistency, the study required that armed robbery appear as the principal offence. Secondly, it will be noted that the maximum number of multiple counts of burglary in a case is eleven, and this is for burglaries in which approximately $10,000 is stolen in each count; the total amount taken in the burglaries in these cases is, therefore, of the order of $110,000. This figure for the total value of the theft is approaching what might be regarded as the upper limit of seriousness of this offence factor (see the earlier discussion), and a comparatively small percentage of cases of burglary of a private home comprise more than eleven counts (see Lovegrove's, 1989, archival analysis of the sentencing of cases of burglary). Thirdly, multiple counts of the burglaries in Cases 9 and 10 would have appeared artifactual – the actual manifestation of organization in the former and the personal confrontation in the latter are unlikely to occur in a series of burglaries. Fourthly, the burglary in Case 10 has an element of violence and is, accordingly, more similar in character to armed robbery than the three other burglaries and, indeed, the typical burglary. Now, it is possible that had it been combined alone with an armed robbery, the offender would have been treated as an armed robber rather than as an armed robber and burglar. Fifthly, it will be recalled, in order to increase the number of combinations of armed robbery and burglary which could be made without loss of realism, in

Table 8.7   *Structures of the combined cases of armed robbery and multiple secondary counts of burglary in the fictitious cases*

Case no.	Armed robbery[a]	Burglary[a,b]	Case no.	Armed robbery	Burglary
11	1	7	24	3	8(3)
12	1	7(3)	25	3	8(7)
13	1	7(7)	26	3	8(11)
14	1	7(11)	27	3	9
15	1	9	28	3	9+10
16	2	8	29	3	9+8(3)+10
17	2	8(3)	30	4	8
18	2	8(7)	31	4	8(3)
19	2	8(11)	32	4	8(7)
20	2	9	33	4	8(11)
21	2	9+10	34	4	9
22	2	9+8(3)+10	35	4	9+10
23	3	7	36	4	9+8(3)+10

Note: [a] The case numbers under armed robbery and burglary refer to the cases as they are defined in Tables 8.1 and 8.6, respectively.
[b] The figures in parentheses denote the number of counts of the case of burglary in the combined case.

the two serious armed robberies in which there were multiple offenders (Cases 3 and 4), the offender being sentenced was made a major player but not the principal one.

There were two cases in which the majority of the multiple secondary counts were armed robbery so as to ensure that there were several instances in which the sum of the sentences appropriate to the additional counts was very substantial. Since these multiple secondary counts had of necessity to be significant, it seemed that the principal offence of armed robbery would need to be around the upper limit of the seriousness of a single count. Case 4, the payroll, appeared to satisfy this condition. Yet, to have presented a case comprising multiple secondary counts of the payroll robbery would have strained the judges' credulity over the realism of the exercise. For this reason, building societies were chosen as an alternative, for the secondary counts. Now, from the previous discussion, a level of twelve counts was considered to be approaching an upper limit for a case comprising multiple armed robberies. In view of this, the more serious of these two combined cases (Case 38) consisted of, in respect of the armed robberies, the payroll armed robbery, as the principal offence, plus eleven counts of armed robbery of building societies. In the robberies of the building societies, organization could reasonably be expected to be maintained more or less at a characteristic level by a group of offenders across a series of armed robberies, and so it was here. Accordingly, the level of the offenders' organization in the payroll armed robbery was adapted to fit the armed robbery of a building society in respect of most of the components but did not, of course, include employment at the building societies. For violence, it did not seem realistic to maintain across the twelve counts the same very high level displayed in the payroll armed robbery. Surely the circumstances would not arise often in which the offenders would decide to shoot or seriously injure a victim? But they might arise in one or two of the counts. Accordingly, it was decided that in one of the eleven building-society counts – the third – the offenders would shoot a security guard to make good their escape and in another of those counts – the seventh – it seemed not unrealistic that the offender taking the victim aside might become impatient or panic and hit him with the gun. Of course, the potential for violence and the lesser aspects of violence, which were gratuitous or designed to terrorize the victims, were maintained at a similar level across the twelve counts; to achieve this, the building-society counts were presented with the modification that the offenders fired shots into the roof on entering and at the security cameras on leaving the premises. Regarding the value of the cash stolen in each of the building-society counts, it seemed that the amount considered to be appropriate in Case 3, the single count of armed robbery of a building society, was similarly appropriate here for each building-society count. It follows, then, that the total amount stolen in the armed robberies in this case was approximately $170,000 ($60,000 + (11 × $10,000)), a very substantial amount, but not an unrealistically high amount for a series of armed robberies of substantial targets (see the earlier discussion). (This series of armed robberies is identified as Case 6, when itself comprising a separate case.)

The less serious of the two combined cases (Case 37) consisted of, in respect of the armed robberies, the payroll armed robbery, as the principal offence, plus three counts of armed robbery of building societies. In this case, the circumstances surrounding the commission of the principal count remained identical, and the offence factors relating to the armed robbery of the building societies were treated as for the more serious combined case; this leaves only one aspect requiring elaboration: in none of the three building-society counts was a security guard shot to make good the offenders' escape, but in one of those counts – the third – the threat to the victim taken aside was carried out. (This series of armed robberies is identified as Case 5, when itself comprising a separate case.)

The two combined cases for which the majority of the multiple secondary counts comprised armed robberies also each had one count of burglary. The reason for including a count of burglary was to ensure that the offender in these two cases, as in the twenty-six other combined cases, would be treated as an armed robber and burglar, not as a specialist armed robber; to strengthen the generalist character of the offender in these two cases, one of the more serious individual counts of burglary, Case 9, was used as the count of burglary.

Case 37 is presented in Appendix 1 for illustrative purposes.

Of course, it was not possible in advance to ensure that the considerations underlying the construction of the combined cases – substantial range with fine discriminations and multiple instances in respect of the levels of seriousness of the multiple secondary counts; the realism of the cases; and armed robbery as the principal offence and covering the range of offence seriousness for this legal category – had been satisfied. These points could be checked only at the completion of the exercise: the first was assessed by an examination of the sentences imposed; the second, by asking the judges whether any of the cases had struck them as unrealistic and improbable; and the third, by the questioning of the judges.

Offender characteristics of the cases

Since this study focused on offence characteristics, the offender characteristics were held constant across all the cases of armed robbery and burglary, presented separately and in combination. This section describes how the biography and circumstances of the offender, covering material relevant to the history of prior convictions and the plea in mitigation, were formulated.

HISTORY OF PRIOR CONVICTIONS To maintain consistency with the earlier empirical work, the cases had to be characterized by an extensive record of prior convictions, especially in relation to convictions for offences of dishonesty (see Chapter 4). Since an offender's record comprises not only offences but also sentences imposed judicially, the safest means of ensuring the realism of an extensive record is for the criminal history to be based substantially on an actual case. And so it was here. The author had composed in this way a criminal history reflecting an extensive record of relevant prior convictions for his study of judicial sentencing of fictitious cases of burglary; for that study, an actual record was selected from one of the cases in the author's archival study of burglary, to which minor changes were made so that it satisfied his requirements (Lovegrove, 1989). In the present study the author took this criminal history and, in the light of his reading of the several very serious criminal histories of offenders in his archival studies of armed robbery (Lovegrove, 1983, 1988), he modified it somewhat further so that it could act as a very serious record of relevant prior convictions for an offender convicted of armed robbery and/or burglary. The criminal history developed for the present study is shown in Table 8.8.

Table 8.8   *The criminal history for the fictitious cases*[a]

1.	Children's Court 17/12/73	Theft of a motor car	7 days Youth Training Centre (YTC)
		Armed with an offensive weapon	7 days YTC
		Unlicensed driver	Fine $14 in default 7 days Total: YTC 14 days
2.	Children's Court 24/1/74	Unlawful assault	Fine $20 in default 10 days
		Indecent language	Fine $20 in default 5 days
3.	Children's Court 7/2/74	Theft of a motor car (2 charges) Larceny (2 charges) Schoolhouse breaking and stealing (2 charges)	YTC 12 months on all charges
4.	Magistrates' Court 7/4/75	Shopbreaking and stealing	YTC 3 months on each of charges 1–5
		Schoolbreaking and stealing Theft of a motor car (3 charges) Larceny (5 charges) Dangerous driving Unlicensed driver	Convicted without penalty on charges 6–10 and 12 YTC 1 month on 11th charge Total: YTC 16 months
5.	Magistrates' Court 15/6/75	Theft of a motor car Escaping from legal custody	2 months 1 month (concurrent) Total: 2 months
6.	Magistrates' Court 20/1/77	Assault occasioning actual bodily harm (2 charges)	6 months on each charge (concurrent)
7.	County Court 28/5/78	Burglary (3 counts) Theft (2 counts)	Probation 2 years
8.	Supreme Court 18/5/82	Armed robbery (4 counts)	3 years on each of counts 1–3 and 2 years on count 4 (2 years 6 months of counts 2 and 3 concurrent with each other and with count 1, and count 4 concurrent with counts 1–3) Total: 4 years Minimum: 3 years

| 9. | Magistrates' Court 11/5/85 | Assault with a weapon Assaulting a member of the police force in the lawful execution of his duty Being drunk and disorderly | 7 days on each of charges 1 and 2 (concurrent) Convicted without penalty on charge 3 |
| 10. | County Court 27/8/87 | Burglary (3 counts) | 2 years 6 months on count 1 and 12 months on each of counts 2 and 3 (concurrent with each other and with count 1) Total: 2 years 6 months Minimum: 18 months |

Note: [a] The offence, or first offence, relating to the current appearance was committed in February 1990.

A criminal record which, when considered in its totality, is serious in terms of features like the number of court appearances and the severity of the sentences imposed on those occasions, does not ensure that, in respect of this record, the court has no alternative but to impose a quantum of sentence proportional to the seriousness of the case. Even under these circumstances, a non-custodial sanction or a custodial sentence less than fully proportionate to seriousness, may be considered appropriate when certain features characterize a criminal history. To avoid the possibility of one of these courses being open to a judge, it was necessary to ensure that there was not a substantial gap between the date of the present offending and the last prior offence, that the offender had already been subject to a substantial term of imprisonment, and he had already been given the opportunity of a non-custodial sanction specifically assisting rehabilitation (see Thomas, 1979; and also, Fox and Freiberg, 1985).

To check that this criminal record satisfied the requirements of the study, the judges were asked whether a more severe sentence would have been imposed in any of the cases if the offender's history of prior convictions had been more extensive or serious.

MITIGATING OFFENDER CHARACTERISTICS Again, to give effect to the previously stated requirements of the study, in these cases the characteristics of the offender offered no more than minimal credit by way of mitigation, except that there was a plea of guilty but with no evidence of contrition (see Chapter 4). In the burglary study (Lovegrove, 1989) the author composed for the offender a biography and circumstances covering the type of information which, where applicable, would be brought before a court at the time of the plea. These offender characteristics were based on the factors identified in the archival burglary study (Lovegrove, 1989) and used in the archival armed robbery study (Lovegrove, 1988) to describe the variation found in actual cases. Since the set of offender characteristics used for the fictitious cases in the burglary study was intended to offer little if anything by way of personal mitigation, it was also used in the present study, with only minor changes. Table 8.9 presents the biography and circumstances forming the offender's plea in the present study; no reference is made to those factors not applicable or covered in the description of the offence.

To check that this plea in mitigation satisfied the requirements of the study, the judges were asked whether, apart from the plea of guilty, there was any mitigation associated with the offender's plea in any of the cases, after allowance had been made for the criminal record.

The case presented in Appendix 1 incorporates the offender characteristics.

The administration of the fictitious cases

Procedure – separate cases of armed robbery and burglary – third sentencing exercise (Part A)

This exercise comprised the separate presentation of four single-count cases of armed robbery (Cases 1–4; see Table 8.1), two multiple-count cases of armed robbery (Cases 5 and 6; see the text associated with Table 8.7) and four single-count cases of burglary (Cases 7–10; see Table 8.6). The ten cases together with the instructions were presented to the judges in a booklet with the cover title "Sentencing Research Exercise – Part 3A." The instructions were on the first page, followed by the descriptions of the fictitious cases, with each case beginning on a new page. The form in which the cases were presented was almost identical with that which was used in Lovegrove's (1989) study of the judges' sentencing of fictitious cases of burglary. The description of each case included: (1) the number and nature of the counts, with a list of the value of the money (and goods) stolen in each count, a description of the nature and value of property stolen, and the period of offending; (2) information from the statement(s) of the victim(s); (3) information from the interview with the offender(s); (4) record of the offender's prior convictions; and (5) the plea in mitigation. (The history of prior convictions and the plea in mitigation were presented only once; they were inserted in the booklet, immediately following the instructions, unbound, so that the judges could transfer them from case to case.) The lengths of the descriptions of the burglary cases ranged from approximately three A4 pages for the case with the least serious combination

Table 8.9 *Analysis of the offender characteristics in the plea in mitigation for the fictitious cases*[a]

Factor	Description of category
Age	The offender was 32 years old (born: 15/9/57) at the time of the offending related to the current appearance.
Previous good character	The offender left school at 16 years of age; he had a series of jobs as a laborer; his longest continuous period of employment was twelve months; most of the periods during which he was out of work occurred because there was no available employment; he was not employed for one month just prior to the offence(s).
Reason for the offence	The offender felt financially insecure.
Remorse – confession	Before the trial the offender indicated his intention to plead guilty; he admitted the charge(s) to the police during the interview, which he signed; initially he denied knowledge of the charge(s) to the police but changed his position when confronted with the evidence.
Remorse – reconciliation	The offender says he has spent the proceeds, although it would appear that he has little if anything to show for the money.
Remorse – current character	Since the current offence(s), the offender has not committed any offences, and there are no matters outstanding.
Remorse – rehabilitation prospects	The offender was looking for work at the time he was arrested but had been unsuccessful.
	He has a girlfriend, who is employed as a shop assistant; they have been living together for eighteen months.
	There is no obvious medical or psychological condition motivating his criminal behavior.
Deprived family background	The offender lived at home until 16 years of age when his mother died; he then drifted, staying with various friends and acquaintances; his father disappeared when he was 12 months old; he married at 22 but has been separated five years (he is now divorced); his wife has remarried and has taken responsibility for the care of their two children, girls aged 8 and 10.

Note: [a] The plea was dated April 1991.

of levels – Case 7 – to approximately four pages for the case with the most serious combination – Case 10. For armed robbery the descriptions of the cases ranged from approximately three pages for the least serious case – Case 1 – to approximately nine pages for the most serious case – Case 6. Regarding the case descriptions: in each of the cases comprised of multiple armed robberies, the first secondary count of armed robbery was approximately three months after the principal count, and the subsequent counts of armed robbery averaged about two weeks apart; the value of the theft in each of the secondary counts of armed robbery was varied across the counts, but in the majority of the counts was not substantially different from the mean for these counts; the descriptions of the secondary counts of armed robbery were presented together – one statement covering all the victims and one record of interview with the offenders.

In most of the case descriptions some information was added to the descriptions of the levels/components of the case factors so as to set the scene fully (e.g., state what the victims were doing just before the offence) or to indicate precisely the level of a factor (e.g., describe the victim's characteristics). Of course, this additional information was kept constant across equivalent cases, and was intended to be neutral regarding the offender's culpability, being neither aggravating nor extenuating: for example, the description of the victim as a 45-year-old male where there was violence in the burglary was intended to connote that the victim was not frail; similarly, in the case where a small amount of money was taken in the burglary, the house was two-storeyed to indicate that the victim was not financially vulnerable.

The sample of judges used here was the same as in the previous two exercises. One booklet was assigned unsystematically to each judge, and in each booklet the fictitious cases were presented in a different random order. (So that the author's view of relative case severity was not conveyed to the judges, the numbers used to identify the cases in the booklet were randomly allocated, but were the same for all the judges.) This was done in early November, 1991, three to four months after the judges had undertaken the second exercise. The judges were left to work through the exercise in their own time. The following instructions were set out at the beginning of each booklet.

This exercise is Part A of the third in the series of three designed to investigate how judges determine what is appropriate by way of an effective (maximum) sentence for a multiple offender. You are reminded that the information gathered in this exercise will be analyzed for that purpose and that your responses will not become part of a system of sentencing guidance.

The booklet contains six case descriptions of armed robberies and four case descriptions of burglaries of private homes. These cases of burglary and armed robbery vary in terms of the following four offence factors: total value of the cash and merchandise stolen; number of counts of armed robbery; amount of violence inflicted on the victim(s); and degree of organization/scale of the offending. (The descriptions also include a common history of prior convictions and plea in mitigation.) Each case is described separately, and your task is to determine a sentence for the individual referred to as "the offender" (cf. co-offender) in the record of the interview(s) in each case. It is inevitable that there will be a lot of repetition among the elements of the case descriptions, although for each case the combination of the case factors is unique. Remember, treat each case as independent of the others and assume that each of the cases relates to a different offender.

You are asked to determine an appropriate sentence – effective (maximum) sentence – for each case; as well, please fix a sentence for each count and concurrency orders, where appropriate. Exercise your discretion in accordance with sentencing law and sentencing policy (and practice) as it is currently to be found in the relevant statutes and appellate judgments: fix each sentence as though you were making the determination for an actual case being heard by you in your Court. You may assume that you have been presented with all the information which is required to fix a just sentence: no material case information has been omitted. Please write your sentence at the end of the description of each case. You are not required to give reasons for your decisions. You are not required to fix a minimum sentence for any of the cases.

Please complete the cases in the order in which they appear in the booklet. When determining a sentence for a particular case, you may refer to cases for which you have already fixed sentences. And you may subsequently change the sentence for a case which upon reflection you think is not correct. Do not feel under any obligation to complete the task without a break, although it is advisable not to spread the whole task over too long a period. Finally, I should be grateful if you would refrain from discussing this exercise with your brother judges. They are fixing sentences for the same cases.

N.B. The history of prior convictions and the plea in mitigation, which are common to all the cases, are presented only once; they have been inserted in this booklet, immediately following these instructions, and are unbound so that you can transfer them from case to case.

Before starting this exercise each judge was given the opportunity to have confusing points clarified.

Judges were allowed to refer to cases for which sentences had already been fixed, when determining a sentence for a particular case, because in practice they do this in order to maintain consistency of sentence across cases. Also, the judges were allowed subsequently to change the sentence for a case, because in practice judges do change their initial view of what is appropriate by way of sentence in the course of contemplating a punishment; moreover, it was thought this may minimize the effects of errors which might arise were a judge to take some time to adapt to the fictitious case procedure.

On returning the booklet, each judge was interviewed by the author and asked: (1) whether he had found any of the case descriptions to be unrealistic and improbable; (2) whether the cases of armed robbery as principal offence covered the range of offence seriousness for this legal offence category; (3) whether, apart from the plea of guilty, there was any mitigation associated with the offender's plea in any of the cases, after allowance had been made for the criminal record; (4) whether a more severe sentence would have been imposed in any of the cases if the offender's history of prior convictions had been more extensive or serious; and (5) whether the sentences had been discounted for the plea of guilty. Each judge was also given the opportunity of making comments on any other aspect of the exercise considered by him to be relevant to the interpretation or validity of his sentences.

Procedure – combined cases of armed robbery and burglary – third sentencing exercise (Part B)

This exercise comprised the presentation of ten cases of armed robbery and burglary in combination (Cases 11, 15, 16, 20, 23, 27, 30, 34, 37 and 38; see Table 8.7 and the associated text); in each case there was a single or multiple armed robbery and a single count of burglary, the count of burglary always being presented after the armed robbery(ies). These cases together with the instructions were presented to the judges in a booklet with the cover title "Sentencing Research Exercise – Part 3B". The comprising counts of a single or multiple armed robbery and a single burglary in these cases were taken from the cases presented in Part 3A. The sample of judges and the form and manner in which the cases were presented to them were the same as in that exercise. There were only two changes in the instructions: in the first paragraph "Part A" became "Part B"; and the first sentence in the second paragraph was changed to read, "This booklet contains ten case descriptions: each case comprises one or more counts of armed robbery and one count of burglary of a private home." Regarding the case descriptions: the date of the count of burglary was approximately six weeks after the count, or last count, of armed robbery.

On returning the booklet, each judge was interviewed by the author and asked: (1) whether he had found any of the case descriptions to be unrealistic and improbable, and (2) whether armed robbery was the principal count in each of the cases. Each judge was also given the opportunity of making comments on any other aspect of the exercise considered by him to be relevant to the interpretation or validity of his sentences.

Procedure – combined cases of armed robbery and burglary – third sentencing exercise (Part C)

This exercise comprised the presentation of eighteen cases of armed robbery and burglary in combination (Cases 12–14, 17–19, 21, 22, 24–26, 28, 29, 31–33, 35 and 36; see Table 8.7); in each case there was a single count of armed robbery and multiple counts of burglary, the count of armed robbery always being presented first. These cases together with the instructions were presented to the judges in a booklet with the cover title "Sentencing Research Exercise – Part 3C." The comprising counts of armed robbery and burglary in these cases were taken from the cases presented in Part 3A. The sample of judges and the form and manner in which the cases were presented to them were the same as in that exercise. There were only three changes in the instructions: in the first paragraph "Part A of" became "Part C of and completes"; the first sentence of the second paragraph was changed to read, "This booklet contains eighteen case descriptions: each case comprises one count of armed robbery and two or more counts of burglary of a private home"; and in the second sentence of the same paragraph "number of counts of armed robbery" was changed to "number of counts of burglary." Regarding the case descriptions: the date of the first count of burglary was approximately six weeks after the count of armed robbery, subsequent burglaries of a different character were separated by about two weeks and when of the same character were spread over a period for which the length in weeks equalled the number of counts; the descriptions of counts of the same character were presented together – one statement covering all the victims and one record of interview with the offender – and descriptions of counts of a different character were presented separately; and in multiple burglaries of the same character the total value of the theft was set at the value for the single count times the number of counts, with the values varying across counts but each count not being substantially different from the mean (the value for the single count), and the value of each type of merchandise was the value for the single count multiplied by the number of counts.

On returning the booklet, each judge was interviewed by the author and asked: (1) whether he had found any of the case descriptions to be unrealistic and improbable, and (2) whether armed robbery was the principal count in each of the cases. Each judge was also given the opportunity of making comments on any other aspect of the exercise considered by him to be relevant to the interpretation or validity of his sentences.

Statutory changes to sentencing law

The sentencing problems forming the first two exercises were done by the judges under the *Penalties and Sentences Act* 1985 (Vic.). In April 1992 this Act was repealed and the *Sentencing Act* 1991 (Vic.) came into operation. The significance of this is that the commencement of this new statutory framework fell in the period during which the judges were undertaking the three parts of the third sentencing exercise comprising the fictitious cases. So that the judges' performances were comparable across the study, they were instructed to approach the task of sentencing in the part-exercises administered after that commencement date as they would have under the previous Act.

In fact two changes to sentencing of potential significance to this study were introduced under the new legislation. The first matter of possible significance arises from the fact that remission for good behavior while in custody was abolished (see Freiberg, 1992). Remission provided for up to one-third of the maximum and minimum terms of imprisonment imposed on an offender to be deducted from the sentence by the correctional authorities; accordingly, for an effective sentence of nine years with a minimum of six years the effect of remission was that these terms became six years and four years, respectively. The *Sentencing Act* 1991 required that courts make allowance for this change when sentencing offenders, such that the period for which an offender was subject to the sentence would be the same as it would have been if the offender had been sentenced under the old Act and had received the full entitlements to remission: for example, where a court thought that a term of nine years with a minimum of six years would have been appropriate under the old Act, the prisoner should be sentenced to an effective sentence of six years with a minimum of four years. In respect of this change, in the period immediately following the commencement of the new Act it could be confidently assumed that the judges could faithfully follow the instruction to continue sentencing as under the previous Act; this assertion could be made because the new Act did not require the judges otherwise to alter the way in which they had exercised the sentencing discretion under the old Act for the levels of seriousness/types of offence in the cases in the fictitious exercise. It follows that to fix a sentence in court according to the new Act the judges had, in effect, first to determine what would have been appropriate under the old Act. With the passage of time, however, there could be less confidence over the judges' capability to follow the instruction. It was certainly considered necessary where a judge had completed one of the part-exercises after the old Act had been repealed to ask him, in addition to the questions set out in the preceding sections outlining the procedure, whether he had experienced any difficulties in determining sentence according to the levels of sentence established under the *Penalties and Sentences Act* 1985.

The second change concerns new statutory maximum penalties for the offences of armed robbery and burglary (see, again, Freiberg, 1992). With the introduction of the *Sentencing Act* 1991 the maxima for these two respective offences were reduced from 25 and 14 years to 20 and $12\frac{1}{2}$ years. The purpose of these amendments was not to signify a change to the relative seriousness of armed robbery and burglary but merely to reduce the gap between the statutory maxima and the levels of sentence considered by the courts to be appropriate to the worst forms of these two offences; these two new maxima remained comfortably above the quanta of sentence which, according to the analysis of sentencing statistics in Chapter 4, had been imposed previously in the courts for these two offences (see also, Sentencing Task Force, 1989). Accordingly, there is no reason to believe that these changes had any significance for the present study.

Towards a requisite decision model for sentencing the multiple offender

The fictitious cases were formulated and administered, as described in the previous chapter, with two ends in mind: (1) the delineation and quantification of the functions relating the variables in the alternative decision model; (2) the testing of this model's validity. Now, the strategy adopted to do this depends on the nature of the model under test – specifically, what is being claimed for it (the knowledge it represents) and what is required of it (the role it has to play). The purpose of the present chapter is to develop and justify an appropriate notion of model and apply it, within the limitations of the study, so as to move towards the above two goals.

The idea of requisite modelling

It will be recalled that only two of the judges in the present sample were able to articulate a relevant, general and coherent policy in considerable detail and with some consistency across the sentencing problems; moreover, from the manner in which these two judges gave their responses even they appeared to a significant extent not to be applying a ready solution but to be formulating on the spot what seemed appropriate by way of approach. And, in this respect, the best that can be said of the other judges is that, to the extent and on the occasions that it was possible to discern elements of a general approach to this type of sentencing problem in their responses, they were consistent with those of the former two (see Chapter 7). It is clear from the results of the analysis of the judges' responses to the sentencing problems that in relation to the sentencing of the multiple offender there is not a well-established, comprehensive and coherent policy to which the judges give detailed effect deliberatively and consistently. Under these circumstances, what is the appropriate notion of model?

An assumption underlying much behavioral science research, whatever the area of study, is that the decision making follows well-established processes which can be represented by a quantitative model, and the task of research is to analyze a data base of attributes and judgments or decisions – in this study case facts and imposed sentences – (1) to discover the model best fitting the data or (2) to test whether a particular model, selected because it is related to a theory of interest, is consistent with the data. A model satisfying the criterion of goodness of fit is regarded as a valid representation of that aspect of decision making, although, of course, is always open to further test and refinement. The theory and methods developed by Anderson (1981, 1982) for the understanding of information integration are in this tradition. What follows is not to deny that this is often a reasonable assumption. However, the evidence in the present study clearly reveals that the judges do not have a well-established policy-based approach to this type of sentencing problem and, accordingly, it follows that the forced use of this notion of model development and validity here would strain the logic underlying its application to breaking point. The error would have practical consequences; if this notion were held to be appropriate in these circumstances, the modeller would be constrained either (1) to continue searching for a model, failure after failure or (2) to accept a model at best no more than crudely fitting the data and representing an over-simplification of the decision problem. There is a second difficulty associated with this approach in the context of the present problem. It is that the holistic assessments on the dependent variable in judgment studies (here, the judges' sentences imposed for the fictitious cases) are regarded as the appropriate criterion of the decision makers' behavior, i.e., the decision to be explained. Now, this is appropriate when the model is to be used as a representation of actual decision making, but is not suitable as a basis for the testing of an ideal model of decision making, where distortions arising from the limitations of human information processing are not wanted in the representation of the decision.

Since, in the present study of judicial decision making, there is no well-established policy to discover, something much more fundamental must be done: the judges must first formulate a set of principles and rules that they believe should be applied and followed in the sentencing of the multiple offender. Clearly, these circumstances are incompatible with the assumption underlying the previous notion of model development and validity and require something quite different by way of approach. Helpful to developing an appropriate notion of model development and validity for this type of problem is Phillips's (1984) concept of the "requisite" decision model. In requisite modelling, where a group of individuals share a decision problem, these decision makers set about formulating a common approach to the decisions required of them, and in the process they develop a greater understanding of the basis of their decisions and new insights into the decision problem, this being done with a view to providing themselves with guidelines for future decisions. A requisite model is a simplified representation of a shared social reality of what is correct by way of approach for a decision problem. This position has several important consequences. (1) There are aspects relevant to the decision which are not incorporated in the model: in the early stages of model development they are the more contentious and idiosyncratic elements, and perhaps the more detailed and less obvious matters, ones yet to be covered; in the final stages of development they are the elements whose effects are so complex as to make more than an approximate account of their influence impossible, and the factors and relationships not lending themselves to ready articulation. (2) Some of the group of decision makers, inevitably, do not agree totally with the final common view, accepting it only in the interests of uniformity or under authority, and there are those who have a higher level of understanding of the decision problem than that represented in the model. (3) The model is, notwithstanding the preceding two considerations, a representation of the group's policy and how it ought to be applied in regard to the decision problem; it is not a description of how the decision is actually made, which description would necessarily cover distortions induced in thinking and arising from the limitations of the decision makers' capacity to process information. (4) As a consequence of the preceding three points the model is prescriptive, but this can never be more than conditional, because it does not cover all elements relevant to a decision and it is always open to change and further development. The point is, requisite models do not exist ripe for discovery; there is no commonly agreed approach to a decision problem and, indeed, the individuals may be yet to develop a clear and detailed approach. Accordingly, requisite models must be generated; they necessarily must come from the decision makers themselves, with the assistance of a decision analyst. Phillips's notion of requisite model clearly applies to the understanding of judicial decision making in sentencing and carries implications for the course the development and validation process should take in the present study. Other decision analysts, such as French (1989), have presented the idea of the decision model as created (cf. discovered) by way of an analysis in which the decision makers come to understand their thinking and the decision problem. But Phillips's article represents the seminal work.

In Phillips's (1984) account, the developmental process is an iterative one.

The analyst first seeks by one data-gathering process or another to ascertain the decision makers' current understanding of and approach to the decision problem, and on this basis suggests a form (e.g., algebraic) which may serve profitably as a framework for representing the problem, and then helps them to establish its content, namely, to identify what they believe are the material factors in the decision and to delineate and quantify the functions relating these variables. The present study does not move beyond this initial step along the course of model development. Indeed, the model produced represents no more than a first draft of the decision model, and without the benefit of judicial reflection, the next step in the developmental process; in fact, it can be regarded as no more than a prototype, since it was not born of the responses of a representative sample of judges experienced in the criminal jurisdiction. And the test of validity goes no further than examining the extent to which the judges gave effect to the alternative decision model. Nevertheless, a brief discussion of the subsequent steps in the developmental process is necessary to set the present work in context and to explain and justify the full notion of validity applicable to a requisite model as a veridical representation of the judges' view of how they want to address the decision problem of the multiple offender. Development is considered first, then validity.

In Phillips's (1984) analysis, the assessment of the adequacy of the first draft (and subsequent drafts) of a requisite model – and, hence, the catalyst to development – comes by way of the level of agreement between the decision makers' holistic assessments on the criterion and the assessments generated from the model (in terms of this study, the extent to which each judge's effective sentences are consistent with the cumulation of the corresponding comprising sentences, according to the alternative decision model); in requisite modelling, low correlations are expected at the start of the modelling process, with high correlations necessarily emerging at the end. In view of Phillips's account of the developmental process, it is important to make the point that a correlation statistic is a weak and potentially misleading index of the level of agreement and that holistic assessments are a flawed criterion of model adequacy. Each of these matters is explained, since it affects the way in which the level of agreement is assessed and interpreted in regard to its consequences for model development.

The argument has been well made that a correlation is not a valid test of the significant variables underlying a decision or of the way in which variables are combined to produce a decision (see Anderson, 1982). The reason is that the correlation statistic is a global measure and brings into prominence the degree of agreement between predicted and observed values, and its pictorial representation, the scatterplot, confounds systematic and error variance; it is because of this orientation of a correlational analysis that near-perfect correlations can be obtained where models seriously misrepresent the decision process; for example, a very high correlation may be found though a linear model be used to represent a decision in which there is a significant interaction. The effect is that the nature of the decision process is obscured. Rather, a rigorous test of the validity of the representation of a decision requires that the measure of the degree of correspondence between the observed and expected values (the holistic and model-generated assessments, respectively) be in terms of an analysis of the deviations between the expected and observed values by way of a factorial-type analysis; it is only in this way that the underlying processes can be revealed. As far as was permitted by the case structures (see Chapter 8), the present analysis of the sentencing data was in accordance with this prescription.

The use of holistic assessments on the criterion as the standard of the model's validity (e.g., Fischer, 1977) has been correctly rejected where the purpose of the model is to improve on the acknowledged flaws in holistic judgments (e.g., Humphreys and McFadden, 1980; Slovic, Fischhoff and Lichtenstein, 1977; Stillwell, Barron and Edwards, 1983). Nevertheless, it would seem that Phillips (1984) in his apparent acceptance of holistic assessments as the measure of the clarity and coherence of the decision makers' understanding of a decision problem (cf. current decision making) has left himself open to a related error. The significance of this point can be seen in the following proposal for the development of a requisite model.

The first draft of the decision model – the product of the present study – would be put before the judges with a view to their gaining a greater understanding of the basis of their decisions and greater insight into the decision problem. Where there was a high degree of agreement between the holistic assessments on the criterion and the model-generated assessments, the possibility arises that the judges have a good understanding of the basis of their decisions, but not a sufficiently complex view of the decision problem. An obvious candidate for inclusion in the alternative decision model is a variable relating to the number of secondary counts; presently this model does not distinguish between the sum of the sentences appropriate to each of the multiple counts being made up of, say, two or four counts. If this variable was considered by the judges to be of potential relevance, it would be incorporated in the model so that they could see how it affected the determination of the effective sentence. A policy decision in regard to its status would be made on the basis of this analysis, but not governed by it; a relevant factor may not actually influence the decision because of the limitations of information processing. Similar comments are applicable in respect of the delineation and quantification of the functions relating the variables in the model. There is the possibility that when the judges saw in a systematic way and across a representative sample of cases the pattern of sentences consequent on decisions made in accordance with this decision model, they would want to restructure their decision, including the variables and their interrelationships.

Where there was a low degree of agreement between the holistic assessments on the criterion and the model-generated assessments, it would be an indication that the judges may not have a good understanding of the basis of their decision making. One possibility is that their decision is based on a factor which they do not regard as relevant – its role would be demonstrated if it was incorporated in the model and the result was greater agreement. If this were found to be the case, it would fall to the judges to decide whether it should be regarded as relevant or whether its apparent effect was an artifact of the limitations of information processing. In the event of the former outcome, it would represent an increase in the judges' understanding of their decision making, and the factor would then be added to the model. Since the model is to represent what sentencing policy ought to be, the decision to include it must have a sound policy basis, regard being paid to the factor itself and its effect on the pattern of sentences in a representative sample of cases. The other possibility is that a factor which they believe to be relevant is in fact not influencing their determination of sentence – this would be demonstrated if it was deleted from the model and the result was greater agreement. Again, if this were found to be the case, the judges would have to decide as a matter of policy whether it should be regarded as irrelevant or whether the absence of its effect was an artifact of information processing. Then, of course, a low level of agreement may arise from the way in which the variables are combined in the decision; accordingly, this aspect, too, requires a similar critical analysis. Finally, it must be remembered, a low level of correspondence can be found where a model is requisite; this may occur where the decision is so complex that the effects of information overload seriously distort the decision making.

Decisions about the development of the model, in the present approach, are considered to be necessarily policy based, the judges' views being definitive; the results of the data analyses are no more than grist for the mill, merely stimuli to hard judicial thinking. In these analyses as long as a factor or a relationship between factors is believed as a matter of policy to be important to a decision it can be put forward and accepted as relevant. Development may be taken to be complete when the judges do not have any further insights into the basis of their decision or the nature of the decision problem and the model in that state is considered by the judges to provide a veridical representation of those agreed elements of sentencing policy capable of being modelled and articulated.

In regard to the final requisite model (and, indeed, each draft of the model), there is the question of whether the traditional concept of model validity can be applied to this model as a veridical representation of the judges' view of how they want to address the decision problem. It is suggested that the answer is no. There cannot be here, as there can be in a model of well-established behavior, external and independent criteria against which to validate the model; it follows that the standard of validity must be so different and, more importantly, so very much weaker, that to classify it as model validity would be a serious misrepresentation of the degree of rigor implied by that term. In requisite modelling the judges are shown the extent to which they gave effect to their policy – in the first draft this is the main principles in the alternative decision model – and the assessment of validity comes down to the judges' considered opinion of the relevance of each factor included in the model, in regard to the factor itself and its combination with the other factors, and the putative irrelevance of those factors left out of the model. The assessment of the validity of the requisite model must rest with the problem owners, in this case, the judges, and them alone, and cannot be otherwise. In view of this, the issue of validity turns on whether the techniques used to elicit the judges' responses might distort their views on elements incorporated in the model, or fail to stimulate their thoughts on other aspects of potential relevance to the decision problem, or not elucidate for them the full implications of the elements of the model in combination. The problem of validity, then, cannot be about the validity of the model but must be seen in terms of the weaker notion of the validity of the modelling procedures, the latter being a necessary condition but not a sufficient criterion for determining rigorously that the model is, within the meaning of the term requisite, a veridical representation of the judges' view of the decision problem. Specifically, validity is a matter of the extent to which what could be called a code of good practice was followed and the adequacy of this code. Of course, a further weakness of this approach is that what might be called good practice itself cannot be assessed against external criteria but for determination can rely on no more than face validity, regard being paid to theory and experiment (sometimes), and to experience and intuition (most often). While there are general standards of practice for some techniques, specific practices vary in potentially significant ways; and, then, there is often information required from subjects for which there are no general standards of practice or even available professional techniques for eliciting it. The method in regard to the present decision problem, unfortunately, primarily falls in the latter category; for example, in the task of eliciting from the judges potentially relevant factors for inclusion in the model, and this covers their identification and the way in which they are construed in the model, there is too much room for initiative and creativity for comfort; and, in respect of sensitivity analyses, techniques are not available which permit more than a small number of factors to be varied at any one time. One final point requires mention. This sort of analysis is vulnerable to the error of the incorporation in the model of irrelevant and, particularly, unreliable details. This problem arises because of the absence of an error theory and appropriate statistical methods applicable to the data. Nevertheless, the fact that the present decision model, at least as it now stands, is not very detailed is a factor militating against these potential effects.

The necessary pre-eminence and decisiveness of the problem owner's judgment regarding the adequacy of a decision model generated by this type of analysis is well recognized by those working in the area (e.g., Howard, 1980); also acknowledged is the implication of this role of the problem owner in the matter of validity (e.g., Bunn, 1984; von Winterfeldt and Edwards, 1986). And there can be no question of this approach to validity not being a tenable position where the model was of actual decision making. The present approach to validity in this sort of problem is consistent with Watson and Buede's (1987) formulation of a standard, at least as far as their criterion goes: to them, a decision model is valid if its implications are consistent with the decision maker's understanding of his/her beliefs and value judgments. However, it would appear from Watson and Buede's subsequent discussion of their definition that it cannot be interpreted as conveying the spirit of the approach taken in the present study. For in that discussion they seem to imply that, first, where the model-generated assessments are inconsistent with the holistic assessments on the criterion, it is the beliefs and value judgments about the elements of the model which require change and, secondly, where model-generated and holistic assessments are congruent, these two authors make no mention of the fact that the problem owners may be capable of further insights and of understanding the decision problem at a much greater level of complexity.

The idea of a modeller overriding the data, in the sense of incorporating variables with no discernible effects, excluding factors related to the criterion, and specifying the nature of the function, may seem heretical and a course antithetical to the veridical representation of a process. Yet it is not a novel one, and has been applied even in the development of models of real-life processes for the purpose of forecasting the outcomes of these processes (see Belsley, 1988); the point made by Belsley is not merely that it is a legitimate or desirable strategy, but that it is a necessary one for sound and successful forecasting. This approach is seen as particularly relevant where there are a priori (data-independent) grounds for regarding a factor as relevant and its relationship taking a particular form, and the data are seriously limited (namely, characterized by substantial unreliability, represent a significant distortion of the effects of the actual process, or are quite unrepresentative of or do not incorporate many of the possible outcomes of the process being modelled). It should be noted that these conditions hold in the problem under investigation in the present study: sentencing principle is policy based and its application by judges subject to the limitations of human information processing. Under these conditions, the variables in a model developed according to the present approach – fitting data to the model – would be correctly specified, but be poorly quantified. By way of contrast, in the traditional approach where the model – the specification of the variables and the quantification of the parameters – is constructed by searching the data for the best-fitting model, under the conditions assumed here, the product would be a well-estimated but incorrect model. The point of the argument is that quality forecasting depends more on correct specification of the model than on accurate estimates of its parameters. The extension of this line of reasoning to the present study is that for the specification of the decision model the judges' policy deliberations and not their sentencing data ought to be decisive. To Belsley, this is the *sine qua non* of quality modelling.

Results: fictitious cases

In this section the judges' responses to the fictitious cases are examined and analyzed. The data are in the form of an effective (maximum) sentence for each of the cases and, where appropriate, sentences for the counts comprising the cases. Consequent on the notion of model considered to be relevant to the present study, the point of this analysis is twofold. First, to examine the extent to which the judges gave effect to the main principles in the alternative decision model. Secondly, to translate the principles into a quantitative form so that the model can be used to generate effective sentences for cases from the sentences appropriate to the counts comprising those cases; in this form the model can be the basis for the development of a detailed, common policy and a system of numerical guidance. Prior to addressing these two matters, there is an analysis of the individual counts of armed robbery and burglary comprising the fictitious cases, comparing the sentences considered appropriate to them as single-count cases with the sentences imposed for them as individual counts in cases comprising multiple counts. But first it is necessary to address several matters concerning the administration of the third exercise.

Methodological considerations

Four matters relating to the methods adopted for the fictitious cases require additional information and discussion: (1) the administration of the cases; (2) the judges' comments on the third sentencing exercise; (3) the size of the sample of judges on which this part of the study is based; and (4) the distribution of the sums of the sentences imposed for the secondary counts of burglary. Most of these matters were raised in Chapter 8.

THE ADMINISTRATION OF THE CASES Four judges (nos. 1, 4, 5 and 7) completed the three parts of the third sentencing exercise.

The first part was given to the judges at the beginning of November 1991, the year in which they had undertaken the sentencing problems in the first two exercises. These four judges returned this part within three months.

It was early in April 1992 that the second part was ready for the judges. Three returned the completed booklet within three months and one took a little longer, five months. In no instances, then, was this part undertaken more than four months after the *Sentencing Act* 1991 had come into operation.

Part C of the third exercise was sent to these judges in August of the same year. Three of these judges finished this task before the commencement of the 1993 legal year, and within eight months of the introduction of the new Act, while the fourth, Judge 4, did not return the completed booklet until August 1993, sixteen months after the repeal of the *Penalties and Sentences Act* 1985, and by which time it would be likely that a judge's memory of sentencing practice under this Act might have started to fade.

THE JUDGES' COMMENTS ON THE SENTENCING EXERCISE In Part A none of the judges felt that any of the cases represented unrealistic and improbable combinations of the factual circumstances relating to the offence and the offender. There was general agreement that the least and most serious single counts of armed robbery as the principal offence approached, respectively, the lower and upper levels of seriousness for this offence type. Nevertheless, there was a belief that, particularly, more trivial, but also, more heinous instances of this category of offence could be envisaged. There was no dispute that the record of prior convictions was very serious and that, apart from the plea of guilty, there was little if anything by way of mitigation personal to the offender; it was not thought that more severe sentences would have been appropriate had the criminal record been more extensive or serious, but there was recognition that the sentences had been reduced somewhat to give credit for the guilty plea. The conditions for the valid administration of this part seem to have been satisfied. The judges had no other comments of significance.

According to the four judges the air of realism about the cases was maintained in Part B; the judges had either experienced cases similar to the ones represented or could readily anticipate cases like these coming before them. All the judges said that in their view an armed robbery was the principal offence in each of the cases. None of the four felt that he had any difficulties in following the instruction to approach the sentencing of the fictitious cases in this part-exercise as he would have under the previous Act; two of these judges justified this conclusion on the ground that to determine what is appropriate by way of sentence under the new Act it is essential first to have regard to sentencing practice under the old Act. Again, the criteria necessary for the validity of this part appear to have been met. There were no other pertinent comments.

In Part C the view of the judges was again that all of the cases were realistic and probable, and in the judgment of the four the armed robbery was always the principal offence. The three judges who completed the task around Christmas 1992 all believed that the levels of sentence set by them reflected sentencing practice under the old Act. The judge (no. 4) who returned this part sixteen months after the introduction of the new Act was less certain, however; in particular, he believed there was a strong mood throughout the community by mid-1993 that effective sentences for serious multiple offenders should be greater than they had been in the past, and he said he could not be certain that his levels of sentence did not reflect this change. The only other apposite comment was made by Judge 5, when he reminded the author that there is the possibility that his levels of sentence would not have been the same had he been sentencing a real as opposed to a fictitious offender. Neither of these difficulties would appear to have the potential to invalidate the testing of whether the model, as specified in terms of its main two principles, could be fitted to the data, since the possible expansion or contraction, were it an actuality, would be expected to be roughly uniform across the range; but, of course, these two factors have the potential to distort the quantification of the relationship between the variables in the model.

THE SIZE OF THE SAMPLE OF JUDGES Four of the eight judges did not complete this third sentencing exercise. Indeed, two did not commence it, one because he went on extended leave and the other because he had a major report to research and write during this period. Another of the judges completed Part A but did not continue for reasons relating to his disenchantment with the new Act. The fourth judge finished the first two parts and accepted the third but had not returned it by the time the author had completed the manuscript.

It was considered that four judges was an adequate number to satisfy the

Table 9.1 *Distribution of the sums of sentence (years) for the secondary counts of burglary in Exercises 3B and 3C – Judges 1,4,5 and 7*

Count(s) of burglary	Judge			
	1	4	5	7
1	1, 1, 1.5	1.5, 3, 4	1.5, 2/3, 3/4	1.5, 2, 3
2	4	8.5	5.5	5.5^b
3	1.5, 3	7.5, 10.5	2.3, 3.8	4.5, 6
5	7^a	19	9.3	12
7	3.5, 7	17.5, 24.5	8.8, 8.8	10.5, 14
11	5.5, 11	27.5, 38.5	8.3, 13.8	16.5, 22

Note: [a] 10 in Case 29.
   [b] 6 in Case 35.

requirements of the present analysis. The results will show that there was at least one of these judges whose responses were sufficiently consistent with the model that they could be used to illustrate the solution to the problem of quantifying the relationship between the independent variables and the dependent variable. And since the second stage in the building of a requisite model – the correction and development of the first draft by means of judicial reflection – is beyond the scope of the present study, as intimated earlier, responses from a representative sample of experienced judges were not required. Also, four judges was a sufficient number to demonstrate the difficulties some judges might be expected to experience in attempting to give effect to the main principles governing the determination of effective sentences for multiple offenders.

DISTRIBUTION OF THE SUMS OF THE SENTENCES IMPOSED FOR THE SECONDARY COUNTS OF BURGLARY In the planning of the fictitious cases the point was made that for a robust validity test and for quantification of the decision model the total seriousness of the secondary counts should have a substantial range, the discriminations across the range should not be coarse, and as far as possible at each level of seriousness there should be several cases, each comprising a different structure. Table 9.1 shows the relevant data for burglary as the secondary count: what is displayed for each level of the number of multiple secondary burglaries comprising a case are the sentences and sums of sentence considered appropriate to the counts and combinations of comprising counts; the data are presented separately for each of the judges and are from their responses in Exercises 3B and 3C; within a level each entry represents a different count or combination of secondary counts (see Table 8.7).

In view of these data, it can be concluded that for each of the judges in relation to the secondary counts of burglary the sentences and sums of sentence considered appropriate covered an adequate range, that within this range the discriminations were reasonably fine, but the criterion that there be several differently structured cases representing the various levels of sentence across this range was only partially satisfied.

Sentences for individual counts as whole and part cases

In Part A of the third sentencing exercise there were four cases comprising single counts of armed robbery (Cases 1–4), two cases comprising multiple counts of armed robbery (Cases 5–6) and four cases comprising single counts of burglary (Cases 7–10). For Part B of the same exercise each of the cases was made up of one of the counts of burglary in association with one of the single or multiple counts of armed robbery, all counts being taken from Exercise 3A. In Exercise 3C, each of the cases comprised from two to eleven of one or more of the single counts of burglary in association with one of the single counts of armed robbery, again all counts being from Part A of the same exercise. The point of interest in this particular analysis is whether the quanta of sentence imposed for the cases in Part A were what was considered appropriate to them by way of sentence when they were presented in Parts B and C as part of a case comprising multiple counts and for which an effective sentence had to be fixed.

The question of whether the sentence fixed for each of the counts comprising a case of multiple offending is solely determined by what is considered appropriate to each of those counts or is in part a function of the seriousness of the other counts is a significant one for two reasons. First, it is not possible to develop a deliberative and rational set of considerations governing the determination of an effective sentence for multiple offending unless that sentence is constructed from elements and those elements are related to or, for simplicity, are the quanta of sentence appropriate to the comprising counts. Secondly, consider the development of the decision model relating the individual sentences for the counts comprising a case to the effective sentence for that case, the data base being the sentences imposed for each of the comprising counts and determined as part of the process of fixing an effective sentence for the case. Now, if the sentences set for comprising counts in the context of a case were uniformly greater or less than the quanta of sentence imposed for those counts considered alone – presumably the sentences appropriate to those counts – then the estimate of the percentage of

Table 9.2 *Sentences (months) for counts as whole cases (3A) and part cases (3B and 3C) in Exercise 3 — Judge 1*

| | Offence type and case no. in Exercise 3A | | | | | | | | | |
| | Armed robbery | | | | | | Burglary | | | |
Exercise	1	2	3	4	5	6	7	8	9	10
3A	36	60	72	84	120	156	18	24	24	24
3B	60	72	84	96	120	162	12	12	18^a	
3C	48	60	72	84			6	12^b	24	24

Note: [a] 12 in Case 38.
     [b] 24 in Case 29.

the quanta of sentence for the secondary counts made concurrent with the sentence for the principal offence would be an over- or under-estimate, respectively, of the real figure. Clearly, accurate information on this point is important when sentencing policy for the multiple offender is being debated. Moreover, accuracy on this matter would be of great practical significance in the development of a system of numerical guidance for the determination of effective sentences. Consider a value for the degree of concurrence which had been determined in the context of a case and for this reason was an over- or under-estimate of the real value. If, in turn, this figure was used in a system of guidance and, accordingly, was applied to the cumulation of a set of appropriate sentences for the counts comprising a case, then the calculated effective sentence would be, respectively, inappropriately low or high.

Now to the presentation and analysis of the relevant data, which is done individually for each of the judges. Table 9.2 shows, for Judge 1, the sentences he imposed for the cases of single and multiple counts of armed robbery and single counts of burglary when presented alone (Exercise 3A) and in combination with other cases from Part A (Exercises 3B and 3C). (Note: in the analyses in this chapter, where a theft of a motor vehicle was connected with an armed robbery or burglary and the sentence for this former offence was not made fully concurrent, then the cumulated quantum was added on to the sentence imposed for the armed robbery or the burglary and this sum was taken as the sentence appropriate to the armed robbery or burglary, since a connected theft was considered to be part of the organization in the definition of that offence factor – see Tables 8.3 and 8.5.)

For each of the cases in Exercises 3B and 3C the sum of the sentences considered appropriate to the comprising counts was calculated in two ways:

one was based on the sentences imposed for those counts when they were presented in isolation (Exercise 3A), and the other used the sentences fixed for those counts in the course of the determination of effective sentences for the cases of multiple offending in Exercises 3B and 3C; for example, consider a case in Exercise 3B comprising Cases (Counts) 1 and 7 from Exercise 3A, the total for the condition representing *in-isolation* would be 54 (36 + 18) months and for the condition representing *in-context* the total would be 72 (60 + 12) months. The mean sentence across the twenty-eight cases of multiple offending was 164 months in the *in-isolation* condition and 128 months in the *in-context* condition. Evidence, indeed, that the quanta of sentence set for comprising counts in the context of a case are less than the sentences fixed as appropriate to those counts when considered in isolation. To investigate whether this effect depended on the seriousness of the case of multiple offending, the preceding calculation was made for cases for which the sum of the sentences for the comprising counts was low, and separately for the remainder of the cases, where the sum was relatively high. The somewhat arbitrary definition of low case seriousness was that the sum of the sentences imposed for the comprising counts was not greater than ten years, the sentences being for the counts when they were presented in Exercise 3A; on this definition there were eleven low-seriousness and seventeen high-seriousness cases. For low seriousness, the mean sentences were 91 and 94 months for the *in-isolation* and *in-context* conditions, respectively; for high seriousness, the mean sentences for these two respective conditions were 211 and 150 months. It would appear that the sentence fixed for each of the counts comprising a case of multiple offending was not solely determined by what was considered appropriate to each of those counts but was in part a function of the seriousness of the other counts, this factor operating in the more serious cases of multiple offending. A plausible explanation for this phenomenon is that it represents a tendency by the judge to fix lower sentences for counts in cases of multiple offending than would be regarded as appropriate were the counts being considered individually, so as partially to offset the potentially crushing effects arising from the cumulation of the sentences for the counts comprising the case. Of course, the possibility that the effect is in some way artifactual must be considered. The finding for the less-serious cases of multiple offending of similar mean sentences for the *in-isolation* and *in-context* conditions is explicable in a way which does not raise doubts about the above conclusion. The less-serious cases of multiple offending are primarily in Exercise 3B and most of these cases comprise one count of armed robbery and one count of burglary; now, from Table 9.2 it can be seen that the sentences for these counts as part of a case of multiple offending are for armed robbery generally higher and for burglary

Table 9.3 *Sentences (months) for counts as whole cases (3A) and part cases (3B and 3C) in Exercise 3 – Judge 4*

| | Offence type and case no. in Exercise 3A | | | | | | | | | |
| | Armed robbery | | | | | | Burglary | | | |
Exercise	1	2	3	4	5	6	7	8	9	10
3A	36	42	72	120	180	195	12	30	36	42
3B	60	60	84[a]	120	162	237	18	36	48	
3C	54	60	108	156			30	42	48	54

Note: [a] 72 in Case 23.

lower than the sentences for the same counts in Exercise 3A. However, the finding for the more-serious cases of multiple offending of a greater mean sentence for the *in-isolation* condition may be open to an artifactual interpretation. The more-serious cases of multiple offending are primarily in Exercise 3C; now, from Table 9.2 it is apparent that the sentences for the counts as part of a case of multiple offending are for armed robbery approximately the same as the sentences for the same counts in Exercise 3A and are for burglary lower for Cases 7 and 8 and the same for the other two counts. It is these former two counts of which there are multiple instances – in fact, up to eleven – in the cases of multiple offending, and patently it is the sentences for these counts which are the source of the difference between the *in-context* and *in-isolation* conditions. Clearly, to offset the potentially crushing effects of the cumulation of multiple sentences, these two counts would be the prime candidates for the discounting of sentence; it is just that the evidence for this explanation would have been more convincing had the discount been applied to the other counts as well; the influence of chance and sentencing disparity cannot be ruled out. In general, whether this phenomenon occurred and to what extent might have depended in part on whether the judge was first confronted with a case comprising three or eleven of these multiple counts of burglary and a less or more serious principal offence of armed robbery, for he might have felt some pressure to fix the same sentence for a particular count within an exercise.

The responses for Judge 4 are presented in Table 9.3, which shows the sentences he imposed for the cases when presented alone (Exercise 3A) and in combination with other cases from Part A (Exercises 3B and 3C).

The mean sentence across the twenty-eight cases of multiple offending was 192 months in the *in-isolation* condition and 267 months in the *in-context* condition. For cases of low seriousness ($n = 9$), defined as for Judge 1, the mean

Table 9.4 *Sentences (months) for counts as whole cases (3A) and part cases (3B and 3C) in Exercise 3 – Judge 5*

| | Offence type and case no. in Exercise 3A | | | | | | | | | |
| | Armed robbery | | | | | | | Burglary | | |
Exercise	1	2	3	4	5	6	7	8	9	10
3A	42	54	66	78	96	108	9	30	36	42
3B	48	60^a	72	108	144	156	18	36^b	48^c	
3C	42	72	102	120			9^d	15	36	30

Note: ^{a} 48 in Case 16.
  ^{b} 24 in Case 16.
  ^{c} 36 in Cases 15, 20 and 27.
  ^{d} 15 in Case 13.

sentences were 86 and 131 months for the *in-isolation* and *in-context* conditions, respectively; for high seriousness ($n = 19$), again the remainder of the cases, the mean sentences for these two respective conditions were 242 and 331 months. The data here indicate no tendency by the judge to fix lower sentences for counts in cases of multiple offending than would be regarded as appropriate were the counts being considered individually, so as partially to offset the potentially crushing effects arising from the cumulation of the sentences for the counts comprising the case. In fact the opposite tendency is readily discernible: Judge 4 fixed higher sentences for the counts in the context of a case and this effect was greater in Exercise 3C which had most of the more-serious cases of multiple offending. It is not clear what this finding represents: there is no readily apparent decision strategy or artifactual interpretation accounting for it. In his comments on this third exercise, it will be recalled that at the time this judge did Exercise 3C he thought that he might have become more severe in his sentencing in response to his perception of a new mood in the community for more-severe sentences for serious multiple offenders, and it would not be unreasonable to argue that this attitude could have inadvertently influenced his fixing of sentences for the comprising individual counts; but, of course, this would not explain the same observed phenomenon of inflated sentences for the individual comprising counts in Exercise 3B.

The responses for Judge 5 are presented in Table 9.4, which shows the sentences he imposed for the cases when presented alone (Exercise 3A) and in combination with other cases from Part A (Exercises 3B and 3C).

The mean sentence across the twenty-eight cases of multiple offending was

Table 9.5 *Sentences (months) for counts as whole cases (3A) and part cases (3B and 3C) in Exercise 3 – Judge 7*

Exercise	Offence type and case no. in Exercise 3A									
	Armed robbery						Burglary			
	1	2	3	4	5	6	7	8	9	10
3A	51	69	87	147	204	252	15	36	48	54
3B	48	66	96	144	180	222	18	24	36	
3C	42	54	84	132			18	24	36[a]	36

Note: [a] 30 in Cases 21 and 28.

175 months in the *in-isolation* condition and 162 months in the *in-context* condition. For cases of low seriousness ($n = 10$), defined as for Judge 1, the mean sentences were 88 and 103 months for the *in-isolation* and *in-context* conditions, respectively; for high seriousness ($n = 18$), again the remainder of the cases, the mean sentences for these two respective conditions were 224 and 194 months. The data here indicate a tendency by the judge to fix lower sentences for counts in serious cases of multiple offending than would be regarded as appropriate were the counts being considered individually. There cannot be much confidence in the conclusion that this effect represents an attempt by the judge partially to offset the potentially crushing effects arising from the cumulation of the sentences for the counts comprising the serious cases of multiple offending. Considering the results for Exercise 3C, where generally there are the more-serious cases of multiple offending, it is apparent that the sentences for the counts as part of a case of multiple offending are for armed robbery actually higher than the sentences for the same counts in Exercise 3A and are for burglary lower in only one of the two cases (nos. 7 and 8) of which there are multiple instances in the cases of multiple offending; against this, it is the sentence for this count (no. 8) which is the source of the difference between the *in-context* and *in-isolation* conditions and the prime candidate for discounting to offset the potentially crushing effects of the cumulation of multiple sentences.

The responses for Judge 7 are presented in Table 9.5, which shows the sentences he imposed for the cases when presented alone (Exercise 3A) and in combination with the other cases from Part A (Exercises 3B and 3C).

The mean sentence across the twenty-eight cases of multiple offending was 241 months in the *in-isolation* condition and 193 months in the *in-context* condition. For cases of low seriousness ($n = 6$), again defined as for Judge 1, the mean sentences were 98 and 92 months for the *in-isolation* and *in-context* conditions, respectively; for high seriousness ($n = 22$), again the remainder of the cases, the mean sentences for these two respective conditions were 280 and 221 months. The data here reveal a clear tendency by the judge to fix lower sentences for counts in cases of multiple offending than would be regarded as appropriate were the counts being considered individually. It would appear inescapable that this effect represents an attempt by the judge partially to offset the potentially crushing effects arising from the cumulation of the sentences for the counts comprising the cases of multiple offending: in both Exercises 3B and 3C the sentences for the counts as part of a case of multiple offending are for armed robbery and burglary with few exceptions significantly lower than the sentences for the same counts in Exercise 3A. The only possible artifactual interpretation is that the generally lower levels of sentence in Exercise 3B compared with Exercise 3A represent an adaptation effect, in this instance the judge's becoming accustomed to the fictitious procedure and particularly the sentencing of a paper defendant as against flesh and blood; but against this is the generally further and indeed greater reduction in the levels of sentence between Exercises 3C and 3B, an effect consistent with the "discount" explanation, since the cases in Exercise 3C are generally the more-serious cases of multiple offending, but at variance with the "adaptation" explanation, on which basis the rate of reduction would be expected to diminish across the exercises.

The judges' sentencing and the alternative decision model

The analysis now turns to consider the judges' responses (sentences) in regard to the extent to which each judge gave effect to the main principles in the alternative decision model. These principles are:

(1) the higher the sum of the sentences appropriate to each of the multiple secondary counts, then the greater the degree of concurrence for each of these appropriate sentences with the sentence for the principal offence, subject to the constraint that more serious and additional multiple secondary counts require a greater quantum of sentence to be added to the sentence for the principal offence;

(2) the higher the sentence appropriate to the principal offence, then the greater the degree of concurrence for each of the appropriate sentences associated with the multiple secondary counts, subject to the constraint that more serious principal offences require higher effective sentences.

JUDGE 1 The principle to be considered first is the effect of the sum of the sentences appropriate to the multiple secondary counts on the degree of concurrence. The relevant data are in Table 9.6, which shows for various levels of the quantum of sentence appropriate to the principal offence and the sum of the sentences appropriate to the multiple secondary counts, the percentage of the total of the sentences for those secondary counts made cumulative on the sentence for the principal offence and the quantum of sentence that percentage represents. The cases are taken from both Exercise 3B and Exercise 3C, and for simplicity cases are grouped in the table where the sum of the sentences for the multiple secondary counts is common to more than one level of the principal offence and where for a particular level of the principal offence there is variation in the sum of the sentences for the multiple secondary counts. By way of illustration of the information in Table 9.6, the third row reads as follows: there are three cases, with respective sentences for the principal offence of 5, 6 and 7 years, for which in each case the sum of the sentences for the multiple secondary counts is 3 years, the mean percentage of the total sentence for these secondary counts made cumulative was 25, and the mean quantum of sentence added to the sentence for the principal offence was 0.8 years.

There is a clear trend across Table 9.6 in regard to the effect of the sum of the sentences appropriate to the multiple secondary counts on the degree of cumulation of the sentences for those counts on the sentence for the principal offence. In the top and bottom blocks, as the sum of the sentences for the secondary counts increases, so the percentage cumulation decreases, the decrement tempered so that a greater quantum of sentence is added for more serious and additional secondary counts; in the middle block, the latter element of the principle is met, but not the former. The clarity of the trend in the direction predicted according to the alternative decision model must be regarded as quite convincing in view of the hazards besetting the data: namely, the fine discriminations between some of the levels on this factor; the small number of cases in each of the levels; the relatively complex calculations underlying the judgments, especially for the more-numerous-count cases; and the effects, especially significant at low levels of sentence, of a judicial preference for ordering concurrence in terms of sentence lengths, rather than percentages, in conjunction with a possible tendency to favor certain sentence lengths, reinforced by a belief that punishment is not calibrated in scruples – all factors acting alone and together to raise the level of noise in the data. Nevertheless, what did favor the analysis in the top and bottom blocks was the substantial range on this factor of the sum of the sentences for the secondary counts together with the fact that for the more-serious cases the total of this sum and the sentence for the principal count reached high to extraordinarily high levels of sentence.

Table 9.6 *Effect on cumulation of the sum of the sentences for the multiple secondary counts in the fictitious cases – Judge 1*

Case nos.[a]	No. of cases/ level	Sentence(s) for the principal offence (yrs.)	Sum of sentence(s) for the secondary count(s) (yrs.)	Percentage cumulation (mean)	Quantum of sentence cumulated (mean yrs.)
11, 15–29, 31–33, 35–36	3	5, 6, 7	1.0	36	0.4
			1.5	44	0.7
			3.0	25	0.8
			4.0	33	1.3
			7.0	22	1.6
			7.0[b]	22	1.8
			11.0	17	1.8
12–14	1	4	1.5	17	0.3
			3.5	17	0.6
			5.5	17	0.9
30, 34, 37–38	1	8	1.0	33	0.3
			1.5	33	0.5
			25.5[c]	9	2.3
			89.0[c]	6	5.5

Note: [a] Case numbers refer to Exercises 3B and 3C.
[b] 10.0 in Case 29.
[c] Sentences are for multiple secondary counts of armed robbery and one count of burglary.

The conclusion that Judge 1 is reasonably adept at applying the first of the main two principles of the alternative decision model governing cumulation of sentence appears warranted.

The second principle is the effect of the quantum of sentence appropriate to the principal offence on the degree of concurrence. The relevant data are in Table 9.7, which is constructed in the same way as the previous table, except for the obvious necessary modifications, and is to be interpreted similarly; the significant difference is the addition of the column "Effective sentence (mean yrs.)." (Cases 13–14, 30, and 37–38 could not be grouped and for this reason are not in this particular analysis.)

There are no clear trends in Table 9.7 in regard to the effect of the sentence appropriate to the principal offence on the degree of cumulation of the sentences for the multiple secondary counts on that sentence. In respect of the percentage cumulation, a trend favoring the alternative decision model is just discernible: the mean of the mean percentage cumulations for principal offence sentences of five and six years (30) is greater than that for the six- and seven-year comparison ($28\frac{1}{2}$); however, the weakness of this effect is revealed by there being no corresponding decrease in the quanta of sentence cumulated. The predicted effect is to be seen in the results for the principal offences of six and seven years: with the more serious principal offence there is a corresponding decrease in the percentage cumulation and resulting in a quantum of cumulation which is lower but of a sufficient magnitude to ensure a higher effective sentence. Of course, the data described here no more than illustrate the operation of the alternative decision model. Nevertheless, the point must be made that there was nothing acting in favor of this particular analysis of the effect of the sentence for the principal offence. Not only did the previously mentioned hazards besetting the data relating to the effect of the sum of sentences for the secondary counts operate here, but also the saving factor in that analysis – the high range on the independent variable under test – did not apply here, there being in the main block a range of only two years on the independent variable of the sentence for the principal offence.

JUDGE 4 The relevant data relating to the effect of the sum of the sentences appropriate to the multiple secondary counts on the degree of concurrence are presented in Table 9.8. (Cases 20, 23 and 27 could not be grouped.)

There is one clear trend across Table 9.8 in regard to the effect of the sum of the sentences appropriate to the multiple secondary counts on the degree of cumulation of the sentences for those counts on the sentence for the principal offence; within each of the blocks, with the third as the exception, as the sum of the sentences for the secondary counts increases, so there is a general

Table 9.7 *Effect on cumulation of the sentence for the principal offence in the fictitious cases – Judge 1*

Case nos.[a]	No. of cases/level	Sum of sentence(s) for the secondary count(s) (yrs.)	Sentence for the principal offence (yrs.)	Percentage cumulation (mean)	Quantum of sentence cumulated (mean yrs.)	Effective sentence (mean yrs.)
11, 15–29, 31–33,35–36	7	1,1.5, 3, 4, 7, 7,[b],11	5.0	29	1.1	6.1
			6.0	31	1.3	7.3
			7.0	26	1.1	8.1
12,34	1	1.5	4.0	17	0.3	4.3
			8.0	33	0.5	8.5

Note: [a] Case numbers refer to Exercises 3B and 3C.
[b] 10 in Case 29.

Table 9.8 *Effect on cumulation of the sum of the sentences for the multiple secondary counts in the fictitious cases – Judge 4*

Case nos.[a]	No. of cases/ level	Sentence(s) for the principal offence (yrs.)	Sum of sentence(s) for the secondary count(s) (yrs.)	Percentage cumulation (mean)	Quantum of sentence cumulated (mean yrs.)
17–19, 21–22, 24–26, 28–29, 31–33, 35–36	3	5, 9, 13	8.5	29	2.5
			10.5	14	1.5
			19.0	18	3.5
			24.5	10	2.5
			38.5	9	3.5
12–14	1	4.5	7.5	13	1.0
			17.5	11	2.0
			27.5	11	3.0
11, 15–16	1	5	1.5	33	0.5
			3.0	33	1.0
			4.0	38	1.5
30, 34, 37–38	1	10	3.0	33	1.0
			4.0	38	1.5
			26.0[b]	17	4.5
			84.0[b]	13	10.5

Note: [a] Case numbers refer to Exercises 3B and 3C.
[b] Sentences are for multiple secondary counts of armed robbery and one count of burglary.

decrease in the percentage cumulation. In respect of the quantum of sentence cumulated, in the bottom three of the four blocks a greater quantum of sentence was added for more serious and additional secondary counts. Both these findings are, of course, consistent with the alternative decision model's predictions. However, in view of the fact that there is no systematic increase in the quantum of sentence cumulated within the first block, where the discriminations on this factor of the sum of the sentences for the secondary counts are comparatively fine, yet across a substantial range and with several instances contributing to the estimate for each level, the evidence here for more than a rough-and-ready effect of the sum of the sentences for the secondary counts must be regarded as uncertain.

It can be reasonably concluded that Judge 4's thinking is influenced by the first of the main two principles of the alternative decision model governing the cumulation of sentence but that he cannot give effect to it with precision and consistency.

The second principle is the effect of the quantum of sentence appropriate to the principal offence on the degree of concurrence. The relevant data are in Table 9.9. (Cases 12–14, and 37–38 could not be grouped.)

It is clear from the data in Table 9.9 that in the general run of cases, even where the sentence for the principal offence is substantial, Judge 4 does not apply the second of the main two principles of the alternative decision model governing cumulation of sentence. Of course, it is possible that in cases characterized by very high levels on this factor of the sentence for the principal offence it would influence this judge's thinking in the predicted way. If, in fact, it were found to influence his thinking under this latter condition, then the conclusion could be no more than that in respect of this element of policy Judge 4's decision making is not finely honed.

JUDGE 5 The relevant data relating to the effect of the sum of the sentences appropriate to the multiple secondary counts on the degree of concurrence are presented in Table 9.10. (Case 20 could not be grouped.)

There is no clear trend across Table 9.10 in regard to the effect of the sum of the sentences appropriate to the multiple secondary counts on the degree of cumulation of the sentences for those counts on the sentence for the principal offence. In the top block, as the sum of the sentences for the secondary counts increases, there is no concomitant decremental trend in the percentage cumulation nor incremental trend in the quantum of sentence added for more serious and additional secondary counts, as would be expected under the alternative decision model. And there is little in the intermediate three blocks. Nevertheless, the bottom block does show substantial agreement with the

Table 9.9 *Effect on cumulation of the sentence for the principal offence in the fictitious cases – Judge 4*

Case nos.[a]	No. of cases/level	Sum of sentence(s) for the secondary count(s) (yrs.)	Sentence for the principal offence (yrs.)	Percentage cumulation (mean)	Quantum of sentence cumulated (mean yrs.)	Effective sentence (mean yrs.)
17–19, 21–22, 24–26, 28–29, 31–33, 35–36	5	8.5, 10.5, 19, 24.5, 38.5	5.0	16	2.7	7.7
			9.0	16	2.7	11.7
			13.0	17	2.8	15.8
11, 23	1	1.5	5.0	33	0.5	5.5
			6.0	33	0.5	6.5
15–16, 30, 34	2	3, 4	5.0	36	1.0	6.0
			10.0	36	1.0	11.0
20, 27	1	4	5.0	38	1.5	6.5
			7.0	38	1.5	8.5

Note: [a] Case numbers refer to Exercises 3B and 3C.

Table 9.10 *Effect on cumulation of the sum of the sentences for the multiple secondary counts in the fictitious cases – Judge 5*

Case nos.[a]	No. of cases/ level	Sentence(s) for the principal offence (yrs.)	Sum of sentence(s) for the secondary count(s) (yrs.)	Percentage cumulation (mean)	Quantum of sentence cumulated (mean yrs.)
17–19, 21–22, 24–26, 28–29, 31–33, 35–36	3	6, 8.5, 10	3.8	18	0.7
			5.5	29	1.6
			8.8	9	0.8
			9.3	20	1.8
			13.8	6	0.8
12–14	1	3.5	2.3	11	0.3
			8.3	6	0.5
			8.8	6	0.5
11, 15–16	1	4	1.5	33	0.5
			2.0	50	1.0
			3.0	50	1.5
23, 27	1	6	1.5	33	0.5
			3.0	33	1.0
30, 34, 37–38	1	9	3.0	33	1.0
			4.0	50	2.0
			28.0[b]	18	5.0
			93.0[b]	6	6.0

Note: [a] Case numbers refer to Exercises 3B and 3C.
[b] Sentences are for multiple secondary counts of armed robbery and one count of burglary.

prediction. The significant differences between this and the other blocks are its coarse discriminations between the levels and the great width of the range on the factor of the sum of the sentences for the secondary counts.

The inescapable conclusion is that in the general run of cases Judge 5 does not apply the first of the main two principles of the alternative decision model governing cumulation of sentence; however, in cases characterized by high levels on the factor of the sum of the sentences for the secondary counts it does influence this judge's thinking in the predicted way. One plausible resolution of this apparent contradiction is that this factor is relevant to this judge's decision making, but in respect of this element of policy Judge 5's mind is roughly honed.

The second principle is the effect of the quantum of sentence appropriate to the principal offence on the degree of concurrence. The relevant data are in Table 9.11. (Cases 12–14, 16, 34, and 37–38 could not be grouped.)

There is no clear trend across Table 9.11 in regard to the effect of the sentence appropriate to the principal offence on the degree of cumulation of the sentences for the multiple secondary counts on that sentence. Nevertheless, the bottom two blocks do show a tendency towards a pattern of judgments consistent with the prediction: with the more-serious principal offences there is a corresponding decrease in the percentage cumulation and resulting in a quantum of cumulation which is lower but of a sufficient magnitude to ensure a higher effective sentence. There are no such trends in the top block. The level of discrimination and range on the factor of the quantum of sentence for the principal offence are not insignificant in the top block and are of a similar magnitude to the second and third considered together. In view of the fact that the number of cases is greater in the first than in the second and third blocks and the totals of the sentences for the principal and secondary counts for the former cases are generally significantly higher, the evidence there for the effect of the sentence for the principal offence on cumulation must be regarded as somewhat uncertain.

The strongest statement that can be made about Judge 5's application of the second of the main two principles of the alternative decision model governing cumulation of sentence is that its influence on his thinking is weak and inconstant.

JUDGE 7 The relevant data relating to the effect of the sum of the sentences appropriate to the multiple secondary counts on the degree of concurrence are presented in Table 9.12.

There is one clear trend across Table 9.12 in regard to the effect of the sum of the sentences appropriate to the multiple secondary counts on the degree of

Table 9.11 *Effect on cumulation of the sentence for the principal offence in the fictitious cases – Judge 5*

Case nos.[a]	No. of cases/level	Sum of sentence(s) for the secondary count(s) (yrs.)	Sentence for the principal offence (yrs.)	Percentage cumulation (mean)	Quantum of sentence cumulated (mean yrs.)	Effective sentence (mean yrs.)
17–19, 21–22,	5	3.8, 5.5, 8.8, 9.3, 13.8	6.0	17	1.2	7.2
24–26, 28–29,			8.5	16	1.1	9.6
31–33, 35–36			10.0	16	1.2	11.2
11, 15, 23, 27	2	1.5, 3	4.0	42	1.0	5.0
			6.0	33	0.8	6.8
20, 30	1	3	5.0	50	1.5	6.5
			9.0	33	1.0	10.0

Note: [a] Case numbers refer to Exercises 3B and 3C.

Table 9.12 *Effect on cumulation of the sum of the sentences for the multiple secondary counts in the fictitious cases – Judge 7*

Case nos.[a]	No. of cases/level	Sentence(s) for the principal offence (yrs.)	Sum of sentence(s) for the secondary count(s) (yrs.)	Percentage cumulation (mean)	Quantum of sentence cumulated (mean yrs.)
17–19, 21–22,	3	4.5, 7, 11	5.5[b]	53	3.0
24–26, 28–29,			6.0	42	2.5
31–33, 35–36			12.0	32	3.8
			14.0	19	2.7
			22.0	15	3.3
12–14	1	3.5	4.5	44	2.0
			10.5	24	2.5
			16.5	21	3.5
11, 15, 23, 27	2	4, 8	1.5	67	1.0
			3.0	59	1.8
16, 20	1	5.5	2.0	50	1.0
			3.0	50	1.5
30, 34, 37–38	1	12	2.0	50	1.0
			3.0	67	2.0
			31.0[c]	13	4.0
			104.0[c]	8	8.0

Note: [a] Case numbers refer to Exercises 3B and 3C.
[b] 6.0 in Case 35.
[c] Sentences are for multiple secondary counts of armed robbery and one count of burglary.

cumulation of the sentences for those counts on the sentence for the principal offence; within each of the blocks, with the fourth as the exception, as the sum of the sentences for the secondary counts increases, so the percentage cumulation decreases. In respect of the quantum of sentence cumulated, in the bottom four of the five blocks a greater quantum of sentence was added for more serious and additional secondary counts. Both these findings are, of course, consistent with the alternative decision model's predictions. However, in view of the fact that there is no systematic increase in the quantum of sentence cumulated within the first block, where the discriminations on this factor of the sum of the sentences for the secondary counts are comparatively fine, yet across a substantial range and with several instances contributing to the estimate for each level, the evidence here for more than a rough-and-ready effect of the sum of the sentences for the secondary counts must be regarded as uncertain.

It appears that Judge 7 applies the first of the main two principles of the alternative decision model governing cumulation of sentence but that its influence on his thinking at more than a coarse level is at best weak and inconsistent.

The second principle is the effect of the quantum of sentence appropriate to the principal offence on the degree of concurrence. The relevant data are in Table 9.13. (Cases 12–14, and 37–38 could not be grouped.)

There is no trend across Table 9.13 in regard to the effect of the sentence appropriate to the principal offence on the degree of cumulation of the sentences for the multiple secondary counts on that sentence. Within each block, with the more-serious principal offences there is not a corresponding decrease in the percentage cumulation and resulting in a quantum of cumulation which is lower but of a sufficient magnitude to ensure a higher effective sentence, as would be expected under the alternative decision model; although it may be said that perhaps there is a hint of the predicted pattern for the levels of sentence for the principal offence of seven and eleven years, in the top block. In relation to this finding the point should be made that the range on the factor of the sentence for the principal offence and the quantum of sentence marking its upper level are not insignificant here.

It is clear from these data that in the general run of cases Judge 7 does not apply the second of the main two principles of the alternative decision model governing cumulation of sentence. Of course, it is possible that in cases characterized by very high levels on this factor of the sentence for the principal offence it would influence this judge's thinking in the predicted way. What can be concluded with some confidence, however, is that in respect of this element of policy Judge 7's decision making is not finely honed.

Table 9.13 *Effect on cumulation of the sentence for the principal offence in the fictitious cases – Judge 7*

Case nos.[a]	No. of cases/level	Sum of sentence(s) for the secondary count(s) (yrs.)	Sentence for the principal offence (yrs.)	Percentage cumulation (mean)	Quantum of sentence cumulated (mean yrs.)	Effective sentence (mean yrs.)
17–19, 21–22,	5	5.5[b], 6, 12, 14, 22	4.5	33	3.1	7.6
24–26, 28–29,			7.0	35	3.3	10.3
31–33, 35–36			11.0	29	2.8	13.8
11, 15, 23, 27	2	1.5, 3	4.0	59	1.3	5.3
			8.0	67	1.5	9.5
16, 20, 30, 34	2	2, 3	5.5	50	1.3	6.8
			12.0	59	1.5	13.5

Note: [a] Case numbers refer to Exercises 3B and 3C.
[b] 6 in Case 35.

In summary, the four judges varied in regard to the degree of precision and reliability with which they applied the factor of the sum of the sentences for the multiple secondary offences to the degree of cumulation. At one extreme, Judge 1 was able to make quite fine and consistent discriminations; at the other extreme, Judge 5's thinking was apparently influenced only at high levels of this factor; while the performances of Judge 4 and Judge 7 fell between these two. In regard to the effect of the sentence for the principal offence on cumulation, it showed no influence on the thinking of Judges 4 and 7, its effect for Judge 5 was uncertain, and the variance on this factor for Judge 1 was too narrow to provide a valid test of its role in his thinking. The point should be made that for the four judges there was not a very substantial range on this latter factor. In fact had the variation on the former factor been as restricted, the evidence for its effect on the degree of cumulation would not have been strong.

This is as appropriate a point as any in the presentation of the results to show for the record the effective sentences imposed by these four judges for the twenty-eight cases of multiple offending comprising Exercises 3B and 3C. They are presented in Table 9.14. The table also presents the range of sentence for each case. As well, it shows the mean of each column of sentences for each of the judges; it is apparent from the sentences in the table that the left-hand set of cases was generally regarded as less serious and the right-hand set as more serious. The first point to note is that the judges differed between themselves in regard to the severity of the punishments they were prepared to impose; the rankings of the judges in this matter are not inconsistent across both sets of cases, but the variation is particularly marked for the more serious set. The immediate mechanism for this disparity must be the sentences considered appropriate to the counts comprising the cases and/or the degree of cumulation of the secondary sentences. In respect of Judge 4's levels of sentence, it should be recalled that he undertook Exercise 3C much later than did the other judges and thought that by then he might have become more severe in his approach to sentencing in response to his perception of a new mood in the community for more-severe sentences for serious multiple offenders. This factor may explain all or part of his apparent greater severity. Nevertheless, the previous comment on the extent of the disparity between the judges still holds good, since this judge alone was not responsible for the variation observed. And in view of this observation it is not surprising that the diversity in the levels of sentence across the judges for each of the cases is generally not inconsequential for the less serious set of cases and is somewhat alarming for the more serious set; no doubt, the variation characterizing each range represents individual differences in the judges' assessment of offence seriousness and within-judge inconsistency in the determination of sentence.

Table 9.14 *Effective sentences (years) for the fictitious cases of multiple offending – Judges 1, 4, 5 and 7*

Case no.[a]	Judge 1	4	5	7	Range	Case no.[a]	Judge 1	4	5	7	Range
11	5.3	5.5	4.5	5.0	1.0	25	7.8	11.5	9.3	10.0	3.7
12	4.3	5.5	3.8	5.5	1.7	26	7.8	12.5	9.5	10.5	4.7
13	4.6	6.5	4.0	6.0	2.5	27	7.5	8.5	7.0	10.0	3.0
14	4.9	7.5	4.0	7.0	3.5	28	7.0	11.5	10.0	10.0	4.5
15	5.8	6.5	5.5	5.5	1.0	29	8.5	12.3	10.0	11.0	3.8
16	6.5	6.0	5.0	6.5	1.5	30	8.3	11.0	10.0	13.0	4.7
17	5.8	6.5	6.8	7.0	1.2	31	7.8	14.5	10.5	13.0	6.7
18	6.2	7.5	6.8	7.5	1.3	32	8.8	15.5	10.8	13.0	6.7
19	6.8	8.5	6.5	8.0	2.0	33	8.8	16.5	11.0	14.0	7.7
20	6.8	6.5	6.5	7.0	0.5	34	8.5	11.5	11.0	14.0	5.5
21	7.0	7.5	7.8	7.5	0.8	35	8.0	15.5	11.5	14.0	7.5
22	6.2	8.3	8.0	8.0	2.1	36	8.8	17.0	12.0	15.0	8.2
23	7.3	6.5	6.5	9.0	2.5	37	10.3	14.5	14.0	16.0	5.7
24	6.8	10.5	9.3	10.0	3.7	38	13.5	20.5	15.0	20.0	7.0
Mean	6.0	7.1	6.1	7.1			8.7	13.8	10.8	13.1	

Note: [a] Case numbers refer to Exercises 3B and 3C.

Quantifying the alternative decision model

What follows is a conceptual and empirical analysis aimed at translating the main two principles of the alternative decision model into a quantitative form capable of generating effective sentences for cases from the appropriate sentences for the counts comprising those cases. According to the model, the dependent variable is the proportion of the sentences appropriate to each of the secondary counts made concurrent with the sentence for the principal offence, and the independent variables are the sentence appropriate to the principal offence and the sum of the sentences appropriate to each of the multiple secondary counts.

On both theoretical and empirical grounds there are powerful reasons for proceeding on the assumption that the functions relating the two independent variables to the dependent variable are the same. The model postulates that both variables must provide for cumulation by way of decreasing gains, but does not otherwise discriminate between their effects; in such circumstances the principle of parsimony requires one rather than two functions. This is the theoretical consideration. The empirical ground relates to the fact that it is difficult to get much of a range of sentence on the principal offence; this holds true even for an offence like armed robbery, varying as it does in its individual circumstances from relatively minor to very serious, not the least reason being that most combinations of minor or very serious cases of armed robbery with other offences, say multiple burglaries, appear to be improbable in real life. Yet this variable must be incorporated in the model and quantified, since according to the model to the extent it does vary it is important; in view of its narrow range, this can be done only if the functions relating the two independent variables to the dependent variable are treated as the same so that the data relating to the estimation of the function governing the sum of the sentences appropriate to the multiple secondary counts can be used to estimate the effect of the sentence appropriate to the principal offence.

The sentencing data from Exercises 3B and 3C show that the range on the principal offence for Judges 1, 4, 5 and 7 was, respectively, only 4, 8.5, 6.5 and 8.5 years; this, despite the fact that the previously reported interviews after Exercise 3A revealed general agreement among the judges that the least and most serious single counts of armed robbery approached, respectively, the lower and upper levels on the dimension of offence seriousness for this offence. This is to be contrasted with the range on the sum of the sentences for the multiple secondary counts for the same judges of, respectively, 88, 82.5, 91.5 and 102.5 years. In view of this it would be expected that the effect of the former variable would be comparatively small, given its range; indeed, hard to detect, considering the imprecise nature of decision making. One conclusion following from these two points is that the assumption of equality of the two functions is empirically necessary for the analysis to proceed. The second conclusion is that this assumption is reasonable: should there be a theoretical difference between these two variables in terms of their effect on the dependent variable it would be expected to be of little practical significance in view of the narrow range covered by the sentence appropriate to the principal offence, especially since both independent variables must provide for de-creasing gains; indeed, perhaps the difference would be within the magnitude of the error for their estimation.

In line with the approach to modelling adopted in this study, it is preferable that the data used to quantify the functions relating the variables in the model and the model be compatible: in the present context this means that a judge's sentencing practice gives effect to the main two principles of the alternative decision model. The earlier analyses showed that it was only Judge 1 who satisfied this criterion: in respect of the sum of the sentences for the multiple secondary counts, as the value of this factor increased, so this judge ordered a lower percentage cumulation, the decrement being tempered so that a greater quantum of sentence was added for more serious and additional secondary counts; this is an outcome consistent with the model; in respect of the sentence for the principal offence, this judge's range on this factor was minimal and, accordingly, the absence of a relationship between it and the percentage cumulation could not be regarded as sentencing behavior inconsistent with the model. It follows that the responses of Judge 1, and the responses of this judge only, could be used to quantify the alternative decision model.

The first step in this process was to quantify the relationship between the degree of cumulation and the sum of the sentences for the multiple secondary counts. It is apparent from Table 9.6 that while the trend is strong, it is a relationship characterized by irregularities; these had to be removed. To do this, the mean percentage cumulation was calculated for each level of the sum of the sentences for the secondary counts; this was not done separately for the various levels of the sentence for the principal offence, since this factor had no effect on the degree of cumulation. (Thus, for the sum of sentence equal to one year, the mean was based on four cases.) Next, these mean percentage cumulations were plotted against the corresponding ten levels of the sum of the sentences for the multiple secondary counts. Finally, a curve of apparent best fit was drawn for these data, from which the adjusted percentage cumulations could be derived for the ten levels.

There was now the data for a graph of the relationship between the degree of cumulation, the sentence for the principal offence and the sum of sentences for the multiple secondary counts; it had to show the degree of cumulation for all of the likely combinations of the sentence for the principal offence and the sum of sentences for the secondary offences. This raised the problem of how this graph should be constructed. The solution was that it be done in accordance with the decision structure, including the components and sequence, inherent in the alternative decision model. It will be recalled that the judge first considers the sentence fixed for the principal offence and this determines what scope is left for the quantum of cumulation upon this sentence to reflect the seriousness of the multiple secondary counts as defined by the sum of the sentences appropriate to them – the higher the sentence for the principal offence, the less scope there is for cumulation. Accordingly, the sentence for the principal offence must be the first of the two factors to be incorporated in the graph. This was done by assuming a multiple-count case in which there is a quantum of sentence (P) associated with the principal offence and the sum of sentences for the secondary counts is infinitesimally small $\left(S_{S\rightarrow 0} \right)$. The graph would show the degree of cumulation (C) appropriate to $S_{S\rightarrow 0}$ for the given P. Now, assume a second multiple-count case in which the sentence for the principal offence is greater (P′) and again the sum of

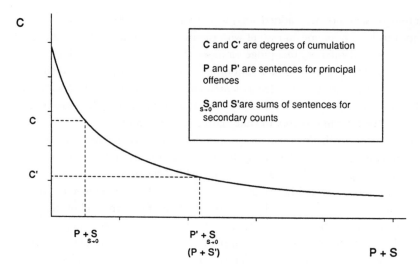

Figure 9.1 Schematic representation of the alternative decision model

sentences for the secondary counts is infinitesimally small $\left(\underset{S\to 0}{S}\right)$. In this case, by way of comparison, the degree of cumulation for the same sum of sentences for the secondary counts $\left(\underset{S\to 0}{S}\right)$ would be lower (C′), since the sentence for the principal offence is greater (namely, P′). This is shown in Figure 9.1, with its curve of decreasing returns as required by the alternative decision model.

This step having been taken, the judge then determines the quantum of cumulation to reflect the seriousness of the multiple secondary counts – within the constraint on cumulation imposed by the first decision, the higher the sum of the sentences for the secondary counts, the less the degree of cumulation on the sentence for the principal offence for those counts. Now, since it may be assumed that the functions for the two independent variables are the same, the effect of the sum of sentences for the multiple secondary counts on the degree of cumulation can be represented on the above curve showing the effect of the sentence for the principal offence on the degree of (scope for) cumulation for those counts. It follows that for a multiple-count case in which the sentence for the principal offence is P and the sum of the sentences for the secondary offences is S′, where S′ is equal to P′ − P, the degree of cumulation appropriate to the sum of sentences for the secondary offences would be C′, as it was for the above case in which the sentence for the principal offence was P′ and the sum of sentences for the secondary counts was infinitesimally small. In terms of the above diagram, the point P′ + $\underset{S\to 0}{S}$ is the same as the point P + S′.

The procedure can be described in terms of the decision process. Consider a

Table 9.15 *Prototypic relationship between the total sentence for a case (years) and the percentage cumulation – Judge 1*

Total sentence for a case (yrs.)	Percentage cumulation
7.0	37
7.5	35
9.0	26
10.0	24
13.0	19
17.0	15
5.5	35
7.5	25
9.5	21
9.0	37
9.5	35
33.5	9
97.0	6

case in which the sentence for the principal offence is P. According to Figure 9.1, the scope for cumulation – the degree of cumulation where the sum of sentences for the secondary offences is insignificant $\left(\underset{S\to 0}{S}\right)$ – is C. Now, where the sum of the sentences for the secondary offences is not insignificant (S'), the degree of cumulation for these sentences must be reduced and would be C'.

In the light of this analysis, the graph showing the degree of cumulation for all of the likely combinations of the sentence for the principal offence and the sum of sentences for the secondary offences should be constructed by plotting the degree of cumulation against the total of the sentence appropriate to the principal offence and the sum of the sentences appropriate to the multiple secondary counts. It will be recalled that the degree of cumulation is made on the basis of the total seriousness of the case viewed globally; Figure 9.1 sets the scene for the numerical operationalization of this concept.

The relevant data for Judge 1 are in Table 9.15. The figures for the composite independent variable – total sentence for the case – are derived directly from Table 9.6; and the figures for the dependent variable – proportion of the sentences appropriate to the secondary counts made cumulative on the sentence for the principal offence – are the adjusted percentage cumulations, derived as described above. Each row in Table 9.6 provides one entry for Table 9.15; for example, in the first, the sum of sentences for the secondary counts is 1.0 year and the sentence for the principal offence is 6.0 years (the

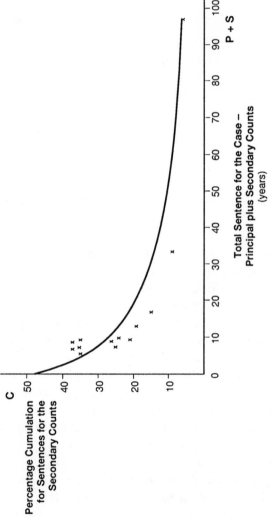

Figure 9.2 Prototypic relationship between the Percentage Cumulation and the Total Sentence for a Case – Judge 1

mean of the sentences for the principal offences), the total sentence for the case being 7.0 years; the corresponding adjusted percentage cumulation is 37. The graph of these data is presented in Figure 9.2.

Finally, to quantify the functions relating the total sentence for a case to the degree of cumulation for the sentences for the secondary counts, in line with requisite modelling it was necessary to find an algebraic model which was consistent with the main two principles of the alternative decision model – it is in this sense that the data are fitted to a model – and then to fit *this* model to these data. It follows from the decision model that the algebraic function must satisfy the following three requirements:

(1) provide for cumulation of sentence by way of decreasing gains;
(2) cross the C axis and at a value of C of not more than 100 percent;
(3) be asymptotic on the P + S axis.

There are two algebraic models satisfying these three theoretical criteria – the negative exponential function and the reciprocal function – and they are defined respectively by the following two formulae:

$$C = ae^{-b(P+S)} \quad C = \frac{a}{1 + b(P + S)}$$

where C is the proportion of the sentences appropriate to each of the multiple secondary counts made cumulative on the sentence for the principal offence, as a percentage; P is the sentence appropriate to the principal offence, in years; S is the sum of the sentences appropriate to each of the multiple secondary counts, in years; and a and b are constants, determined in the process of fitting the model to the data set.

These two models were fitted to the data in Table 9.15.[2] In regard to these data considered as a whole, both models provided reasonable degrees of fit, as shown by an inspection of the graphs. (The residual sums of squares for the negative exponential and reciprocal curves were, respectively, 316 and 288.) In the interpretation of the adequacy of a model's fit, it must be understood that comparatively small deviations between the values of the degree of cumulation (C) in the data and those generated by the model are of little consequence at low levels of the total sentence for a case (P + S) but assume critical significance at high levels of this latter variable. (For example, for $P = 2$, $S = 5$, it makes little difference to the quantum of sentence cumulated whether C is 31 or 34; but for, say, $P = 12$, $S = 100$, the difference between

[2] Appreciation is due to Dr Pip Pattison, Department of Psychology, University of Melbourne, for running this analysis. She used the modified Gauss-Newton algorithm and the BMDP 3R program (Dixon, 1990).

a C of 3 and a C of 6 is substantial not only in regard to the quantum of sentence cumulated but also in view of the already long sentence to which it is being added.) In this respect, for the value of P + S = 97 months, the value of C on the exponential curve was 0.1 percent and for the reciprocal curve was 3.7 percent, against the data figure of 6 percent. Thus, the reciprocal function provided not only a better overall fit, but also a better approximation to the data at the upper levels on the composite independent variable. Now, one of the problems in fitting a model to these particular data so that it provides a veridical representation of the judge's decision making is that the critical high levels on the composite independent variable are represented by just one point, in comparison with the multiple values at the lower levels, and accordingly are underweighted in the curve-fitting process. For this reason the model providing the better fit – the reciprocal function – was refitted to the data with the comparatively loose constraint that for the value of P + S = 97 the value of C must lie within the range not greater than 7.0 or less than 5.0. The curve fitted to the data according to this process is shown in Figure 9.2; the values of the constants a and b are 47.9 and 0.0737, respectively, and the residual sum of squares for this model is 360.

This model is the numerical representation of the main elements of Judge 1's determination of effective sentences for cases comprising multiple counts from separate transactions, once appropriate sentences have been fixed for these counts; it shows the degree of cumulation of the sentences for the secondary counts on the sentence for the principal offence, and does this for all possible combinations of the sentence appropriate to the principal offence and the sum of the sentences appropriate to the secondary counts. By way of illustration of its application, consider a case comprising three counts for which the appropriate sentences are 5, 4 and 4 years: the sentence for the principal offence is 5 years, the sum of sentences for the secondary counts is 8 years and, from the formula, the degree of cumulation for these secondary counts is 24.5 percent, i.e., 1.96 years, making an effective sentence for the case of 6.96 years.

Consonant with the idea of requisite modelling, the now quantified decision model of Judge 1 represents a prototype of a first draft of this element of sentencing policy; had it been born of a representative sample of experienced judges this product could have been regarded as functional rather than merely illustrative and in that capacity put before the judges with a view to their developing a greater understanding of the basis of their decision and greater insight into the sentencing problem. It would be important to test the reasonableness of the effective sentences generated by this model for a comprehensive range of realistic combinations of sentences for the principal offence and sums of sentences for the secondary counts.

Several points must be made about the algebraic model used to describe Judge 1's sentencing behavior. First, it is not a necessary requirement that the curve fits the data closely. The reason for this is that the judge may not have given logical and consistent effect across the range of the composite independent variable to his stated approach to this sentencing problem. Indeed, an inspection of the data points in Figure 9.2 suggests that he did not: if a curve of best fit were drawn for these data, either it would be asymptotic on the dependent variable or it would cross the C axis at a value much greater than 100. Now, so as to be consistent with the idea of requisite modelling, the criterion adopted here for the process of curve-fitting was not simply one of best fit, but of best fit within the constraint that it be consistent with the prescriptions of the decision model. The second point is that the reciprocal model as quantified here may not be a veridical representation of this judge's sentencing, even to the extent that he applied his policy coherently; the reason for this is threefold. The first two components relate to the complete absence of data at the lowest levels of the composite independent variable and the paucity and, accordingly, likely unreliability of the data at the higher levels. The third is less obvious. It will be recalled that in an earlier analysis for this judge (see Table 9.2 and the associated discussion) there was evidence in the sentencing data that where the total sentence for a case was high he may have imposed somewhat lower than appropriate sentences for the secondary counts partially to offset the potentially crushing effects of cumulation. If, indeed, the judge did adopt this strategy, the values for the degree of cumulation would be greater than they would have been with appropriate sentences. Now, the effect of this on a curve showing the relationship between cumulation and appropriate sentences, the purpose of Figure 9.2, is that the data points representing the more serious cases would be artifactually low on the composite independent variable and high on the dependent variable.

The product of the preceding theoretical and empirical analyses associated with the earlier sentencing problems and the later fictitious cases is an outline of a proposal for guidelines taking the form of written policy statements – the principles of the alternative decision model set out in Chapter 7 – and the just-derived numerical decision aid for the sentencing of the multiple offender. These guidelines are a manifestation of a model of judicial decision making in sentencing, a model accurately described by two epithets, ideal and created – its formulation being based on what judges believe upon reflection should be the main principles of proper policy and how they should be applied, the judges' view of their application being modified only to an extent necessary to ensure a logical, coherent and precise approach.

As a complement to this, the alternative decision model, as operationalized in Figure 9.1, can be applied to archival data in order to describe judicial sentencing practice. To illustrate this, Lovegrove (1996) analyzed cases determined in the Victorian Court of Criminal Appeal over a ten-year period. For each of the sixty-nine offenders whose case was included in the study, an armed robbery was the principal offence. Again, a reciprocal function was found to provide the better fit to the data, further supporting this general algebraic model as a valid description of the judicial decision strategy for sentencing the multiple offender.

It is appropriate to close this chapter with a brief overview of relevant algebraic models to be found in psychological contributions to the study of the legal system. The reciprocal function is a mathematical (algebraic) representation of a cognitive process governing the determination of an effective sentence for a multiple offender once sentences have been fixed for the individual counts. At this point in time it does not appear to have a competitor. Indeed, the development of algebraic models of decision making in sentencing is a largely unexplored field.

There have been, as discussed in Chapter 1, attempts to quantify the relationship between case fact and sentence using multivariate analyses such as multiple regression. However, these were not attempts to represent algebraically the judges' underlying decision process and, since no thought was given to this, not surprisingly, the implicit structure of these statistical models is incompatible with the structure of judicial thought.

The exploratory nature of psychology's contribution to the study of decision making in sentencing can be seen in the thoughtful contribution of Hommers and Anderson (1989). Their purpose was to consider possible algebraic schemes for the integration of information in the process of determining deserved punishment. The components of the assessment of deserved punishment were assumed to be the offender's culpability, the harm suffered by the victim and the recompense by the offender to the victim, and the problem was to discover how assessments made in regard to these three factors are integrated. The proposed solution was underpinned by Anderson's theory of information integration and the associated methodology of functional measurement. The authors in illustrating the approach asked specifically: does recompense reduce deserved punishment by subtraction or by multiplication, or by some other operation?

There appear to be four general problems associated with this proposal. First, the conceptual framework is so general as to be little more than schematic. Indeed, what is required is account to be taken of relevant sentencing law and principle, but for this advance the analysis would need necessarily to be jurisdiction specific. For example, in Victoria remorse, which may well be related to recompense, may reduce the severity of what would otherwise be the deserved sentence by mitigating the offender's culpability and, under certain circumstances, also by enhancing the offender's claims to rehabilitation (see Lovegrove, 1989). Secondly, the three component factors of culpability, harm and recompense are treated as unidimensional for the purposes of assigning values to them. Yet these factors are multidimensional, the comprising components themselves requiring assessment and integration, a difficult theoretical and empirical problem in itself, as the work of Lovegrove (1989) demonstrated (see Chapter 2). The preceding applies to single counts; multiple offending adds further to the complexity as the present study shows. Thirdly, Hommers and Anderson explicitly assume that judges' cognitive processes are highly structured, on the ground that legal thought is a well-developed system of knowledge. The empirical work in the present study provides strong evidence against the validity of this assumption. Fourthly, functional measurement for its implementation requires that the case factors be incorporated in factorial designs. The problem here is that many of the offence–offender combinations would be unrealistic or improbable, and the responses to them, even if judges are prepared to enter into the spirit of the exercise and make them, would be of questionable validity (see Chapter 8). Moreover, there would appear to be limits to the applicability in practice of functional measurement; for example, with greater complexity, the number of cases required to satisfy a factorial design would probably become prohibitive. There is a fifth problem, specific to the present study. Research according to the theory of information integration has demonstrated that the weighted average of the relevant evaluative components and the initial impression describes the process of combination in a variety of judgment tasks. Although this scheme could be readily applied in principle to the problem of relating offence facts to quantum of sentence for single-count cases (see Chapter 2), it is difficult to conceive that it could ever rival the reciprocal function in the multiple-count case.

A more specific and direct example of the application of psychological theory to decision making in sentencing is to be found in the research of McKnight (1981). He adapted two psychological theories and applied them in a complementary way to predict sentence. The two theories, multi-attribute utility theory and personal construct theory, were used to identify and link sentencing objectives, their importance, and the extent to which a particular sentence would achieve an aim. The former theory was used to quantify the relationship between sentence and how the case was construed according to its components. These components, the aims of sentencing and their assessment in regard to a case, were elicited according to the latter theory. It was predicted that judges would impose the sentence with the highest subjective expected utility. The utility of a sentence was defined as the rating of a sentence in relation to a goal of sentence (i.e., the extent to which a sentence would achieve a goal for the case under consideration) multiplied by the weight assigned to that construct (i.e., the importance of that goal for that case). This product was added to similarly derived products for each goal of possible significance, and the utility of a sentence was the sum of these products. This calculation was repeated for each of the possible sentences. McKnight elicited this information from sentencers in a simulation exercise and found that he was able to predict the sentences imposed there with a high degree of accuracy. However, Lovegrove (1989) concluded that in order to be useful for guidance it would be necessary (1) to establish the grounds relied on by judges in their assessment of the extent to which a sentence would achieve a particular goal for a given case and in their assessment of the importance of that goal for that case and (2) to quantify these assessments in relation to the facts of the offence and circumstances of the offender in a particular case. In regard to the present project, which assumes only one goal of sentence – proportionality according to seriousness – McKnight's analysis fails because it could not be used to quantify the relationship between the component sentences and the effective sentence, but would leave it as an intuitive decision. It should be noted here in parenthesis that Fitzmaurice and Pease's (1986) important analysis of the nature of the proportionality between case seriousness and sentence in terms of psychophysics and the power function similarly does not deal with the construction of seriousness from the elements of the case.

A second major weakness of McKnight's (1981) analysis would appear to lie in the implied nature of the decision process, namely the strategy of moving backwards from the sentence to the case. Surely, this begs the question of how judges select which sentences are to be tested for their appropriateness? Now, it may (or may not) be a reasonable representation of the process for the decision as to type of sanction (e.g., imprisonment or a probation-type measure), but would appear to be highly contrived where the task is to fine-tune sentence within a particular sanction (e.g., setting a quantum of imprisonment so that its severity is proportional to case seriousness). Indeed, the judicial decision strategy discerned in the present study implies a process of moving forwards from the components of the case – the quanta of sentence appropriate to the comprising counts – to the effective sentence.

In stark contrast with the position in sentencing research, psychology's contribution in the form of algebraic representations of cognitive processes is well advanced in the area of juror decision making (see, particularly, Hastie, 1993, and, also, Pennington and Hastie, 1993). In this development, Anderson's (1981) theory of information integration has played an important role. This body of research is of only limited interest to the present study, since there are significant differences between the two areas in respect of both decision and decision maker. However, two matters are of interest to the study of multiple-offender sentencing. First, the usefulness of the weighted averaging model in juror decision making (see Hastie, 1993) is unlikely to hold for the judicial sentencing of multiple offenders, as intimated above. The second point arises from the fact that there are two general algebraic processes proposed for juror decision making (see Hastie, 1993). One is a global strategy, in which the final judgment is the weighted average of an initial opinion and evaluations from subsequent evidence, the process being performed as a one-step calculation once all the evidence has been presented. The second is a sequential strategy, in which each new piece of evidence is evaluated and on this basis the running judgment is revised, again by a rule of weighted averaging. The difficulty with this latter strategy, according to Hastie (1993), is that often the relevant questions or dimensions of the judgment are not known to the juror until the presentation of the evidence has been concluded. This distinction has its parallel in the sentencing of the multiple offender. In the alternative decision model (see Chapter 7) the determination of an effective sentence is made globally in regard to the component sentences. This must be, since, to fix a quantum of sentence appropriate to the seriousness of the case as a whole, regard must first be paid to all the quanta of sentence of which account must be taken; a sequential strategy, in which a degree of cumulation was determined for the sentence for the first of the secondary counts without consideration being given to the sentences appropriate to the other secondary counts would not permit the required proportionality to be achieved.

CHAPTER TEN

The armature of judicial sentencing

To this point in the current study two quite conceptually distinct decision models of sentencing in cases comprising multiple counts, properly regarded as separate transactions, have been proposed: one model applies where all the offences belong to the same legal offence category and the other covers circumstances where at least two of the offences belong to different statutory offence categories. The task of this chapter is to integrate these two models in order to complete the decision framework underpinning the judicial determination of sentence, and to consider how this decision structure is to play its role as a numerical guideline.

Now, the decision model for multiple offences of the same type cannot be applied to the problem of determining the effective sentence for a case comprising separate types of offence, since the parameters of this model are defined in terms specific to a particular type of offence and treat the series of offences globally (see Chapter 3). So, for example, the measure of organization as an offence factor is not aggregated across each of the counts but is measured in terms of what is the characteristic level for that series of offences; now, clearly, this definition cannot be applied where the comprising offences belong to different offence categories, since the way in which organization is manifest varies with the type of offence. However, the decision model for multiple offences of a different type can be used to determine the effective sentence for a case comprising offences belonging to the same offence category, since it operates by way of the aggregation of the appropriate sentences for the comprising counts. The point should be made parenthetically that only the former model – the model for multiple offences of the same type – can be used to determine the quantum of sentence appropriate to single counts; of course, the offence factor relating to the number of counts is not then relevant and, even though the structure of the model is invariant across offence types, the constituent offence factors, and particularly the operational definition of these factors, are specific to a particular legal offence category.

Consider a case comprising a series of offences belonging to the same legal offence category, say multiple counts of burglary, and there is information about the facts of the offences covering the violence to the victims, the value of the theft in each of the counts, the organization of the offences, and the number of counts; assume also that sentencing policy in regard to the elements of the decision model is known, i.e., there is a seriousness scale for each factor, the relative weight of each of the offence factors in the determination of total seriousness is known and the scale showing the relationship between case seriousness and effective sentence has been established (this last element being for an assumed criminal history and mitigation of the offender). In these circumstances the effective sentence appropriate to the case can be determined in one of two ways. First, the decision model applying to multiple offences of the same type could be applied directly to this information to calculate the effective sentence appropriate to the total seriousness of this series of burglaries (see Chapter 2). Alternatively, the same decision model could be used to calculate the sentence appropriate to the seriousness of each of the counts of burglary comprising the case; then, with this information (set of quanta of sentence) the alternative decision model for multiple offences of a different type could be used directly to calculate the effective sentence appropriate to this series of burglaries. To do this, one of the counts would be deemed to be the principal offence (the count with the highest sentence) and the sentences for the other counts would be partially cumulated on it, according to the formula representing the alternative model (see Chapter 9).

When one of the two decision models for cases comprising multiple counts covers counts belonging both to the same and different legal offence categories, whereas the other can be applied only to multiple counts of the same type, a question arises over whether the latter model should be retained for the task of aggregating sentence across counts of the same type. There are two grounds for answering this question in the negative. The first is the principle of parsimony. Simplicity is to be preferred to complexity, and the maintenance of two models when one would suffice is in this context an unjustifiable extravagance. This conclusion is warranted, of course, only where there is little or nothing to be gained from the greater complexity. This leads to the second point. Not only does the model covering multiple counts of the same kind not offer advantages, it is actually inferior to the other as a basis for the cumulation of sentence across counts of the same type, the problem to which it applies. This arises from the way in which this decision model conceptualizes the total seriousness of a case: specifically, the seriousness of organization and violence are viewed globally as the seriousness of the level of organization characteristic of the counts and the seriousness of the most violent of the counts, respectively (see Chapter 2). Consider two cases, each comprising four counts; in one, each of the counts is characterized by a high level of violence, whereas in the other only one of the counts could be described as violent, the two cases being similar in all other material respects. Now, justice would seem to require that a higher sentence be passed in the former instance, but the model applying only to counts of the same kind would not distinguish the total seriousness of these two cases. By way of comparison, effective sentences calculated on the basis of the model applying to both same and different counts would not be the same in the two cases in this illustration, since cumulation is by way of the sentence appropriate to each of the comprising counts, hence account would be taken of the disparity in the seriousness of the individual counts in respect of violence and this would be reflected in a higher calculated effective sentence in the first example. A similar illustration could be given for the offence factor of organization. Accordingly, it follows that the model applying only to cases comprising counts of the same type should be disposed of for the purpose of calculating effective sentences. (Of course, this model, minus the factor relating to the number of counts, would still be required to calculate the sentence appropriate to each of the counts comprising a case.) From this it can be concluded that the other model (labelled in Chapter 7 as the alternative decision model), applying as it does to cases comprising multiple counts belonging both to the same and different legal offence categories, can be regarded as a general model for determining effective sentences in all cases comprising multiple counts properly regarded as separate transactions.

The conclusion having been reached that the decision model applying only to cases comprising counts of the same kind is of no practical use in determining effective sentences, it might be presumed that it can be regarded as no more than a relic of the quest to understand the sentencing process for the multiple offender and to develop a sound policy and system of numerical guidance for this sentencing problem. Nothing could be further from the truth. But first, before this can be explained, a preamble is necessary to set the scene. There is a serious conceptual gap in the alternative decision model. While it provides for cumulation of custodial sentences for multiple counts, but by way of decreasing gains, this decision model has no framework for determining as a matter of principle the appropriate degree of constraint on the cumulation of sentence (see Chapter 7). For an assumed case comprising multiple counts of a given number and level of seriousness, any one of an infinite number of effective sentences within the range from almost full to just short of zero concurrency could be constructed so as to be consistent with the principle of decreasing returns, the variation in the actual value calculated for the effective sentence depending, in terms of Figure 9.2, in effect, on the degree of concurrence of the sentence for the first secondary offence and, across the remainder of the counts, the rate of increase in the percentage made concurrent. One justification for the use of decreasing returns – the reason coming most readily to the minds of the judges in this study (see Chapter 6) – is that it makes possible effective sentences which are not crushing. This concept is not helpful in respect of the problem of quantifying the degree of constraint on the process of aggregation because it is generally not determinative on this matter; it can be advanced as a reason whenever something less than full cumulation is ordered. Indeed, within the normal working range in sentencing, it is applied to cases comprising counts of an order of seriousness warranting moderate custodial sentences as well as to cases comprising relatively serious counts. Yet the constraint on cumulation of sentences in the middle of the range on the grounds that the outcome would otherwise be crushing is as far as it goes inconsistent with the same courts' not uncommonly approving very substantial sentences. No, the connotation of the notion of crushing is one of moderation, its significance increasing with the seriousness of the case. It is only at uncommonly very high levels of sentence, perhaps twenty-five years, that the notion of crushing becomes determinative, its import then shifting to that of a general absolute ceiling. (This argument holds only when, as in the present study, the notion of the crushing sentence is given as a reason for constraint on cumulation of sentence but without consideration being given to specific characteristics of the offender. By way of contrast, this notion can be determinative for the purposes of sentencing in discriminating between cases in respect of certain offender characteristics, such as age.)

Nevertheless, there is a second justification for the principle of decreasing returns and, fortunately, it appears to offer a framework from which a principled solution can be found for the problem of determining the appropriate degree of constraint on the cumulation of sentence: it is that cumulation by way of decreasing gains at once permits more severe effective sentences for more serious and numerous counts and yet makes it possible to avoid violating the principle that the severity of the effective sentence be appropriate to the seriousness of the legal category of the offences comprising the case – the thrust of the totality principle (see Chapter 1). How can this justification be used to determine constraint on cumulation in the alternative decision model? Its application is better illustrated with offences of low or moderate seriousness, since violations of the principle are probably more readily sensed on intuitive grounds at these levels of sentence. Burglary as a principal offence was chosen for this purpose, because the conceptual analysis of offence seriousness upon which the solution depends has already been made in Lovegrove's previous study of judicial decision making (see Chapter 2).

A rule that the sum of the individual appropriate sentences for the counts comprising a case may be excessive if its severity is appropriate to an offence belonging to a significantly more serious class of crime would provide guidance only when the total warranted the epithet egregious. Thomas (1979), in formulating working rules for the determination of the limiting quantum of sentence for a case, expressed his approach in several ways (see Chapter 1): presented in the terms used in this study, one is that the effective sentence may be longer than the appropriate sentence for the most serious of the offences comprising the case but must bear some recognizable relationship to it; a second version is that the effective sentence should not be above the upper limit of the normal range of sentence appropriate to the legal category of the most serious of the comprising counts. Again, the violation of the first rule could be detected only if the effective sentence was manifestly excessive. In respect of the second rule, the standard for the appropriateness of an effective sentence could be sentencing statistics of actual court practice: for a case comprising multiple counts of, say, burglary, or comprising a principal offence of burglary together with multiple secondary counts less serious than the burglary (seriousness being defined by quantum of sentence), the imposed effective sentence would come under suspicion of being excessive if it was above the range of effective sentences imposed in the courts for cases in which the principal offence is burglary. As a basis for ascertaining a rough guide to the upper limits on aggregation in current practice this rule is satisfactory. Alas, it is devoid of normative content; it provides no conceptual grounds for determining whether the courts lack sufficient restraint, or perhaps are too timid, in their approach to the cumulation of sentences for multiple counts in cases to which the totality principle applies. Moreover, it offers no guidance for cases where the total severity of the comprising appropriate sentences places them well below the upper limit of the category of offence to which the principal offence belongs.

To infuse some precision into these rules as a basis for guidance on the constraint of cumulation, the conceptual framework developed for the offence seriousness of the legal offence category of burglary was applied to these rules. It will be recalled that the total seriousness of the offence characteristics of a case was scaled in terms of a dimension representing the possible range of seriousness of the offending associated with this legal offence category, partitioned into a composite component available to the seriousness of the offence characteristics used to define the circumstances surrounding the commission of the individual counts (for burglary: violence, organization, and value of the theft) and a component available to the seriousness associated with the number of multiple counts of that offence (here: number of counts of burglary). And Thomas's (1979) "recognizable relationship" between the sentence for the principal offence and the effective sentence for the case was quantified by weighting the dimension of seriousness representing the number of multiple counts in terms of the dimensions of seriousness defining the circumstances of the individual offences. It is this weighting which is the critical element in determining whether the effective sentence bears some recognizable relationship to the quantum of sentence for the most serious of the offences comprising the case; and whether the severity of the sentence falling at the upper limit of the normal range of sentence for the legal category of the comprising counts (the quantum of sentence deemed appropriate to the upper limit of the dimension representing the possible range of seriousness of the legal category of the comprising counts) is excessive. Again, it will be recalled that the weighting was made in terms of a formal decision model and this provided for a rational and coherent relationship between the seriousness of the principal offence and the overall seriousness of the counts comprising the case. This step – the conceptual analysis and the associated judgments required of the judges in respect of seriousness – rests on the validity of the global approach to the determination of sentence in cases comprising multiple counts, and can be entertained only when the multiple counts are of the same kind; hence, the earlier statement that the decision model covering this type of case is vital to understanding the sentencing of the multiple offender.

Discussion now turns to explain how the weighting for the component relating to the number of multiple counts could play a role in quantifying the constraint on cumulation of sentence. Assume that there is an agreed sentencing policy in respect of the elements comprising the decision model conceptualizing seriousness for the offence characteristics of a case comprising multiple counts of burglary. Moreover, for the purposes of the present discussion, assume that total offence seriousness is defined by the components organization, violence to the victims, total value of the theft and the number of multiple counts; that the 0–100 seriousness scales for total value of the theft and the number of multiple counts show that the seriousness of $10,000 and twelve counts is 34 and 55, respectively; that the relative contributions of organization, violence, value and counts to total seriousness are 25, 25, 20 and 30, respectively; and that the relationship between the total seriousness of a single count of burglary (the sum of the offence's scores on the seriousness scales of organization, violence and value, modified by .25, .25 and .20, their

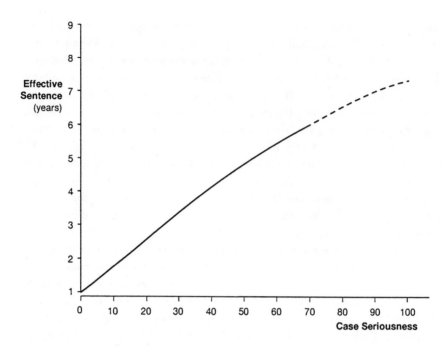

Figure 10.1 A hypothetical relationship between Case Seriousness and Effective Sentence

respective weights) and the quantum of sentence is as shown in Figure 10.1, by the unbroken line (this is, as before, for an offender with an extensive record of relevant prior convictions and very little credit available by way of a plea in mitigation). The horizontal axis represents the dimension covering the possible range of seriousness of the offending associated with the legal offence category of burglary. In view of the weights of the three components used to define the circumstances surrounding the commission of the individual counts, a single offence characterized by a set of facts placing it at the assumed upper limit on each of the three components (e.g., $120,000 for the value of the money and merchandise stolen) would have a total seriousness of 70 (25 + 25 + 20) and warrant a sentence of 6 years' imprisonment, and 1 year would be appropriate to an offence falling at the lower end of this dimension of offence seriousness of burglary. (To formulate the policy, judges would undertake the exercises described in Chapter 2, developing seriousness scales and assessing the relative weights for the four offence factors and determining appropriate sentences for *single* counts of burglary of varying seriousness.)

Once a sentencing policy for a single count of burglary had been established, together with a weight for the component available to the seriousness associated with the number of multiple counts of that offence, then the constraint on cumulation of sentence for multiple counts of burglary could be set in place as a consequence. The total seriousness of a case comprising multiple counts of burglary is the sum of the case's scores on the seriousness scales of organization, violence, value and counts, modified by .25, .25, .20 and .30, their respective weights. The seriousness associated with the counts additional to the principal offence cumulates through the factors of value and counts, the degree to which the seriousness of these counts adds on to the seriousness of the principal offence being constrained by the seriousness scales and weights of these two factors. Assume that the total seriousness of a case comprising multiple counts was 90. The effective sentence appropriate to this particular case could be derived by extrapolating the curve showing the relationship between offence seriousness and sentence for single counts of burglary and then reading off the graph the sentence appropriate to a calculated case seriousness of 90 – 7 years (see Figure 10.1). What is the justification for extrapolating the curve as the means of setting the ceiling? Sentences falling above this line would be prima facie evidence of a change from a policy of decreasing gains towards one of increasing gains in sentence for the additional seriousness arising from extra and more serious multiple counts, a position consistent with an untrammelled approach to the cumulation of sentence. Conversely, sentences falling below this line would be suggestive of an approach in which the additional seriousness associated with multiple counts was not being adequately punished. In this way, then, the decision model relating to counts of the same kind provides a rational basis for quantifying the constraint upon cumulation of sentence in cases of this kind. On a similar basis, the unbroken curve could be used to determine effective sentences for cases of multiple offending whose total seriousness fell below the assumed range of seriousness for single counts of burglary.

The next step is to apply this conceptual framework to determining constraint on cumulation for multiple counts of a different kind. Now, using this decision model for counts of the same kind, it is possible to calculate not only an effective sentence appropriate to a case comprising multiple counts belonging to the same offence category but also sentences appropriate to each of the comprising counts in the case. The following illustration is based on the preceding hypothetical sentencing policy. Consider a case comprising twelve counts of burglary. The seriousness of the offence characteristics of the principal count in regard to the components of organization, violence and value are 50, 50, and 34 on their respective 0–100 seriousness scales; allowing for the weights of the components, the total seriousness would be 32, for which a sentence of $3\frac{1}{2}$ years is appropriate (see Figure 10.1). Since the value stolen in the principal count is \$10,000 (the amount equivalent to a seriousness level of 34), the case can comprise eleven additional counts each involving the same amount stolen before reaching the assumed upper limit of \$120,000 on this component. Furthermore, assume organization is constant across the twelve counts, but the level of violence associated with each additional count is zero on its seriousness scale. Therefore, the total seriousness of each of the additional eleven counts would be 19, for which the appropriate sentence on each count is $2\frac{1}{2}$ years (see Figure 10.1). Now consider the appropriate effective sentence for this case on the basis of the global approach to the determination of case seriousness: the seriousness of the offence characteristics of the case in regard to the components of organization, violence, value and counts would be 50, 50, 100 and 55; allowing for the weights of the components, a total seriousness of 61, for which the corresponding sentence is $5\frac{1}{2}$ years (see Figure 10.1). This is two years greater than the sentence for the principal offence. Accordingly, an additional quantum of sentence of two years would be considered an appropriate degree of cumulation for the eleven multiple secondary counts and the effective sentence of $5\frac{1}{2}$ years would not be deemed to bear an unrecognizable relationship to the sentence of $3\frac{1}{2}$ years for the principal offence. The way in which this decision model, relating to multiple counts of the same kind, can be applied to determine the appropriate degree of constraint on the cumulation of sentences for multiple counts of a different kind follows readily.

   In the alternative decision model, relating to cases comprising multiple counts belonging to different legal offence categories, the effective sentence is dependent on the quantum of sentence appropriate to the principal offence and the sum of the quanta of sentence associated with the multiple secondary offences; moreover, this model does not discriminate between cases comprising counts of the same kind and cases comprising counts of a different kind (see Chapter 7). It follows that the effective sentence for a case comprising one count for which the appropriate sentence was $3\frac{1}{2}$ years and eleven other counts for which the appropriate sentences were $2\frac{1}{2}$ years each would be the same whether or not the counts belong to the same legal offence category or different categories. The problem, intimated above, is that this model provides no rational basis for determining the extent to which cumulation should be constrained; there is no way of deciding whether the constraint according to the function relating the sentence for the principal offence and the sum of the sentences for the multiple secondary offences to the effective sentence (illustrated in Chapter 9) is appropriate. It is the decision model relating to counts of the same kind that provides the standard. In regard to the case illustrating the present discussion, the alternative decision model, covering counts of a different kind, would be regarded as giving valid effect to the totality principle if the calculated effective sentence was of the order of $5\frac{1}{2}$ years. Of course, more than one combination of comprising sentences would be required to determine the appropriate degree of constraint on sentence, a curve of best fit for combinations reaching the medium and upper levels of case seriousness being particularly significant.

In relation to this analysis three points must be recognized. First, the standard calculated for the purposes of the above illustration is derived from a hypothetical sentencing policy. While, in the light of Lovegrove's (1989) analysis of judges' responses in respect of the decision model relating to counts of the same kind, it could not be considered to be an eccentric policy, it nonetheless has no significance outside of the present discussion. Secondly, the standard determined from the decision model relating to counts of the same kind should not be regarded as beyond question. This is because the element of policy covering the relationship between case seriousness and effective sentence (as illustrated in Figure 10.1) might be regarded as inappropriate when its effect in respect of cumulation was viewed in terms of the relationship between the effective sentence for a case and the sentences appropriate to the counts comprising a case (as illustrated in Figure 9.2). Thirdly, this analysis makes no allowance for the effect on the effective sentence of the principle, espoused by the judges in responding to the sentencing problems, that a case comprising counts reflecting variety in the nature of the criminality requires a somewhat higher effective sentence in comparison with an equivalent case comprising counts of the same kind (see Chapter 7). Of course, once quantified, this factor could be readily incorporated in the present analysis.

In applying the decision model relating to counts of the same kind as the touchstone, it must be remembered that under certain factual circumstances its validity as a basis for calculating effective sentences becomes untenable; namely, (1) where the counts comprising a case vary so markedly in the level of the sophistication behind their planning and execution that there is not a characteristic level of organization; and (2) where the violence in one of the counts arose in unusual circumstances and was so extreme that it is not an appropriate index of the offender's propensity to violence in the other counts comprising the case (see Chapter 2 and the earlier discussion in this chapter).

The alternative decision model is intended to apply across the sentencing range, all categories of offence, and all combinations of levels of offence seriousness within these categories, considered. Accordingly, its normative validity in respect of constraint on cumulation would require testing at all levels of total case seriousness – low, medium and high. Burglary is appropriate as a basis for a series of tests for cases, no matter what the category of offence, of moderate seriousness, but less and more serious categories of offence would be required for cases of low and high seriousness, respectively. The various levels of offence category are required for this purpose for two reasons. One consideration is that it is only sentences for serious offences that cover the upper reaches of the sentencing range. The second relates to the fact that the parameters (e.g., the seriousness of the number of multiple counts of, say, burglary) of the decision model acting as the standard are not measured without error; when a category of offence at an appropriate level of seriousness was used, the values quantifying the seriousness of the factual circumstances of the comprising counts would to a lesser extent have to be taken from the more unreliable parts of the seriousness scales – the sections just above and just below the lower and upper levels, respectively.

In attempting to develop a decision structure for an understanding of the application of the totality principle to the sentencing of the multiple offender, it was necessary to address the problem, posed by Ashworth (1983, 1992a), of integrating the seriousness of two or more offences of the same or of a different kind into a coherent system of proportionality principally related to the seriousness of single (principal) offences or classes of (principal) offence. This is the theoretical puzzle which has given direction to the present study. The preceding analyses offer an interpretation of that problem and give rise to the armature as a solution to it.

But how is the armature as a decision framework to play its role as a numerical guideline? Guidance is said to be necessary because for high quality sentencing the demands of the task exceed the limits of human information processing, even those of the expert, the consequence of intuition therefore being error and a coarseness of judgment. The role of the numerical guideline, then, is to reduce the demands of the task by showing the combined effect on sentence of the more important and common relationships and case character- istics; the net sentence acts as a precise reference point against which the judge individualizes sentence further. In this process, the judge extrapolates from the factors in the guidelines to allow for the effects on the reference sentence of the less significant and the new (see Chapter 1).

Although, in the analytic tradition considered generally, the idea that judgment based on a model of decision making in some way combined with the decision maker's intuition may be superior to that based on a model or intuition alone is not new (see, for example, Peters, Hammond and Summers, 1974), it would appear to be a view gaining increasing attention in recent years (see, for example, Blattberg and Hoch, 1990; Bunn, 1992; and Johnson,

1988; this literature concentrates on forecasting/prediction, but can be considered with profit in the present domain). The advantage of mechanical combination over intuition is that the elements in the model – typically the important and common factors and their interrelationships – are combined with consistency and without error. Against this, significant decision elements are omitted from consideration: novel factors and relationships, rare factors and levels of factors, qualitative factors and those recognized at a less conscious level and, for simple linear models, interactions and non-linear relationships. Intuition has the potential to take account of these elements, although the limitations of human information processing ensure that the accuracy of the judge's thought is diminished where these elements assume a significant proportion of the material circumstances; notwithstanding this potential advantage, intuition carries the danger that too much weight may be given to the unique elements at the expense of the common elements.

While the stage has been reached where the potential value of a decision incorporating both sources has gained prominence, how these two sets of judgments should be brought together is very much an open question. Blattberg and Hoch (1990) suggest the simple heuristic of 50 percent model plus 50 percent decision maker; they recognize that it is almost certainly a sub-optional solution but consider it reasonable in the absence of an adequate understanding of the problem. By way of contrast, Johnson (1988) proposes that the process should be one of adjustment: the model provides an estimate of the impact on the decision of the important factors, and the decision maker then adjusts this initial estimate to account for information not incorporated in the model. Bunn (1992) has considered the problem more broadly. He argues that whether combination or adjustment is the more appropriate procedure depends on circumstances relating to the model's development and application. In the process of adjustment – presumably it would be akin to the process of calculative intuition described in Chapter 1 – the statistical model provides a structure in relation to which the decision maker extrapolates, considering the new information in relation to the elements in the model; and adjustment is appropriate where: (1) the model describes an organizationally established policy; (2) the factors and associated rules incorporated in the model normally account for an overwhelming proportion of the variance of the decision; and (3) it is proper that the organization's policy and its application in particular cases be open to scrutiny. These three criteria would be satisfied in regard to the task of sentencing only where there was a detailed and expressly stated policy and judges applied it to particular cases in a deliberative and open fashion. It is only with a process of adjustment that the final decision could be the coherent product of a single set of internally consistent and compatible principles and working rules, some of which were to be found in the model and others in the decision maker. But this would require the first two of the just-stated conditions to apply. Where they were not characteristic of the sentencing system, sentencing judgments might be in effect no more than an unknown and pragmatic mixture of several perspectives, as indeed they would be with the mechanical combination of the two sets of overall judgments of model and decision maker.

Were guidance to be incorporated in the sentencing process in this way, judges would not be absolved from their duty in law of globally, qualitatively and subjectively assessing the seeming rightness of a sentence arrived at by this means. The High Court of Australia in *Mill* (1988) approved Thomas's (1979) statement of the totality principle. In one of the English cases cited by Thomas, *Holderness*, the appellant had been sentenced to a total of four years' imprisonment for a series of offences, mainly relating to driving; the Court of Appeal (Criminal Division) stated that the sentencer had failed to reflect on the overall effect of the sentence, and noted that had this been done it would have immediately been realized that this level of sentence is appropriate to a serious crime. Common experience would recommend the wisdom of this final step of intuitively contemplating the overall result of a series of discrete moves so as to ensure there was no obvious sign that there had been a compounding of errors of omission or commission. And where there was a discrepancy between the global impression of what was correct by way of sentence and the decision-aided sentence the judge would then re-examine the intuitive extrapolation in an attempt to identify possible error.

In view of this discussion on the role of the armature as a decision framework, the provenance of the armature would better be seen as not in the physical sciences but in the fine arts.

With the completion of this second study, the conceptual exploration of the judicial determination of sentence has taken another step forward. The first monograph (Lovegrove, 1989) developed a framework for the scaling of offence seriousness and the determination of sentence for each of the individual counts comprising a case; this second book covers the aggregation of sentence according to the totality principle for these individual counts. The role of circumstances peculiar to the offender remains to be explored. And it may be necessary to incorporate the aggregation of seriousness for counts individually not warranting a custodial sentence. But sufficient ground has been covered for the final form of the armature of judicial sentencing to be apparent. This provides a sound basis for a detailed review of the structure and content of current judicial sentencing policy, the formulation of more detailed principles and working rules, and the development of a system of numerical guidance for the determination of quantum of sentence according to policy. These steps must be taken before there can be quality sentencing; for this assertion the evidence from this study is compelling. "Armature" is offered here as, in the words of Gould (1987), a metaphor to inform theory and (one may add) understanding.

Case 37 from Sentencing Research Exercise – Part 3B

New case

Date of Plea: April 1991

Presentment: 4 counts Armed robbery

                            4 counts Theft of a motor vehicle

                            1 count Burglary

                            1 count Theft of a motor vehicle

Plea: Guilty

Count 1(a.r.) and Count 5(theft m.v.)

Date of Offence: 2 February 1990

Statements of Victims

The armed robbery occurred at approximately 2.30 pm one Friday as several of the office-staff of four – two men and two women – were arranging the distribution of the employees' wages, which had been delivered to the factory a short time earlier by a security van.

The receptionist reported that two men burst through the main door; they were wearing overalls and gloves, and had pulled on beanies with eye-slits as they entered the building; they took from the bags they were carrying what appeared to be a hand-gun and a sawn-off shotgun. They waved their guns in the air, told the young woman it was a hold-up, and ordered her to walk ahead of them into the pay-office area. One of the offenders pushed past the young woman and ran into the office.

The office-staff heard a shout of "hold-up" from the corridor and almost immediately a man ran into the room shouting obscenities and waving his gun around, and then ordered everyone to stand together. This offender grabbed one of the staff, a man aged 45, pulled him to one side, held a gun at his head, and shouted that if all the pay-packets and money in the office were not handed over quickly, then the man would be shot. At this point another man entered the room. The two threw down their bags and ordered two of the employees to open the safe and help load the pay-packets and loose cash into their bags. The second offender waved his gun around, pointing it at the two employees who were loading the bags and shouting at them to hurry. When all the money had been handed over, the two offenders ran out the door; as they were leaving they pulled the telephone cords from the wall-sockets and warned that anyone who attempted to follow them would be shot. The office-staff said that they had not attempted to leave the office as the men left; but when the men were in the corridor they heard a shot fired. As soon as it was clear the men had left the building they went into the corridor and found the security officer lying in the corridor, bleeding from a wound in his left leg.

The security officer, aged 55, said he had heard a commotion from the main-office area, and went to investigate; as he entered the main corridor he saw two men running past the front desk and dressed in overalls, wearing beanies and carrying bags. The officer said he instinctively drew his service revolver; as he was drawing his gun, one of the offenders, who was carrying a hand-gun, shot at him and hit him in the left leg; the officer collapsed, and the two offenders ran out the front door. The security officer suffered severe internal bleeding and underwent an operation to have the bullet removed. He has since recovered.

The unarmed attendant, a man aged 50, in the security office at the gate of the factory, about 50 metres from the main office, who was on duty that afternoon, said that at about 2.30 pm shortly after the wages had been delivered by the security van, a car pulled up just outside his office. As he looked up he was confronted by a man carrying a bag and wearing overalls and gloves; as he entered the office the offender had pulled on a beanie with eye-slits; he took a sawn-off shotgun from the bag he was carrying. At this time the attendant noticed two other men walking quickly towards the main office; the men were wearing gloves and overalls and carrying bags. The offender pointed the gun at the attendant and told him that he would shoot him if he moved or attempted to set off the alarm; the offender then pulled the telephone cord from the wall-socket. The attendant said that he was held at gunpoint until the two partners arrived back at their car. At this point the offender ran to the car; as he turned and left the office, he warned the officer that if he attempted to follow him he would be shot; he then pulled off his beanie and put his gun in the bag. This man was the driver of the get-away car. The attendant said that the two other men were not wearing beanies when they returned to the car but he did not get a good look at them. The man taken aside by the offender in the main office was not physically injured.

The company stated that the offenders had stolen $60,985 in cash.

Record of Interviews (all signed)

According to the offender, some months before the robbery, he and two of his friends were drinking one evening at his mate's flat. One of the two friends suggested that they do a robbery to get a lot of money easily; they decided that a payroll of a large factory would be a great idea. The offender said that his mate knew of one large factory (it had well over 100 employees) at which it was easy to get casual work, especially at certain times of the year when production was high; he knew that there the employees' wages were paid in cash and the payroll, he thought, would be delivered at a regular and known time to the main office from where the wages would be distributed to the various sections of the factory for collection by the employees. The offender's mate decided to get a job there to find out how the office was set out and payment of wages was organized; he was able to get employment within a month and worked there for about six weeks, leaving just four weeks before the robbery. The offender reported that two days before the robbery he persuaded a friend of his to take part, his job being to act as the observer for the security van and help them escape. One of the co-offenders admitted that he owned a hand-gun and used this in the robbery, and that at this time he shortened the barrels of two shotguns he also had at home; as well, he bought three beanies and three pairs of gloves for himself and two of the three other offenders (including the driver); furthermore, he admitted that on the same day he and one of the co-offenders (the driver of the get-away vehicle) searched for a car-park from which they could steal a car on the morning of the robbery; they decided on a car-park at a railway station – this car-park was quiet at off-peak times and most of the vehicles there were left by their owners for at least several hours. The driver said that about one hour before the robbery he went to the car-park and stole a car; he immediately drove to the flat of a girlfriend of the offender several kilometres away, where the offender and one of the other co-offenders were waiting, hiding the car at the back of the flats. The third co-offender said that at about this time he drove in his own car to the factory, and parked about 400 metres away so that he could see when the security van had delivered the money; as soon as the van left he drove to the flat, told the other three, who were drinking, had a few drinks himself, and then drove to the park where he was to meet the others after the robbery. Upon being alerted, at about 2.00 pm, the offender, the driver of the get-away vehicle and the other co-offender immediately drove to the factory – about a half-hour drive – and stopped at the security office at the gate. The driver said he went straight to the security office, took out his gun – a sawn-off shotgun – and pointed it at the attendant and told him that he would shoot him if he attempted to set off the alarm; and he pulled the telephone cord from the wall. The offender and other co-offender said that they went quickly to the main building; they admitted to waving their guns around in front of the receptionist and ordering her to walk ahead of them into the main office. The co-offender also admitted that on entering the pay-office area he waved his gun in the air, and then ordered the staff to stand together; he also agreed that he grabbed one of the staff, took him aside, pointed his gun at the man's head, and threatened to shoot him if the pay-packets and any cash on hand were not handed over quickly. Both offenders said they ordered two of the staff to open the safe and fill their bags. The co-offender further admitted that as they were leaving the building a security officer drew his gun and that in defence he fired his hand-gun at him. The offender admitted to waving his sawn-off shotgun around and pointing it at the two employees who were loading the two bags, telling them to hurry. They both said that they grabbed the pay-packets which were being sorted on the table. When all the money had been put in their bags they ran out of the office, admitting that they first pulled out the telephones in the office. The three offenders left in the stolen get-away car, which had been left with the engine running, and drove to a quiet parkland, about two kilometres away, got out of this car and walked through the reserve and met the fourth offender who was waiting for them in his own car; they all then drove to the flat of one of the co-offenders. The offender and co-offenders stated that they took off their overalls in the car as they left the factory and put them in their bags; the driver took his gloves off after leaving the get-away vehicle; the three later burnt their bags, disguises and the clothes which they wore during the robbery. The offenders admitted that the two sawn-off shotguns had been loaded.

Counts 2–4(a.r.) and Counts 6–8(theft m.v.)

Dates of Offences: 10 May–25 June 1990

Statements of Victims

The premises in these three robberies were building-society branches. Each branch had approximately half a dozen staff, and at the time of the robbery there were two to four tellers on duty and several customers. Each robbery occurred mid-morning during a lull in business. The staff and customers in each of the three branches gave similar evidence about the circumstances of the robberies.

In each case it was reported that two men ran into the building, both wearing gloves and beanies with eye-slits, which they had pulled on as they had entered; they shouted obscenities at the staff and customers and pulled out what appeared to be sawn-off shotguns from the bags they were carrying. The staff and customers stated that the two offenders waved their guns around, fired several shots into the roof, and ordered everyone to lie on the floor. In each case it was reported that one of the offenders grabbed one customer, a man apparently in his mid-forties, pulled him to one side, held a gun at his head, and shouted that if all the money on the premises was not handed over quickly or if the alarm was set off, then the man would be shot; at this point he threw the bags he was carrying across the counter and ordered the staff to fill them up. In one of the counts (Count 4) the offender appeared to become impatient and hit the man taken aside across the face once or twice with the handle of his gun; the man groaned, clutched his jaw and then fell to the ground, clearly suffering much pain. The offender then said to the tellers that if they didn't hurry and hand over all the money others would be hurt. Meanwhile, the other offender jumped over the counter and waved his gun around, pointing it first at one teller then another and telling the staff to hurry; he threw his bags at one of the tellers and ordered him to go to the safe. When it appeared that all the money had been handed over, the two offenders ran out the door; as they were leaving the premises they fired shots at the security cameras and warned that anyone who attempted to follow them would be shot. The staff and customers reported that as the offenders were leaving they removed their beanies and put them and their guns in the bags with the money; it was also reported that the man hit by the offender suffered a fractured jaw, but has since recovered; none of the staff or other customers was hurt in the three counts.

According to the managements of the three building societies, the offenders stole amounts in cash of $10,100, $8,470 and $15,750 in the three counts, a total of $34,320.

Record of Interviews (all signed)

According to the offender, about three months after the payroll robbery, the four of them who did that were drinking one evening at his mate's flat, when one of the three others suggested that they could get themselves a lot more money easily by robbing several banks or building societies. The offender said that over the next week or so his mate searched around Melbourne suburbs for banks or building societies with low security and easy access, such as a car-park next to the premises; he also suggested that one of them should visit those premises which appeared suitable to look over the inside of the buildings and assess security; they found several building societies which seemed to be what they wanted. The four decided to do the robberies at times when they thought there might be a lot of cash on the premises. In these robberies they used the sawn-off shotguns and hand-gun from the previous robbery. One of the co-offenders said that a couple of days before the first building-society robbery he bought two beanies, a pair of dark glasses for the driver, and three pairs of gloves for himself and two of the three other offenders (including the driver); furthermore, he admitted that on the same day he and another of the co-offenders (the driver of the get-away vehicle) searched for car-parks from which they could steal a car on the morning of the robbery; they decided upon car-parks at railway stations – these car-parks were quiet at off-peak times and most of the vehicles there were left by their owners for at least several hours. The driver said that on the morning of each robbery he went to one of the car-parks, stole a car, and drove it directly to the flat of a girlfriend of the offender, several kilometres away, where the offender and the two others were waiting, hiding the car at the back of the flats. The offender said that they would have a few quick drinks, then three of them would drive to the building society. On entering each of the premises the offender and the co-offender with him admitted to waving around sawn-off shotguns, firing shots into the roof and ordering the staff and customers to lie on the floor. The offender admitted that at each branch he had pointed his gun at several of the tellers when he demanded the money and that he had ordered at least one teller to go to the safe. The co-offender agreed that at each branch he had taken one of the customers aside, pointed his gun at the man's head, and threatened to shoot him; and that at one of the branches he had become nervous and hit the man across the face once or twice with the handle of his gun, and threatened to do the same to others if the staff did not hurry and do what they were told. The two said that when the tellers had filled their bags with all the money which appeared to be in the building, they fired shots at the security cameras and then ran out of the building to the get-away car, which was parked just at the back of or outside the premises, with the engine running and one of the co-offenders, who admitted to carrying a hand-gun on each occasion, at the wheel; they would drive to a quiet parkland within easy reach of the premises they had just robbed, get out of this car and walk through the reserve and meet the fourth offender who was waiting for them in his own car (when the three left for the building society, this co-offender would drive from the flat to the park where he was to meet them after the robbery); they all then would drive back to the flat of one of the co-offenders. In each case the offender and co-offender who entered the building society changed their clothes in the car as they left and put them in their bags; the driver would take his gloves off after leaving the get-away vehicle; the three hid their bags, disguises and the clothes which they wore during the robbery at the flat of the girlfriend of one of the co-offenders.

Count 9(burg.) and Count 10(theft m.v.)

Date of Offence: 2 August 1990

Statement of Victim

The owner, a man aged 45, had been out for part of the night and, on his return home around midnight, entered through the front door to find that the contents had been slightly disturbed and that property and valuables had been stolen. Entry had been made by the back door, which had been forced open.

Missing property: cash $750, jewellery $16,550, silverware $3,120, electrical equipment $8,400, cameras $1,830
Total value: $30,650

Record of Interview (signed)

The offender stated that about one week before the offence he decided to do a "break-in" to get some money easily. He said several days later he had driven around one morning in a well-to-do area, and picked out a house – he knew the people who lived there were very wealthy, the house was partly hidden by a bushy garden, and the couple of times he had gone past the house during the day and at night everything seemed quiet as though they were away. The offender added that also on that day he had got in touch with a friend and asked him to help with a burglary for some "easy" money; his friend said he would be in it; he said he had asked that friend because he knew a lot about alarm systems and the house he had specially picked had a burglar alarm. They did the burglary at night, between about 9.00 pm and 10.00 pm. The offender wore gloves and took a jemmy, which he had owned for some time, in a bag, and on his way he stole a panel van from a hotel car-park near his home, then met the co-offender, who brought an extension ladder, and drove to the house he had picked, parking the van in the street by the driveway. He knocked at the door to check that no one was home; he said they went around to the back door, and knocked again. The friend then climbed on to the roof, using the ladder, removed tiles, and disconnected the alarm in the ceiling.

Once this was done, the offender entered the house by forcing the back door. The offender admitted that they had searched the house well for cash and goods they could sell. When shown the list of items allegedly stolen, he agreed that they probably had taken it all. After the burglary the offender took the goods straight to a fence he knew, took his friend home, and then left the vehicle in a suburb several kilometres from his own home and walked back; he left the bag and jemmy with the fence.

PRIORS:
(Presented exactly as in Table 8.8.)
PLEA:
The offender was born on 15.9.1957 and was 32 years old at the time of the first offence (February 1990) being dealt with by this Court.

His father disappeared from the family home when the offender was twelve months old and he lived at home with his mother until he was sixteen when his mother died, after which he moved from place to place staying with various friends and acquaintances. He left school at this age and had a series of labouring jobs, with the longest continuous period of employment being twelve months. Most of the periods when he was out of work occurred because there was no work available.

When he was twenty-two years of age the offender married and there are two children of this marriage, girls aged 10 and 8. He has been separated from his wife for five years and they are now divorced. His wife has remarried and has taken responsibility for the care of the two children.

Just prior to offending he had been out of work for one month and felt financially insecure. He was looking for work when he was arrested but had been unsuccessful. He says he has spent the proceeds, although it would appear that he has little, if anything, to show for the money.

Since the offending which has brought him before this Court he has not committed any offences, and there are no matters outstanding.

The offender has been living with his girlfriend for the past eighteen months. She has regular employment as a shop assistant.

Initially the offender denied knowledge of these matters to the police, but changed his position when confronted with the evidence; he signed the police interview, admitting his guilt; before the trial he indicated his intention to plead guilty.

References

Abernathy, C.M. and Hamm, R.M. (1995). *Surgical intuition*. Philadelphia: Hanley and Belfus.

Advisory Council on the Penal System. (1978). *Sentences of imprisonment: A review of maximum penalties*. London: Her Majesty's Stationery Office.

Anderson, N.H. (1981). *Foundations of information integration theory*. New York: Academic Press.

Anderson, N.H. (1982). *Methods of information integration theory*. New York: Academic Press.

Aramah. (1982). *Criminal Appeal Reports (Sentencing)*, *4*, 407–410.

Aroyewumi and others. (1995). *Criminal Appeal Reports (Sentencing)*, *16*, 211–219.

Ashworth, A. (1983). *Sentencing and penal policy*. London: Weidenfeld and Nicolson.

Ashworth, A. (1984). Techniques of guidance on sentencing. *Criminal Law Review*, 519–530.

Ashworth, A. (1992a). *Sentencing and criminal justice*. London: Weidenfeld and Nicolson.

Ashworth, A. (1992b). The Criminal Justice Act 1991. In C. Munro and M. Wasik (eds.), *Sentencing, judicial discretion and training* (pp. 77–103). London: Sweet and Maxwell.

Ashworth, A. (1994). Editorial. Elephants and sentencing: A duty unfulfilled. *Criminal Law Review*, 153–155.

Ashworth, A. (1995). Reflections on the role of the sentencing scholar. In C. Clarkson and R. Morgan (eds.), *The politics of sentencing reform* (pp.251–265). Oxford: Clarendon Press.

Ashworth, A. and Gibson, B. (1994). Altering the sentencing framework. *Criminal Law Review*, 101–109.

Attorney-General's Department – Victoria. (1987). *Sentencing statistics: Higher criminal courts Victoria 1986*. Melbourne: Attorney-General's Department.

Attorney-General's Department – Victoria. (1988). *Sentencing statistics: Higher criminal courts Victoria 1987*. Melbourne: Attorney-General's Department.

Attorney-General's Department – Victoria. (1989). *Sentencing statistics: Higher criminal courts Victoria 1988*. Melbourne: Attorney-General's Department.

Attorney-General's Department – Victoria. (1990). *Sentencing statistics: Higher criminal courts Victoria 1989*. Melbourne: Attorney-General's Department.

Belsley, D.A. (1988). Modelling and forecasting reliability. *International Journal of Forecasting, 4*, 427–447.

Bibi. (1980). *Criminal Appeal Reports, 71*, 360–362.

Blattberg, R.C. and Hoch, S.J. (1990). Data base models and managerial intuition: 50% model + 50% manager. *Management Science, 36*, 887–899.

Breyer, S. (1992). The key compromises of the Federal sentencing guidelines. In C. Munro and M. Wasik (eds.), *Sentencing, judicial discretion and training* (pp. 105–136). London: Sweet and Maxwell.

Bunn, D.W. (1984). *Applied decision analysis*. New York: McGraw-Hill.

Bunn, D. (1992). Synthesis of expert judgment and statistical forecasting models for decision support. In G. Wright and F. Bolger (eds.), *Expertise and decision support* (pp. 251–268). New York: Plenum Press.

Canadian Sentencing Commission. (1987). *Sentencing reform: A Canadian approach*. Ottawa: Canadian Government Publishing Centre.

Chan, J.B.L. (1991). A computerised sentencing information system for New South Wales courts. *Computer Law and Practice, 7*, 137–150.

Chi, M.T.H., Glaser, R. and Farr, M.J. (eds.). (1988). *The nature of expertise*. Hillsdale, NJ: Erlbaum.

Cohen, M.S. (1993). The bottom line: Naturalistic decision aiding. In G.A. Klein, J. Orasanu, R. Calderwood and C.E. Zsambok (eds.), *Decision making in action: Models and methods* (pp. 265–269). Norwood, NJ: Ablex.

Coltman. (1993). Unreported judgment of the Victorian Court of Criminal Appeal, 5th April.

Daunton-Fear, M.W. (1977). *Sentencing in Western Australia*. St Lucia, Australia: University of Queensland Press.

Daunton-Fear, M. (1980). *Sentencing in South Australia*. Sydney: Law Book.

Davies, P. (1983). *God and the new physics*. London: Dent.

Davis, J.H. (1989). Psychology and law: The last 15 years. *Journal of Applied Social Psychology, 19*, 199–230.

Davis, K.C. (1969). *Discretionary justice: A preliminary inquiry*. Baton Rouge: Louisiana State University Press.

Diamond, S.S. (1981). Exploring sources of sentence disparity. In B.D. Sales (ed.), *The trial process* (pp. 387–411). New York: Plenum Press.

Dixon, W.J. (ed.). (1990). *BMDP statistical software manual Vol. 2*. Berkeley: University of California Press.

Dreyfus, H.L. and Dreyfus, S.E. (1986). *Mind over machine: The power of human intuition and expertise in the era of the computer*. New York: Free Press.

Ebbesen, E.B. and Konečni, V.J. (1981). The process of sentencing adult felons. In B.D. Sales (ed.), *The trial process* (pp. 413–458). New York: Plenum Press.

Edwards, W. and Newman, J.R. (1982). *Multiattribute evaluation*. Beverly Hills: Sage.

Elwork, A., Sales, B.D. and Suggs, D. (1981). The trial: A research review. In B.D. Sales (ed.), *The trial process* (pp. 1–68). New York: Plenum Press.

Ericsson, K.A. and Simon, H.A. (1984). *Protocol analysis: Verbal reports as data*. Cambridge, MA: MIT Press.

Fischer, G.W. (1977). Convergent validation of decomposed multi-attribute utility assessment procedures for risky and riskless decisions. *Organizational Behavior and Human Performance, 18,* 295–315.

Fitzmaurice, C. and Pease, K. (1982). On measuring distaste in years. In J. Gunn and D.P. Farrington (eds.), *Abnormal offenders, delinquency, and the criminal justice system* (pp. 91–110). Chichester, England: Wiley.

Fitzmaurice, C. and Pease, K. (1986). *The psychology of judicial sentencing.* Manchester: Manchester University Press.

Fox, R.G. (1988). The killings of Bobby Veen: The High Court on proportion in sentencing. *Criminal Law Journal, 12,* 339–366.

Fox, R.G. (1993). Legislation comment: Victoria turns to the right in sentencing reform: The Sentencing (Amendment) Act 1993 (Vic.). *Criminal Law Journal, 17,* 394–415.

Fox, R.G. and Freiberg, A. (1985). *Sentencing: State and Federal law in Victoria.* Melbourne: Oxford University Press.

Freiberg, A. (1992). Truth in sentencing? The abolition of remissions in Victoria: Sentencing Act 1991 (Vic.). *Criminal Law Journal, 16,* 165–185.

Freiberg, A. and Fox, R. (1986). Sentencing structures and sanction hierarchies. *Criminal Law Journal, 10,* 216–235.

French, S. (ed.). (1989). *Readings in decision analysis.* London: Chapman and Hall.

Gordon, S.E. (1992). Implications of cognitive theory for knowledge acquisition. In R.R. Hoffman (ed.), *The psychology of expertise: Cognitive research and empirical AI* (pp. 99–120). New York: Springer-Verlag.

Gould and others. (1983). *Criminal Appeal Reports (Sentencing), 5,* 72–75.

Gould, S.J. (1987). *Time's arrow, time's cycle: Myth and metaphor in the discovery of geological time.* Cambridge, MA: Harvard University Press.

Greenberg, M.S. and Ruback, R.B. (1992). *After the crime: Victim decision making.* New York: Plenum Press.

Griffiths. (1989). *Australian Law Journal Reports, 63,* 585–597.

Harvey, L. and Pease, K. (1987). Guideline judgments and proportionality in sentencing. *Criminal Law Review,* 96–104.

Hastie, R. (1993). Algebraic models of juror decision processes. In R. Hastie (ed.), *Inside the juror: The psychology of juror decision making* (pp. 84–115). Cambridge: Cambridge University Press.

Hawkins, K. (1986). On legal decision-making. *Washington and Lee Law Review, 43,* 1161–1242.

Hoffman, R.R. (ed.). (1992). *The psychology of expertise: Cognitive research and empirical AI.* New York: Springer-Verlag.

Hogarth, J. (1971). *Sentencing as a human process.* Toronto: University of Toronto Press.

Hogarth, J. (1986a). Computers as an aid to sentencing. Paper presented at the conference on The Role of Courts in Society, Jerusalem.

Hogarth, J. (1986b). Sentencing data base study: Demonstration package. Unpublished manuscript, Law Courts, Vancouver.

Hommers, W. and Anderson, N.H. (1989). Algebraic schemes in legal thought and everyday morality. In H. Wegener, F. Lösel and J. Haisch (eds.), *Criminal behavior and the justice system: Psychological perspectives* (pp. 136–150). New York: Springer-Verlag.

Hood, R. and Sparks, R. (1970). *Key issues in criminology.* London: Weidenfeld and Nicolson.

Houlden, P. (1981). A philosophy of science perspective on the validity of research conclusions: Response to Anderson and Hayden. *Law and Society Review*, *15*, 305–316.

Howard, R.A. (1980). An assessment of decision analysis. *Operations Research*, *28*, 4–27.

Humphreys, P. and McFadden, W. (1980). Experiences with MAUD: Aiding decision structuring versus bootstrapping the decision maker. *Acta Psychologica*, *45*, 51–69.

Jareborg, N. (1993). The role of aggravating and mitigating factors in sentencing: The new Swedish sentencing law. In U. Göranson (ed.), *Modern legal issues: An Anglo-Swedish perspective* (pp. 103–127). Uppsala: Iustus Förlag.

Johnson, E.J. (1988). Expertise and decision under uncertainty: Performance and process. In M.T.H. Chi, R. Glaser and M.J. Farr (eds.), *The nature of expertise* (pp. 209–228). Hillsdale, NJ: Erlbaum.

Judicial Studies Board. (1993). Recent legislation. *Bulletin of the Judicial Studies Board*, No. 2, 2–6.

Judson, H.F. (1979). *The eighth day of creation: Makers of the revolution in biology*. London: Jonathan Cape.

Kahneman, D. and Tversky, A. (1982). On the study of statistical intuitions. *Cognition*, *11*, 123–141.

Kapardis, A. and Farrington, D.P. (1981). An experimental study of sentencing by magistrates. *Law and Human Behavior*, *5*, 107–121.

Keeney, R.L. (1977). The art of assessing multiattribute utility functions. *Organizational Behavior and Human Performance*, *19*, 267–310.

Keeney, R.L. and Raiffa, H. (1976). *Decisions with multiple objectives: Preferences and value tradeoffs*. New York: Wiley.

Klein, G.A., Orasanu, J., Calderwood, R. and Zsambok, C.E. (eds.). (1993). *Decision making in action: Models and methods*. Norwood, NJ: Ablex.

Konečni, V.J. and Ebbesen, E.B. (1979). External validity of research in legal psychology. *Law and Human Behavior*, *3*, 39–70.

Konečni, V.J. and Ebbesen, E.B. (1992). Methodological issues in research on legal decision-making, with special reference to experimental simulations. In F. Lösel, D. Bender and T. Bliesener (eds.), *Psychology and law: International perspectives* (pp. 413–423). New York: de Gruyter.

Lawrence, J.A. (1988). Expertise on the bench: Modeling magistrates' judicial decision-making. In M.T.H. Chi, R. Glaser and M.J. Farr (eds.), *The nature of expertise* (pp. 229–259). Hillsdale, NJ: Erlbaum.

Levin, I.P., Louviere, J.J., Schepanski, A.A and Norman, K.L. (1983). External validity tests of laboratory studies of information integration. *Organizational Behavior and Human Performance*, *31*, 173–193.

Lloyd-Bostock, S.M.A. (1988). *Law in practice: Applications of psychology to legal decision making and legal skills*. Leicester, England: British Psychological Society and Routledge.

Lovegrove, A. (1983). *Towards detailed sentencing statistics: A feasibility study for offence characteristics of armed robbery*. Report to the Victoria Law Foundation, Melbourne.

Lovegrove, A. (1988). *Towards detailed sentencing statistics: A feasibility study for offence and offender characteristics of armed robbery*. Report to the Victoria Law Foundation, Melbourne.

Lovegrove, A. (1989). *Judicial decision making, sentencing policy, and numerical guidance*. New York: Springer-Verlag.

Lovegrove, A. (1995). Structuring the judicial sentencing discretion: Some empirical considerations on reforms. *Law in Context, 13(2),* 143–165.

Lovegrove, A. (1996). Sentencing the multiple offender: Towards detailed sentencing statistics for armed robbers. (Article in preparation.)

Lovegrove, A. (in press). Towards consistency of approach in sentencing the multiple offender (*Criminal Law Journal*).

McCormack and others. (1981). *Victorian Reports,* 104–112.

McKnight, C. (1981). Subjectivity in sentencing. *Law and Human Behavior, 5,* 141–147.

Mill. (1988). *Commonwealth Law Reports, 166,* 59–68.

Monahan, J. and Loftus, E.F. (1982). The psychology of law. *Annual Review of Psychology, 33,* 441–475.

Moxon, D. (1988). *Sentencing practice in the Crown Court.* London: Her Majesty's Stationery Office.

Mussell and others. (1990). *Criminal Appeal Reports (Sentencing), 12,* 607–616.

Newton, J.E. (1979). *Cases and materials on sentencing in Queensland.* Canberra: Australian Institute of Criminology.

Nisbett, R.E. and Wilson, T.D. (1977). Telling more than we can know: Verbal reports on mental processes. *Psychological Review, 84,* 231–259.

O'Brien. (1991). *Australian Criminal Reports, 55,* 410–418.

Palys, T.S. and Divorski, S. (1984). Judicial decision-making: An examination of sentencing disparity among Canadian provincial court judges. In D.J. Müller, D.E. Blackman and A.J. Chapman (eds.), *Psychology and law* (pp. 333–344). Chichester, England: Wiley.

Payne, J.W., Braunstein, M.L. and Carroll, J.S. (1978). Exploring predecisional behavior: An alternative approach to decision research. *Organizational Behavior and Human Performance, 22,*17–44.

Pennington, N. and Hastie, R. (1993). The story model for juror decision making. In R. Hastie (ed.), *Inside the juror: The psychology of juror decision making* (pp. 192–221). Cambridge: Cambridge University Press.

Peters, J.T., Hammond, K.R. and Summers, D.A. (1974). A note on intuitive vs analytic thinking. *Organizational Behavior and Human Performance, 12,* 125–131.

Phillips, L.D. (1984). A theory of requisite decision models. *Acta Psychologica, 56,* 29–48.

Polk, K. and Tait, D. (1988). The use of imprisonment by the magistrates' courts. *Australian and New Zealand Journal of Criminology, 21,* 31–44.

Potas, I. (1990). The sentencing information system of New South Wales: Promoting consistency in sentencing through computerization. Paper prepared for the Australian Delegation to the Eighth United Nations Congress on the Prevention of Crime and the Treatment of Offenders, Cuba.

Robinson, P.H. (1986). Dissent from the United States Sentencing Commission's proposed guidelines. *Journal of Criminal Law and Criminology, 77,* 1112–1125.

Ruby, C.C. (1980). *Sentencing* (2nd edn). Toronto: Butterworths.

Scadden. (1993). Unreported judgment of the Victorian Court of Criminal Appeal, 22nd March.

Sentencing Task Force. (1989). *Review of statutory maximum penalties in Victoria.* Melbourne: Victorian Government.

Slovic, P., Fischhoff, B. and Lichtenstein, S. (1977). Behavioral decision theory. *Annual Review of Psychology, 28,* 1–39.

Smith, E.R. and Miller, F.D. (1978). Limits on perception of cognitive processes: A reply to Nisbett and Wilson. *Psychological Review, 85,* 355–362.

Stillwell, W.G., Barron, F.H. and Edwards, W. (1983). Evaluating credit applications: A validation of multiattribute utility weight elicitation techniques. *Organizational Behavior and Human Performance, 32,* 87–108.

Svenson, O. (1989). Eliciting and analysing verbal protocols in process studies of judgement and decision making. In H. Montgomery and O. Svenson (eds.), *Process and structure in human decision making* (pp. 65–81). Chichester, England: Wiley.

Thomas, D.A. (1979). *Principles of sentencing: The sentencing policy of the Court of Appeal Criminal Division* (2nd edn). London: Heinemann.

Thomas, D. (1982). *Current sentencing practice.* London: Sweet and Maxwell.

Thomas, D.A. (1992). Criminal Justice Act 1991: (1) Custodial sentences. *Criminal Law Review,* 232–241.

Tonry, M. (1992). Judges and sentencing policy – The American experience. In C. Munro and M. Wasik (eds.), *Sentencing, judicial discretion and training* (pp 137–163). London: Sweet and Maxwell.

Tutchell. (1979). *Victorian Reports,* 248–258.

United States Sentencing Commission. (1987a). *Guidelines manual.* Washington, DC: U.S.S.C.

United States Sentencing Commission. (1987b). *Supplementary report on the initial sentencing guidelines and policy statements.* Washington, DC: U.S.S.C.

United States Sentencing Commission. (1994). *Guidelines manual.* Washington, DC: U.S.S.C.

Vining, A.R. and Dean, C. (1980). Towards sentencing uniformity: Integrating the normative and the empirical orientation. In B.A. Grosman (ed.), *New directions in sentencing* (pp. 117–154). Toronto: Butterworths.

von Winterfeldt, D. and Edwards, W. (1986). *Decision analysis and behavioral research.* Cambridge: Cambridge University Press.

Watson, S.R. and Buede, D.M. (1987). *Decision synthesis: The principles and practice of decision analysis.* Cambridge: Cambridge University Press.

Weatherburn, D., Crettenden, I., Bray, R. and Poletti, P. (1988). *New South Wales sentencing information system: Penalty display and sentencing options facilities.* Sydney: Judicial Commission of New South Wales.

White, P.A. (1988). Knowing more about what we can tell: 'Introspective access' and causal report accuracy 10 years later. *British Journal of Psychology, 79,* 13–45.

Wilkins, L.T., Kress, J.M., Gottfredson, D.M., Calpin, J.C. and Gelman, A.M. (1978). *Sentencing guidelines: Structuring judicial discretion. Report on the feasibility study.* Washington, DC: U.S. Department of Justice.

Williscroft and others. (1975). *Victorian Reports,* 292–304.

Young and others. (1990). *Victorian Reports,* 951–967.

Index